# NEGOTIATING FOR THE PAST

*Archaeology,*

*Nationalism,*

*and Diplomacy* **NEGOTIATING**

*in the Middle East,* **FOR THE PAST**

*1919–1941*

James F. Goode

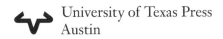

University of Texas Press
Austin

Requests for permission to reproduce material from this work
should be sent to:
  Permissions
  University of Texas Press
  P.O. Box 7819
  Austin, TX 78713-7819
  www.utexas.edu/utpress/about/bpermission.html

⊚ The paper used in this book meets the minimum
requirements of ANSI/NISO Z39.48-1992 (R1997) (Permanence of
Paper).

Library of Congress Cataloging-in-Publication Data
Goode, James F., 1944-
Negotiating for the past : archaeology, nationalism, and diplomacy in
the Middle East, 1919-1941 / James F. Goode. — 1st ed.
      p.    cm.
Includes bibliographical references and index.


ISBN-13: 978-0-292-71498-4


1. Middle East—Antiquities.   2. Archaeology—Middle East.
3. Archaeological thefts—Middle East.   4. Nationalism—Middle
East.   I. Title.
DS56.G55   2007
939'.4—dc22                                    2006037510

To our Arab, Persian, and Turkish friends, for many kindnesses

# CONTENTS

# PREFACE

My introduction to this subject was serendipitous. While doing research in U.S. State Department records at the National Archives, I repeatedly came across references to Persepolis and an ongoing crisis in U.S.-Iranian relations during the 1930s, which aroused my curiosity. As a Peace Corps volunteer in Iran, I had visited Persepolis in 1969 and again in 1971, but I had never connected it in any way to foreign affairs. I decided to investigate once the current research was completed.

That was well over a decade ago, and I have been engaged on this project ever since. I quickly discovered a triad of actors involved in that and other, similar regional crises. There were U.S. diplomats supporting American archaeologists, who encountered increasing challenges from local nationalists. These three groups have provided the subtitle and, more important, the substance of this study.

Originally, I intended to focus on Iran, but gradually the project spread beyond its borders to include Turkey, Egypt, and Iraq, for the more I researched, the more clearly I could see similarities and links between developments in these four countries. My career path led me to three of these nations, first the long residence in Iran, then a yearlong Fulbright grant in Turkey, and finally numerous visits to Egypt as director of study-abroad programs. This has afforded opportunities to visit archives, museums, and sites and to interview several archaeologists. Upon reflection, I suppose the broad scope of this study was almost predestined, for I have always had a keen interest in the various peoples of the Middle East, especially the Arabs, Persians, and Turks, and an appreciation for the many parallels in their histories.

Other works have taken up the subject of the intersection of archaeology and nationalism, but they have done this almost exclusively within the borders of a single nation. Of this genre, Donald Reid's fine study on Egypt, *Whose Pharaohs?* (2002), and more recently Magnus Bernhardsson's *Reclaiming a Plundered Past* (2006) on Iraq come readily to mind.

There are good, practical reasons to narrow one's focus, especially when a scholar considers the multiplicity of languages and historical traditions across the region.

And yet my own broad interests and the many indications from the sources that these nations had experienced remarkably similar developments in the interwar period convinced me to proceed. Here was a subject, it appeared, that would invite comparison and an emphasis on connectedness, that would allow me to focus on similarities across the region. No single author, of course, can know each of these four nations as well as many scholars will know any one of them, and I have relied heavily on the expertise of others, suitably acknowledged. Even then, it has taken more years to complete this study than I could have imagined at the outset.

One of the greatest challenges in writing such a work is to give voice to non-Westerners, especially to local nationalists, who may have left few written records or whose official accounts are not readily available. To overcome this, I have relied heavily on the secondary accounts of other scholars and also on my own translations from Arabic, French, German, and Persian (and on the assistance of former students for Turkish material). These include sections of autobiographies, letters, and, above all, newspaper and journal accounts. From these I have been able to reconstruct the arguments of those nationalists who were most centrally involved with archaeological matters.

I want to be clear about the focus of the work. Within each of the four case studies, I am examining interactions among three groups of participants: archaeologists, nationalists, and diplomats. If the reader will imagine three overlapping circles, representing archaeology, nationalism, and diplomacy, this study concerns especially that limited area where the three intersect. It does not claim to be a comprehensive study of any one of these fields but rather an analysis of how all three intersected, and to what effect, in each of these nations during the interwar years. Much could be written about each of these fields separately, and much has already been written; my objective is less grand, and yet even within these limits, the challenge has been substantial.

The two world wars bracket the study, for together they dramatically influenced the events discussed here. They disrupted normal patterns, especially those established by Western archaeologists in the region, and in so doing hastened processes of change in unimagined and unintended ways. A comparison of the accounts of two leading archaeologists dating from the close of each of these conflicts, one by James Breasted written in 1920, the other by John Wilson written in 1946, provides eloquent testimony of the degree to which Middle Eastern archaeology had changed during the intervening years and of the extent to which local nationalist elites had become empowered.

Given the tendency to ascribe overwhelming agency to Western powers and their institutions in the developing world prior to World War II, it may surprise some to discover just how successful nationalist elites could be in exercising control over archaeological affairs in many parts of the Middle East. This, of course, was a long-term trend; it did not happen quickly, and sometimes there were setbacks. Yet by the end of this twenty-year period of negotiation, nationalist elites had achieved remarkable success in attaining their objectives.

Such a long period of research in an array of archives on four continents could not succeed without the assistance of archivists, librarians, and scholars. I will remain always in their debt. I would like to single out two individuals who assisted this project over long periods and in especially significant ways. Alessandro Pezzati, reference archivist at the University Museum of the University of Pennsylvania, assisted me on three separate occasions during lengthy stays in Philadelphia, guiding me expertly through the voluminous sources. John Larson, archivist at the Oriental Institute of the University of Chicago, did an excellent job of introducing me to the succession of rich materials at his disposal on each of my many visits, and all this at a time when the archive was undergoing a major transformation. He has continued to assist as issues and questions have arisen over the intervening years. Several of my graduate students at Bilkent University, Ankara, especially Mehmet Ergin, Sibel Ertürk, and Fatih Tokatli, helped to translate relevant Turkish materials. Dr. Reza Nezar-Ahari of the Center for Documents and Diplomatic History, Tehran, provided useful published materials from his archive. Interlibrary loan staff at Grand Valley State University have for many years now assiduously tracked down elusive sources at my request. I am grateful to Wendy Moore at the University of Texas Press for her patience and efficiency in bringing this book to publication. Finally, I extend my thanks to a small group of scholars who have taken time to discuss this project with me or have read and commented on parts of the manuscript. These include Majd al-Mallah, Magnus Bernhardsson, Toni M. Cross, Elizabeth Fernea, Bert DeVries, Robert H. Ferrell, Charles Gates, Douglas Little, Ilknur Özgen, Donald Reid, Neil Asher Silberman, Reeva Simon, El-Mubarak Yahya, and the anonymous readers chosen by the University of Texas Press. My colleague

Roy Cole kindly produced the maps for the book. For financial support of my research I would like to thank the Rockefeller Archive Center, the American Institute for Persian Studies, the Fulbright Commission, and, most important, the Research and Development Committee and the Padnos International Center at Grand Valley State University.

**NEGOTIATING FOR THE PAST**

# INTRODUCTION

This study of the Middle East during the two decades after World War I examines events in the region from the perspective of archaeology. This twenty-year period witnessed a major transformation in Middle Eastern archaeology, and such an approach provides a key to understanding many of the important political, cultural, and diplomatic developments during those critical years. The detailed discussion and analysis of archaeological affairs in Turkey, Egypt, Iran, and Iraq, which shared remarkably similar experiences, reveals how intertwined the field had become with the broad agendas of the nationalist elites of the day.

For Western archaeologists the interwar years would prove remarkably different from what had gone before. Prior to World War I archaeologists in the Middle East operated with a minimum of regulation. Even where a strongly worded antiquities law existed, as in the Ottoman Empire after 1906, local officials rarely enforced it, especially at the distant perimeters of the realm. This prewar period, then, became the great age of collection building, when the museums of the West were built and filled with wonderful antiquities from every corner of the world. The Middle East, given its relative ease of access and profusion of ancient sites, contributed more than its share to public exhibition halls and private collections in Europe and the United States.

This monograph examines the middle period, what some have called the years of negotiation, to show how archaeologists, their institutions, and their governments negotiated with local nationalists and how they steadily lost ground in their struggle to avoid stricter controls. Who would excavate, and where and under what conditions? Who would keep the antiquities that were found? Who would write the histories of what was discovered? These questions arose repeatedly over the two decades because newly empowered nationalists in Ankara, Baghdad, Cairo, and Tehran refused to accept the status quo.

This negotiation produced much tension, for it was a time of challenge to established practices and, quite naturally, it contributed to crises that threatened to disrupt peaceable and friendly relations, not only among those directly concerned, but among their governments as well. There is arguably no better way to understand the struggle between rising nationalist movements in the developing world and Western interests than to examine the course of relations in regard to questions of cultural heritage.

In addition to the four case studies—Turkey, Egypt, Iran, and Iraq—this book makes brief references to other parts of the region, especially Palestine and Syria. I have chosen these four countries because they provided the best examples of well-established and successful nationalist movements during these years. In each case the nationalists came to power and steadily spread their ideology to a critical part of the population. In each of these the struggle with foreign archaeologists, who were typically viewed as representatives of Western imperialism, took clearly defined paths. These struggles peaked at slightly different times, beginning with Turkey in the early 1920s, but in each case the nationalists had taken control over archaeological affairs before the outbreak of World War II. Even where foreign archaeologists still served as directors of antiquities, as in Egypt and Iran, they had little freedom of action and operated under the watchful eyes of nationalist officials.

Why focus on these four to the exclusion of others such as Palestine and Syria? In the latter two mandates there were vibrant and complex national movements, it is true, yet in neither did local nationalist elites succeed in imposing control over the Europeans in regard to archaeological affairs as they did in the selected countries. The British high commissioner in Palestine, for example, was able to negotiate with James Breasted for the building of a new museum in Jerusalem using Rockefeller money, without interference from either Palestinians or Zionists. French authorities encouraged European and American expeditions to work in Greater Syria, allowing them to repatriate many of their finds, at a time when such liberality had become a thing of the past in Egypt and Iraq and, of course, in Turkey as well.

In each of the four countries constituting the core of this study, nationalist elites succeeded in establishing control over foreign archaeologists. Such changes did not come immediately, or without periods of tension and crisis, but the process seemed almost irresistible. The transformation happened first in Turkey under Atatürk, where virtually no antiquities left the country legally after the early years of the republic. Next came Egypt, where the Wafd Party under Saʿd Zaghlul challenged Lord Carnarvon and Howard Carter's right to a share of the treasure of Tutankhamun.

Egypt won that important struggle. The nationalists then pressured the French directors of antiquities in Cairo, Pierre Lacau (1914–1936) and his successor, Étienne Drioton (1936–1952), to tighten restrictions generally over the division of antiquities. By the end of the 1930s, most foreign expeditions had withdrawn from the country. In Iran, too, nationalist authorities exploited divisions among the Westerners to get the French monopoly over Iranian antiquities canceled. Later they went on to set the regulations for excavations and to assume control over the nation's premier archaeological site, Persepolis. In Iraq, the nationalist Satiʿ al-Husri, director of antiquities (1934–1941), extended his control over Western archaeologists, severely restricting the terms under which they could excavate in the kingdom. Many of them fled across the border into the French mandate of Syria. In each of these the trend toward greater local control had become clear well before the outbreak of World War II.[1]

Thus the post–World War II era found local national governments exercising almost complete control over their ancient sites and antiquities. They determined who would excavate, where and under what conditions. Often their own archaeologists worked in cooperation with Western colleagues, a practice almost unheard of prior to 1945; in some countries foreign archaeologists were unwelcome, and "native" archaeologists carried out excavations on their own. Antiquities laws, too, had changed. Now export of artifacts was carefully controlled, in many cases forbidden altogether. Most Western archaeologists had come to accept these new conditions almost without complaint.

These countries did not act in isolation but learned from each other's experiences, from their failures as well as their successes. The Turks looked to Greece and other European countries for their models. The Egyptians followed closely developments in the Republic of Turkey, especially in matters of cultural heritage. Officials in both Iran and Iraq knew the details of the struggle that had taken place in Egypt over the tomb of Tutankhamun, King Tut, and modeled their antiquities laws on those of Cairo.

Serving to energize the nationalists and to complicate matters for foreign archaeologists was the fact that some of the most remarkable archaeological discoveries came during this period: Tutankhamun in Egypt (1922), Ur in Iraq (1927), Persepolis in Iran (1932), Daphne in Syria (1936) (annexed by Turkey, 1939). These served as focal points of controversy, bringing an immediacy to the debate over the rights of excavators versus those of host governments. Thus the very success of Western archaeologists exacerbated tensions with local nationalists.

Although there is much in this study about British and French archaeology, and somewhat less on German, which was less active in this period, American archaeology takes center stage. There are good reasons for this. The interwar period saw a dramatic expansion of the discipline in the United States, for this was a time when Americans and their institutions, as in so many other areas of endeavor, including business, communications, and entertainment, dominated the field as never before. Although the most prominent American archaeologists had received their advanced training in Germany, new academic departments were being established in the United States to train students at home. The noted Egyptologist James Breasted persuaded Americans that archaeology was a necessary academic discipline for the study of man. Breasted's importance in this period is hard to exaggerate. With the strong support of the Rockefellers, he established archaeological expeditions throughout the region. He will appear again and again throughout these pages.[2]

Americans such as Breasted had expansive plans for the Middle East, which, they believed, held the secrets of the origin of Western civilization. To decipher these, they introduced new, more sophisticated techniques. They considered themselves scientists, a view that put them in concert with 1920s advocates of technological and scientific advancements in the United States. Breasted's closest friend was George Hale, the well-known astronomer, and Breasted, who wrote history books for the general public and served as president of the American Historical Association (1928), was also inducted with much fanfare into the National Academy of Science in 1920 and the American Association for the Advancement of Science in 1933.

Most important, the Americans had money, and the Europeans, suffering from the tremendous expense and destruction of World War I, did not. They were hard pressed to put expeditions in the field and certainly to supply them as amply as Breasted could. Traditionally, European expeditions had closer ties to their respective governments, receiving much of their funding from public monies rather than from private philanthropies. After 1918 their governments could spare few resources for archaeology, a situation commonly lamented among European scholars. They envied the wealthy Americans, who showed them new ways of organizing and outfitting their expeditions. In these early years there were not enough trained American archaeologists, however, and so American institutions hired British, Dutch, and German experts. These became truly international undertakings.

Americans were also in the vanguard because they had started much later than the Europeans, and they were eager to catch up. European museums already bulged with exquisite antiquities, which they had been collecting since the late eighteenth century. After World War I civic-minded philanthropists in the United States would pay for splendid museum buildings and for expeditions to fill them. There was a sense of urgency in all this, for even the most unenlightened archaeologist or museum director sensed that the day could not be far off when the door to the export of antiquities would be closed, perhaps forever. Struggle though they might against such an eventuality, they wanted to get all they could while law and practice still treated foreigners generously. Their determination often brought them into conflict with local authorities attempting to restrict the flow of antiquities abroad.

As we might expect, American sources for this period are abundant and accessible. Archives contain not only letters, reports, diaries, and journals of Americans but also of many foreign archaeologists, who worked closely with them, such as the Britishers Leonard Woolley, who excavated at Ur, and Howard Carter, discoverer of the tomb of Tutankhamun. European and American institutions often organized joint expeditions; such was the case at Ur in Iraq and Antioch, then in Syria, to cite but two examples. These became more common after the Stock Market Crash in 1929, when many donors stopped contributing. There is in these sources, as well, interesting material from prominent Middle Eastern nationalists, such as Satiʿ al-Husri (Iraq), Saʿd Zaghlul (Egypt), and Halil Ethem (Turkey). Although I have drawn substantial material from archives in Britain, France, Egypt, Iran, and Turkey, that from the United States is the most extensive, showing connections to all the centers of archaeological activity.

The discipline of archaeology was relatively new in 1919. If not quite in its infancy, it certainly had not yet matured. It was a Western invention, growing out of the Enlightenment, the scientific study of the life and culture of ancient peoples based on the excavation of artifacts. Western archaeologists rarely incorporated local people into the story of a site, taking them for granted as foremen, laborers, cooks, and domestics.[3]

For their part, members of traditional societies rarely approached their ancient history and monuments as scientists. They recited mythical tales of glorious ancestors, without the need to tie these to specialized study of surviving sites or monuments. In Egypt, medieval Muslims wrote with wonder of the pyramids and other antiquities. In a cave in southern Iran stood a headless statue of Shapur I, the powerful Sasanian ruler. Local people believed that Iran's greatness had come to an end when the statue

**Figure I.1.** Statue of Shapur I in a cave high on a valley wall at Bishapur, southern Iran. The broken, seven-meter-high statue was reassembled during the reign of the last shah. Photo by author.

was broken and that it would return when it was repaired. From pre-Islamic times beginning with the Sasanian dynasty (226–641 C.E.), Iranians had been moved by the ruins of Persepolis, and in spite of the fact that they had little specific historical knowledge about its builders, the site retained a crucial symbolic value, which was handed down over the centuries, reinforcing it "as a place of spiritual resonance with Iranian traditions of noble greatness."[4]

Generally, intense local interest in antiquities came only in response to a demand for them in the West. Once a market existed, illicit digging followed. Western nations had experienced this pattern as well in the days before their citizens had been taught to protect their own cultural heritage.

Many early excavators were no more than adventurers and treasure hunters; they worked in the region using the most primitive methods, thereby destroying much of the historical record. By the early 1920s, however, new, more effective methods of excavation had been developed. The American archaeologist George Reisner, director of the Harvard–Boston Museum of Fine Arts expedition at Giza in Egypt, was a leader in employing these techniques. Having been influenced early in his career by the great British archaeologist Sir Flinders Petrie, a pioneer in the field, Reisner carefully documented the context in which an object was discovered, keeping detailed records and taking many photographs. These new methods spread quickly, although one could find a mix of the old and the new throughout this period.

Also, there was the perennial question of the propriety of purchasing antiquities from dealers, who usually obtained them from illicit diggers. At the start of this period, it was a common practice, indulged in by almost all archaeologists and museum directors. Only Reisner and one or two others consistently criticized this trade. By the end of the interwar period, many had abandoned the custom, pressed by local governments but also convinced that such a market encouraged illicit digging. According to one expert source, "an example of ancient artistry which is brought to light by ignorant natives in a clandestine dig and is sold to a museum by an antiquities dealer who cannot know the circumstances of its finding . . . may retain its aesthetic appeal, but as an historical document it is worthless."[5]

Archaeologists considered themselves scientists, and their reports and letters are full of references to the scientific nature of their work. This claim put them at the leading edge of development in 1920s America, where scientific and technological advancement seemed to hold endless promise. They called for the continuing export of antiquities in the interest of furthering scientific study.

Archaeologists belonged to an international fraternity, and although they sometimes engaged in nasty exchanges with each other, these tended to be personal disagreements, unrelated to nationality. One should not forget that they often worked together under trying circumstances, plagued by heat, dust storms, floods, primitive living conditions, inadequate budgets, bureaucratic interference. Overall, there was a remarkable amount of cooperation and camaraderie. Where they came from seemed relatively unimportant to most of them. It was not uncommon to have three or four nationalities represented at a single site. How could it be otherwise when American institutions depended on Europe to supply them with experts even into the 1930s? In the mid-1930s, with the rise of anti-Semitism in Germany, American field directors and their sponsoring institutions provided safe haven in the United States for a number of German Jewish archaeologists.

James Breasted, director of the Oriental Institute at the University of Chicago, which sponsored by far the most expeditions in the region, introduced a new model of organization. Whereas the Europeans hired archaeologists and other specialists only for the duration of the season, three or four months at most, Breasted contracted them for the whole year. This guaranteed that virtually the entire staff would return year after year, providing a continuity that had previously been lacking. In the off-season they would gather in Chicago to study their finds, to work on publicizing them, to give lectures, and to prepare for the next season. Breasted was able to implement this practice because of the generous support of John D. Rockefeller Jr.

Breasted had few equals when it came to fund-raising to support his expeditions in the field. He was a wonderful storyteller, a gifted historian, who was able to link the ancient past with the present in ways that allowed him to play upon potential contributors' interest in the Bible. Writing to Rockefeller in May 1925, for example, to seek financial support for an expedition in Palestine, the director conjured an irresistible vision of what this picturesque spot must have meant to an earlier resident:

> It is one of the extraordinary things about Megiddo [Armageddon] that the boyhood village of Jesus is perched upon the hills looking directly down upon the Megiddo plain. He must have looked down upon it every day of His life there. We shall never know how often His own visions of future peace and brotherhood may have been clouded by the contemplation of that great battlefield where the fate of the world empires had been decided for thousands of years by the brutal force of physical power, which He proposed to displace by the rule of love. It is the task of those who look back upon His wonderful life to piece together, without a gap, the marvelous development which culminated in His teaching. And we cannot do this without Megiddo.[6]

Archaeology made front-page news, especially in the 1920s, and Breasted and his colleagues took full advantage of the fact. Amazing discoveries grabbed the public's attention at home. American newspapers were filled with details of the discovery of "Tut's" tomb and the supposed curse of the ancient pharaoh. Those few who could afford the trip booked passage for Egypt's Valley of the Kings; the majority feasted on the special photo sections that appeared in all the popular magazines. This response was repeated again and again over the decade, following subsequent discoveries. Articulate spokesmen, individuals such as Breasted, Woolley, Arthur Upham Pope, and William F. Albright, had larger than life personalities, and they enthralled countless audiences with firsthand stories of adventure and discovery in the Orient. One had to be something of a showman to attract attention and financial support for future or continuing expeditions, and they did not disappoint. To give one example, when Albright, foremost authority on biblical archaeology in Palestine, took home leave in 1927, he was swamped with lecture requests from all over the country. During the winter of 1926–1927, he gave seventy-two formal lectures and slide presentations, and this in a sabbatical year. Breasted constantly referred to his own busy lecturing schedule; he was always in demand.

Archaeologists were not free from the prejudices of their day, of course, and many carried to the Middle East those notions of racial and religious superiority that were common baggage in the West. Their writings overflowed with disparaging references to the "natives," whose abilities they impugned and whom they encountered almost exclusively in their roles as employers and supervisors of local laborers. They seem to have recognized a hierarchy among the various peoples of the region. In Iraq, for example, they considered their imported Egyptian supervisors to be far superior to any workers the local environment could produce. In Iran, some preferred Indians over Iranians; in Turkey, it was Kurds over Turks. Overall their tales were strikingly similar. "Natives" were incapable of respecting the ancient sites and monuments; they could not be trusted with antiquities, nor could they appreciate their artistry, and so on. Even in the rare instance where they were allowed to assume responsibilities usually reserved for Europeans, such as taking photographs or keeping the expedition's diary, a paternalistic relationship existed between the foreign expert and local members of his staff. These attitudes contributed to their difficulties when they began to encounter "natives" in positions of authority.

The education and training of local students as archaeologists was not encouraged. Many Westerners thought they were incapable of taking on such large responsibilities on their own. Then, too, if there were local archaeologists, they would surely challenge foreigners for a share of the field and perhaps come to dominate it. Westerners resisted this possibility well into the interwar period. Even those who accepted the proposition that "natives" could be, perhaps should be, transformed into archaeologists wanted to put off the day, believing it should come gradually at some unspecified time in the future. Thus it was not until very late in this period that a handful of professionally trained archaeologists began to undertake excavations in their own homelands. Turkey and Egypt led the way, and by the late 1930s Iraq and Iran had joined them. Local governments, not Western institutions, sponsored their education.

Surprisingly, Western archaeologists working in the Middle East did not generally view their activities as in any way political. Thus John Wilson of the Oriental Institute could write in November 1937, concerning the ongoing Arab Revolt (1936–1939) in Palestine, "We have every expectation that we may continue without serious difficulty. . . . [M]ost archaeologists feel that they are sufficiently removed from the political scene so that they may continue work in expectation of quiet." Yet everything they did, from the sites selected for excavation to the disposition of antiquities, drew attention to their activities and frequently engaged them in controversy. They seemed largely unprepared to cope with the fact that field archaeology was a highly political practice.[7]

Most archaeologists worked on pre-Islamic sites, ignoring the thirteen centuries since the appearance of the Prophet Muhammad. They knew little about the Arab world or Islam, and many believed that nothing original had come out of the Islamic world, that everything of worth there had derived from earlier civilizations. They searched for the roots of Western civilization and of the Bible, and these they expected to find in excavations at prehistoric sites or in ancient Egypt, Palestine, or Sumer, not in the Muslim dynasties that ruled from Damascus, Baghdad, or Cairo from the seventh century. Many Middle Eastern nationalists resented this neglect.

These resentments increased as both new (Turkey, Iraq) and old (Egypt, Iran) states began to define themselves more clearly. Much has been written recently on the idea of the nation and the special circumstances required to bring such an artificial entity into existence. Benedict Anderson was one of the first to tell us that nations are imagined communities with constructed identities. Citizens were made, not born. An important part of this process involved the creation of a narrative of the nation, which would be told and retold until it became accepted as historical truth. This narrative, rooted in a definite historical perspective, provided common myths and memories that contributed to a sense of community among people within a given territory. This common narrative also justified claims to particular borders.

In recent years, more studies have been written on nationalism, perhaps, than on any other Middle Eastern topic. It has become clear from this large body of work that nationalism is extremely complex and that it always means different things to different people in different contexts. Nationalist identities are not exclusive and absolute; individuals often claim multiple identities. Thus some clarification is warranted regarding the approach used here. This study focuses largely on elite nationalism and on what one scholar has labeled "official memory." It examines nationalism from the top down. It can be characterized, I believe, as part of the "new narrative" on nationalism because it examines elite ideologies in the context of the larger society, suggesting how these ideas permeated the growing middle class in each of the four countries. In each of these states nationalist elites made extensive use of the media and the education system, both of which they controlled, to disseminate their messages.[8]

In these newly constructed or reinvigorated nations, history became one of the primary disciplines, for whoever controlled history controlled the nation's memory. Those who wished to create a national identity saw as one of their most important tasks the rewriting of history to convince their fellow citizens of the glorious achievements of their ancestors and thus to breathe pride and confidence into them. If such glories had once existed, surely with effort and commitment, they could be re-created in the present among the descendants. Writing history became an obligation among nationalists everywhere. This history would serve a clearly political purpose; it was not necessarily a balanced attempt to approach the truth. An Egyptian author, admiring the success of the Turks in this endeavor, called upon his countrymen to write a new history of Egypt. "We must improve on our own self-conception," he advised, "by taking examples from Egyptian history . . . and if we don't find anything we should create something." According to the Iraqi nationalist, Sami Shawkat, "history is made or formulated according to necessity and that is the politics of history." Nationalists placed a high priority on writing history texts for the public schools, which became for them the favored locale for inculcating the narrative of the nation.[9]

In the process of constructing a national identity, archaeology came to play a decisive role. Buried within the national domain lay the remains of the ancestors, and it became the responsibility of archaeology to establish links between the past and the present, to provide the evidence to support the national narrative. Thus modern Turks sought to establish links to the Hittites, Egyptians to the pharaohs, Iranians to the Achaemenids, and Iraqis to the ancient Semites who had migrated out of the Arabian peninsula. Control over archaeology and its discoveries, therefore, became a critical battleground in developing nations. As most work was being undertaken by Western archaeologists, who had quite different agendas, questions arose over how the historical record was to be obtained and interpreted. For Western archaeologists to claim scientific objectivity and a nonpolitical status, with the memory of colonialism still fresh, seemed naive and perhaps disingenuous.

Foreign archaeologists paid scant attention to what their discoveries meant to local people. They saw the ancients as quite distinct from and decidedly superior to the current inhabitants of the territory, who seemed with their dulled senses to have no appreciation for the works of art around them. At the turn of the century one archaeologist lamented the looting of an ancient church, writing that "the miserable Moslems of the present generation have simply destroyed the beautiful relics of antiquity to furnish material for putting together their hideous little hovels." Almost forty years later, also in reference to the plain of Antioch, a publication of the Oriental Institute reported that "the scattered miserable villages in this plain today, with their incredible reed hovels[,] . . . are in striking contrast to the numerous stately city-mounds—the material of ancient civilizations—which are characteristic of the present landscape." They often disparaged the motives of "native" nationalists as being rooted in greed or political chicanery while presenting themselves as representing the higher interests of humankind.[10]

In no other area did the debate become sharper than over the question of the disposition of antiquities. Westerners developed a litany of arguments to support the continued division of finds between the expeditions and the host governments. As the period progressed, nationalists resisted this practice with increasing tenacity and effectiveness, responding with their own justifications.

Foreign archaeologists and museum directors argued that the antiquities would allow them to educate people in the West about little-known areas in the developing world and that their display would encourage tourism—a thriving industry in the 1920s—to those same countries. They believed that the antiquities belonged to humanity and were not the sole property of the nation where they happened to be found. Furthermore, advanced scientific methods in the West could provide more sophisticated facilities for their study, leading to a better understanding of the common past. There would, they observed, be no expeditions without a division at the end of each season, for no one would advance the sizable sums necessary unless guaranteed a return for their museum. As one plainspoken official at the British Museum stated, regarding a proposed expedition in Syria, "the question is, will [it] give the trustees an adequate material return for their money." In addition they claimed that the host country received a fine collection of antiquities at no cost whatsoever. Finally, they argued that there was no interest in the antiquities within the countries where they were discovered, except, that is, as a source of profit. Sites were not adequately protected, and given the political instability, many antiquities would be damaged, destroyed, or stolen if left at the sites.[11]

In response nationalists claimed that the antiquities belonged to their nation and that they constituted an important part of their heritage and would be used to educate future generations on the glorious past of their ancestors. With improved transportation, tourists could now arrive in greater numbers than ever before. Rather than dispersed around the world, antiquities should be kept together in their country of origin, where they could be more easily studied. As local facilities improved, scientists, too, could just as easily undertake their studies in Baghdad or Tehran as in New York or Boston. To insist on a share of antiquities was an attempt by the West to continue its domination; such practices should come to an end. As for security, nationalists pointed to all the antiquities and works of art that had been destroyed in Europe during World War I and also to the considerable amount of loss and damage occurring during the long, frequently hazardous journeys to museums in Europe and America. Finally, they charged, if the West had not provided a market for antiquities, illicit digging would not have become such a problem.

As they debated back and forth, tempers often flared, especially among those archaeologists such as Breasted, Woolley, and Ernst Herzfeld who had established their careers prior to 1914. They found the increasing restrictions insufferable. They were the ones who usually had the greatest difficulty adjusting to the new world of independent nations emerging in the Middle East.

It is easy to see from argument and counterargument the importance each placed on museums. Recently, the study of these institutions and their important role in society has become a burgeoning research field. In each of the four nations studied here, building museums occupied an important part of the nationalist agenda.[12]

The purposes of museums in the West were somewhat different from those in the developing world. Western museums vied with each other to boast the best collections from this or that era or location. Fine collections attracted visitors, but more important, they attracted donors, who would finance new expeditions and purchases. They performed an educational role as well, and here some experts have speculated that by amassing treasures from around the world, Western museums were expressing the continuing domination of the West, both culturally and politically, over less developed and often poorer regions.

For the nationalists, museums became primarily institutions within which "a significant part of national education" could take place. They used them to teach and to inspire citizens of the new nation. The nationalist press was full of exhortations to readers to visit ancient sites and museums to familiarize themselves with the glories that were part of their cultural heritage. Youth and scouting groups made frequent visits to such locations, which for many became places of secular pilgrimage. Going to the national museum became a ritual of citizenship.[13]

Museums were highly politicized. Choosing what objects to display privileged some over others, and the mere act of placing an item in a museum had considerable significance for "such objects expose[d] the power to own as well as the power to construct the [historical] narratives." The French, for example, manipulated museums in Syria and Lebanon to suit their larger purposes. In the museums of the former the Arab roots were emphasized and in the latter the Phoenician era, with its openness to the West, to appeal to a Maronite constituency.[14]

This brings to mind another important point concerning nation building and national identity formation in the Middle East. Many nationalists had come to accept the view promoted by Westerners and their own Westernized fellow citizens that the influence of Islam and the Arabs had been responsible, at least in part, for the decline from former greatness and that to return to that glory and pride in nation, one would have to dismiss the Arab contribution and weaken the deadening hand of Islam. Hence most of these new nations chose to emphasize their pre-Islamic past.

This tendency, however, should not be exaggerated. Many Egyptian nationalists, for example, edged away from pharaonism toward an Arab-Islamic identity in the 1930s. Neither held absolute sway among the elite. In Iraq, the emphasis on cultural heritage was centered more on the Islamic centuries for reasons having to do with ethnic diversity and the non-Iraqi origin of leading members of the elite, but in Iraq, too, history and archaeology became important tools for spreading ideology.

To this day much less archaeological work has been done on the Islamic period in the four countries studied here than on the ancients. Young archaeology students trained in the West studied—and many still do —the traditions and history of the ancient and classical worlds. When they returned home many focused on these same periods in their own excavations.

Many nationalists faced the fundamental question concerning what period of the ancient world should be studied. When archaeological discoveries are used to privilege one national narrative over another, the choice of site and the focus within that site are crucial. The historian Lawrence Davidson has referred to this phenomenon as "archaeological theatre," by which he means the capture of archaeology by ideology. There are countless examples of this phenomenon. Zionist archaeologists, for example, remained fascinated with discovering the origins and history of ancient Israel. They gave scant attention to other levels within the same mound because at best they did not interest the excavators, at worst their tale might conflict with or even challenge the Israeli narrative. Lebanon has witnessed a similar development; Maronite Christians have focused almost exclusively on the Phoenician past, excluding the Islamic centuries, which are of most interest to the country's majority Muslim population. Iranian nationalists likewise emphasized the Achaemenid and Sasanian dynasties, both of which had Persian origins. Turks in the early republic focused on the Hittites, ignoring the Greeks and even the Ottomans.[15]

Although the emphasis here is on archaeology, museums, and history, one realizes that not all nationalists focused so intently on these same concerns. The Iraqi governor of Baghdad, for example, eager to modernize the city in the mid-1930s, wanted to tear down medieval walls and towers to build roads, and he ended up butting heads with the director of antiquities. Yet both were nationalists. There were those who remained suspicious of archaeologists, thinking they were mere treasure hunters and that resources devoted to excavations, antiquities services, and museums might be better spent on factories, modern transportation, and an improved military. Nevertheless, this study shows that in each of these four countries key groups of political leaders, newspaper editors, intellectuals, and educators helped to set nationalist agendas in which archaeology and history were understood to have an important role. Even those not greatly enamored of the work of archaeologists would come to support the campaign to end the division of antiquities; as it became a symbol of the ongoing struggle between the colonizers and the colonized, a vestige of imperialism, they could hardly stand aside.

The nationalist ideology spread slowly among the masses via attendance in the public schools and service in the military. In this period perhaps only a minority had become sufficiently informed to abandon traditional ways of thinking and to embrace wholeheartedly the nationalist agendas. For the majority the conversion to this new, national identity would take decades or longer. It is reported that even in Turkey, a leader in the region, peasant support for Kemalism in the 1920s was limited, with many villagers continuing to identify themselves as Muslims, not Turks. Nadia Abu El-Haj discovered a similar phenomenon among Jews in Mandate Palestine, where "there seemed to be very little widespread popular regard for such an archaeological or national heritage project" as that proposed by Zionist leaders. Lack of interest in archaeology, she concluded, may not indicate a disregard for one's history but rather preference for other ways of relating to it.[16]

The emphasis on pre-Islamic periods, considered by many Muslims the Age of Ignorance (al-Jahiliyyah), caused tensions with orthodox believers and members of the ulama, leading them to dismiss archaeology as a new tool of colonialism and as anti-Islamic in nature. One prominent writer dismissed the art of ancient Egypt as glorifying idolatry and paganism and argued that it had no relevance for modern Egypt. Such ideas could result in violent action wherever mullahs stirred up villagers and local government authority was weak. In the late 1920s at Hadda in eastern Afghanistan where the French were digging, for example, a local mullah led a mob to the site to smash Buddhist antiquities that had recently been excavated. This was not an isolated occurrence.[17]

In the rapidly changing context of the 1920s and 1930s, diplomats had no easy task trying to uphold the rights of their citizens under archaeological concessions that were constantly challenged. Examination of the efforts of this small group of hard-pressed American officials may be one of the most useful contributions of this study. American diplomats in the Middle East had always been few in number, representing the fact that the United States had no major interests there that required establishment of diplomatic posts. Often the government would engage some European or American expatriate to represent its interests on those rare occasions when any appeared. Sometimes this resulted in surprising developments. American missionaries, for example, often doubled as U.S. consuls, with nary a thought for separation of church and state. Then there was the amusing case of Aleppo in 1900 where the American consular agent in that Syrian city was an Italian, who spoke no English.

These casual arrangements worked only because very few Americans visited the region, with the exception of the Holy Land and Egypt, and there were few commercial or other relations. By the end of the nineteenth century, with the expansion of missionary activity and, of course, archaeological expeditions, the United States had exchanged diplomats with the Ottoman Empire and Iran. Still, they were found almost exclusively in the capital cities, and this remained the situation throughout the interwar years, even though U.S. interests were clearly increasing.

Archaeologists, like missionaries, were what the historian Emily Rosenberg has called chosen instruments, that is, semiofficial representatives of the United States, flying the American flag in distant places where diplomats seldom ventured. Archaeologists, in fact, became quasi-diplomats, out of necessity negotiating with officials at all levels. These included kings, presidents, and prime ministers, as well as ministers of education and directors of antiquities. Often they enjoyed more influence in the various capitals than did Washington's official representatives. Usually they worked closely with the heads of American legations to further the interests of both. The archaeologists had important contacts on Capitol Hill and even in the White House, and on occasion they would go over the heads of resident diplomats to get the State Department to act. Sometimes their respective positions became blurred, with archaeologists entering into negotiations with or without diplomatic advice.

To make the relationship even more complex, many diplomats were amateur archaeologists, taking great pleasure in visiting sites during the short excavation season. They purchased antiquities from dealers, and some, such as Burton Y. Berry, who served in Turkey, Iran, and Iraq and left a remarkable collection to his alma mater, Indiana University, became experts in Middle Eastern art. In at least one instance in this period, a junior diplomat regularly purchased antiquities on consignment for a prominent American museum.

There was a significant policy change in these years, which indicated the growing involvement of the United States in the world of the 1920s. In the prewar years, the State Department regularly adopted a hands-off attitude toward American ventures abroad. Breasted complained early in 1914 that "the traditional policy of the State Department has been to refuse all official intervention on behalf of such expeditions. . . . American scientific enterprise in the humanities, therefore, is very much handicapped in the foreign field as over against the expeditions of foreign countries, which receive every assistance from their home governments."[18]

In the postwar period the department became more supportive. This applied particularly to archaeological expeditions. When a disagreement arose between an American group seeking a concession in French-controlled Syria and colonial authorities, Secretary of State Charles Evans Hughes assured them that "the Department of State is in entire sympathy with the view expressed in your letter that the principle of the 'open door' should govern in the granting of concessions for archaeological exploration and as occasion may arise it will be glad to give appropriate support to this policy." Seven years later Assistant Secretary of State William Castle reiterated this assurance in a conference with James Breasted.[19]

We can easily affirm the findings of other historians that in the decade of the 1920s the United States did not pursue an isolationist policy. Even in the decade of the Great Depression, American diplomats struggled to maintain a presence in much of the region. Department policy had changed so dramatically that at times it seemed the diplomats had become the handmaidens of the archaeologists. Time and again the U.S. government came to their support, either alone or in concert with the other Western powers, Britain, France, and, less often, Germany. There were frictions, of course, especially with the French, who devoted themselves to expanding their cultural influence in the Middle East during the interwar years, sometimes to the detriment of American interests. Although the struggle for great power dominance in the region that Neil Asher Silberman has so carefully detailed for the prewar period in his *Digging for God and Country* (1982) was more muted, tensions did develop, especially with France in the 1920s and with Germany after Hitler came to power in the early 1930s.[20]

Even private support for the archaeologists, at least in the decade prior to the Great Depression, was more in evidence than it had been earlier. In May 1907 Breasted had tried to interest John D. Rockefeller Sr. in supporting a continuation of his survey and epigraphic work among the Pharaonic monuments of the upper Nile Valley. The great philanthropist denied his request, saying that this work should be paid for by the Egyptian government, not by private sources. Twelve years later, John D. Rockefeller Jr. gave the money for Breasted's postwar survey of archaeological sites and monuments in the Middle East and went on to contribute many millions of dollars to the Oriental Institute.[21]

With this new policy of support, diplomats became drawn into disputes between local governments and the archaeologists, and much of their time and energy was devoted to smoothing out difficulties. Often they negotiated on behalf of American institutions with archaeological interests, such as the Oriental Institute, the Metropolitan Museum of Art, and Princeton University. It was important for them that Americans succeed for this represented a prime—sometimes the only—area of long-term interest for the United States. They understood also how sensitive this issue had become for the new nationalist governments in the region, and they usually proceeded with great care.

Repeatedly during these years, archaeologists, nationalists, and diplomats clashed over issues that concerned them all. Much was at stake, and the disagreements arising in each of these four nations became drawn out and frequently bitter. In the end, however, despite disparities of power, the nationalists won undisputed control over their cultural heritage. How they succeeded is revealed in the following pages.

# 1. END OF THE OLD ORDER

With the end of World War I and soon thereafter the demise of the Ottoman Empire, a spirit of nationalism slowly spread throughout the Turkish population of Anatolia and Thrace. The courageous exploits and rousing speeches of Mustafa Kemal, later fondly called Atatürk ("Father Turk") enlivened spirits that had suffered through years of war, defeat, and foreign intervention.

Mustafa Kemal had been the hero of successful Turkish resistance at the battle of Gallipoli (March–December 1915), when an Allied army, seeking to seize the Dardanelles to allow passage of the British fleet to Istanbul and the Black Sea, had taken such heavy casualties that it had to withdraw. After the war the decrepit government of Sultan Mehmed VI (1918–1922) staggered from crisis to crisis in the imperial capital, where commanders of an Allied occupation force exercised real power. Mustafa Kemal, refusing to surrender to the defeatism surrounding the court, fled east into the heart of Anatolia to rally Turks to defend their homeland. Assisted in his objective by the misguided irredentist attempts of Greece to seize large portions of western Anatolia (1919–1922) and the Allied imposition of the draconian Treaty of Sevres (1920) on an apparently defenseless government at Istanbul, the nationalist movement took fire, and its forces, under the command of Mustafa Kemal and his able lieutenants, drove out the invaders.

Then, rejecting the Sevres agreement, the new Republic of Turkey, with its capital at Ankara far beyond the reach of Allied gunboats and with Mustafa Kemal as its first president, set about to negotiate a more favorable treaty. Playing skillfully on divisions between Britain and France, the Turks, represented by the president's most trusted supporter, Ismet İnönü, negotiated the Treaty of Lausanne (1924), which gave them most of what they wanted.

For the next fourteen years until his untimely death at age fifty-seven, Atatürk led the nation through a period of intensive reform, which be-

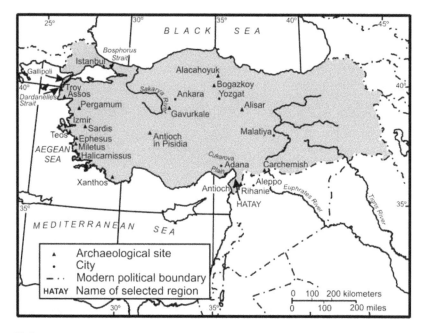

Turkey

came a model for other nations in the region, such as Egypt and Iran. In the early years he focused on consolidating power in the new capital, breaking up the religious brotherhoods, so influential under the late empire, and cutting the tie between Islam and the state.

By the late 1920s Atatürk could turn his attention from practical concerns to those that were more theoretical or ideological in nature. He had long been a student of the works of Mehmet Ziya Gökalp (1876–1924), a key figure in the early years of reform prior to World War I. Gökalp stressed the importance of efforts to awaken and strengthen the national consciousness of the Turks, which was, he believed, the source of all progress and the cornerstone of national independence. In his work Gökalp emphasized the pre-Islamic past of the Turks, the need to modernize the cultural life of Turkey and to purge the language of its Arabic and Persian elements.

These ideas were not original; Europeans, especially Hungarians, had expressed such thoughts as early as the 1840s. The University of Budapest, spurred by the theory of the common origin of Hungarians and Turks and concerned at the rise of Pan-Slavism in the region, established a department of Turcology as early as 1870. Scholars there suggested a link between the Sumerians, Hungarians, and Turks. Such ideas had a strong influence on a young Turkish student in Budapest, Hamit Zübeyr Koşay, who received his Ph.D. in Turcology and philology in 1921. Later he became an important archaeologist and director of antiquities in the republic.[1]

A series of late-Ottoman Turcologists added to these studies, publishing many books and articles. Gökalp acknowledged the influence of one in particular, Necip Asim (1861–1935), who wrote *Turkish History* (1898), which, according to Gökalp, "awakened a tendency to Turkism everywhere." Recent Turkish scholars have concluded that the "bases of modern Turkish intellectual life and ethnic identity," including the ideological ground for what would become the "new" historical thesis of the republic, were laid during the last two decades of the nineteenth century.[2]

While Gökalp preached his reformist ideas to the elite, others, such as the poet Mehmet Emin, took the message of revival to the illiterate masses, reciting his nationalistic poetry to village gatherings, repeating endlessly, "I am a Turk. My race and language are great." Although success came slowly, propaganda at all levels served to strengthen support for the republic during the difficult months and years when the empire was dying and the new nation struggling to be born.

Atatürk worked to the end of his life to make Gökalp's dreams a reality. According to a reviewer in the leading daily, *Cumhuriyet*, "Our great Saviour (Ghazi) made Turkey; now he will make the Turks, as Cavour and Mazzini made Italy and then the Italians." The president of the republic knew how important it was to instill confidence in his people.[3]

For centuries "Turk" had been used as a term of derision, not only by foreigners, but by members of the Ottoman elite as well. To them it had come to mean barbarism and rudeness. Educated Ottomans took offense at suggestions of lineal ties to the nomadic tribes of Central Asia. Westerners peppered their speeches and writings with stereotypical statements, such as George Clemenceau's famous remark at Versailles in 1919 that "there has been no case found in Europe or Asia or Africa in which the establishment of Turkish rule has not been followed . . . by a fall in the level of culture," or Harold Nicolson's observation fifteen years later, when he explained Ankara's rapid recovery from the effects of World War I, "In dealing with highly civilised and therefore sensitive organisms," such as the Central Powers, Allied controls would last for a decade or two, he explained. In contrast, "dealing with purely animal organisms such as Turkey there was no nervous prostration: the victim recovered overnight." Nicolson went on to identify the Turk as that "marauding herd, the only race which in long centuries of opportunity had contributed nothing whatsoever to any branch of human enlightenment or progress."[4]

Faced with such outpourings of Turkophobia from abroad, Atatürk launched a crusade to refute them officially by presenting his own thesis of Turkish history and inserting it in the minds of Turkish youth through the school curriculum. Believing that writing history was as important as making it, he gathered around him sympathetic advisers and scholars, drawn from the membership of the recently founded Turkish Historical Society, whose specific task was to write a multivolume history expressly for use in the public schools. He kept a close eye on their work, meeting with them often, to ensure that the record of the past would support the nationalism of the present. To later generations of Turks and non-Turks alike, many of those early claims would seem exaggerated, and indeed there have been revisions in this official four-volume history, but given the context of the times and the confidence-building purpose of the project, one can better understand—if not wholly accept—the sweeping historical revisionism of the early republic.[5]

Some of these same ideas had appeared earlier in a book titled *The Pontus Issue* (1922), published in Turkish and French to influence the Allied deliberations at Lausanne. The volume's editor, Yilmaz Kurt, argued among other points that Anatolia had been a Turkish land since time immemorial and that the Sumerians and the Hittites had been Turks.[6]

To spread these new ideas, the historical society organized its first national conference, at Ankara in 1932. This was mainly a Turkish affair with only limited foreign participation. Atatürk attended every session. For nine days, speaker after speaker lauded the accomplishments of distant Turkish ancestors and called for pride in a glorious heritage. According to the minister of public instruction, Esat Bey, from then on Turkish children would understand the advanced position of Turkish civilization among all nations, and this would encourage them to make further contributions to world civilization. An elderly teacher, Ihsan Şerif, confessed that until the publication of the first volume of the official history, he had searched in vain for something in writing that could make him proud of being a Turk. Now he enjoyed sharing this work, which reflected his own love of nation, with his students.[7]

At its most expansive, the thesis argued that the Turks traced their ancestry back thousands of years to the earliest inhabitants of Anatolia; that the Hittites—this was the golden age of Hittitology—had been Turks; that Anatolia was the cradle of all major civilizations, including Egypt, Mesopotamia, Greece, and Rome. As a complement, the Turkish Language Society, also newly founded by the president, adopted the sun-language theory, which held that Turkish was the mother of all languages. Many articles filled the pages of Turkish journals claiming the most unlikely connections between Turkish and this or that distant language. Ankara University students—at least until Atatürk's death in November 1938 —were required to take a course extolling the virtues of this new theory. According to one knowledgeable observer, "It was sheer nonsense but thought out beautifully."[8]

Some of the early claims in support of the historical thesis were excessive, even nonsensical, but they were good for the nation's spirit. Often such views were encouraged by advisors, who did not really understand the scientific approach to learning. Nevertheless, the popular press quickly took up the call, claiming that the Turks constituted the first civilized nation in the world. "The masses were deluged with information through books, journals, lectures and radio. From this was born a powerful, living, growing feeling—the people of the new Turkey felt and knew they were Turkish and were confident of their strength."[9]

A few brave intellectuals refused to embrace the new doctrine completely. One such was the historian Mehmet Fuat Köprülü, who raised his concerns at the 1932 conference. Unlike most speakers, he did not exclude the six centuries of Ottoman history from his purview, and he tried to find a balance between the Europeans, who considered the Turks barbarians, and the new nationalist interpretation, which saw them as more civilized than the Europeans. In what was rumored the Gazi's revenge, Köprülü was transferred from Istanbul to Ankara University, which for a sophisticated scholar in the 1930s was a sentence akin to exile.[10]

Gradually, sounder ideas came to predominate and discussion focused less on the Hittites as Turks than on the fact that the Turkish people had inherited all the civilizations, including those of the classical age, that had flourished in Anatolia. One expert, the archaeologist Remzi Öğuz Arik, showed a balance that was lacking earlier when he wrote, "Turkish history is an ocean. We should purify our generations in it at a time when we are in search of ourselves. We should neither abandon ourselves to blind pride in what we did nor deem it worthy to have given up loving one's nation and origins."[11]

Leaders of the republic, none more than the president himself, quickly realized that to substantiate their historical claims, for which there was little hard evidence, they would have to rely on archaeological findings. Suddenly this discipline received a degree of official attention and support unknown under the Ottomans.

In the eighteenth and nineteenth centuries Western archaeologists had come from Austria, Britain, France, and Germany to dig for the treasures of ancient civilizations. In these early years excavations were driven by desire to find objects for collections or for sale; many found their way into museums in Vienna, London, Paris, and Berlin. Excavators had little scientific training—at the time there was little to be had—and their methods were destructive. They tore into ancient mounds, blurring forever the historical record. The age of the stratigraphic approach, recording carefully each layer and the relationship of objects within each level, lay far in the future.

Primarily they focused on classical sites of the Aegean coast and neighboring islands. Heinrich Schliemann's efforts at Troy in the 1870s are probably the most notorious, but from Xanthos, Miletus, Ephesus, Halicarnassus, and elsewhere, Europeans shipped home the finest examples of statues, sarcophagi, pottery, rare metal work, coins, and other antiquities. Their efforts were aided by the fact that most Ottoman officials had little interest in the kind of materials that they discovered, especially if they were "mere" stones. In this age of open looting, the advice from the authorities ran thus: "If you find stones you can keep them, if you find gold we will keep it." Whenever necessary, excavators received assistance and protection from local consuls or from their ambassadors at the Ottoman Porte. During the declining decades of the empire, the sultans had little leverage over the Europeans, who seemed to wander almost at will. A British excavator at Halicarnassus in the 1860s, for example, bought and then tore down peasant houses so he could excavate under them; railroad concessions gave the grantee rights to discoveries made along the right-of-way, which must have pleased the British, French, and German contractors who built railways throughout the empire in the late nineteenth and early twentieth centuries.[12]

In her popular novel, *The Other Side of the Mountain*, the Turkish author Erendiz Atasü compares these Ottoman practices to the more enlightened policies of the republic. Writing about the travels of two young, patriotic Turkish women, she remarks, "They went to Berlin in 1932 . . . saw the wide avenues, the smart cafes, the magnificent Brandenburg Gate, the Palace of Charlottenburg, the Pergamon Museum. They shook their heads knowledgeably before the Altar of Zeus, the gift of Sultan Abdulhamid the Second to the Germans; they were completely agreed that such an insensitively conceived gesture would never have occurred under the Republic."[13]

The German excavators had obtained the magnificent altar by maintaining strict secrecy about their work at Pergamon. Ottoman law in the late 1870s decreed that one-third of any finds should go to the excavator, one-third to the property owner, and one-third to the state. The Germans convinced the Porte to sell them the land and also to relinquish its own share for a small sum. Only when sizable fragments went on display at the Royal Museum in Berlin in 1880 did German officials boast that they now possessed Greek works of art to rival those in the British Museum.[14]

Beginning in 1881 there was an attempt to exercise more control over antiquities in the empire with the appointment of Osman Hamdi Bey as director of antiquities (1881–1910). He came from a prominent family, and his father had once served as grand vizier; he was an accomplished artist who had studied for several years in western Europe. In 1884 new regulations governing excavations and antiquities were issued and an archaeological museum was inaugurated in Istanbul. But the new director and his brother, who assisted him, Halil Ethem Bey (1861–1938), faced an uneven struggle against foreign interests, who often complained at the Porte about a too-rigorous enforcement of the regulations. As the empire's fortunes declined toward the end of the century, Sultan Abdul Hamid II (1876–1909) used gifts of antiquities to win European support; large numbers went to Germany in the late 1880s.

Up to the outbreak of World War I in 1914, antiquities were regularly exported. The Germans, who began excavating at Boğazköy, the ancient Hittite capital in central Anatolia, in 1906, were assigned among other items a share of the cuneiform tablets and a stone sentinel from one of the city's many gates. Likewise, the British archaeologist David Hogarth, assisted by T. E. Lawrence and Leonard Woolley, had exported many antiquities from Carchemish, a Hittite center located on the upper Euphrates River.[15]

This briefly was the situation in the world of Ottoman archaeology to the outbreak of war: a few hardworking officials trying, without much support and with only limited success, to stop the loss of ancient antiquities, which occurred through the activities of foreign expeditions or the clandestine digging by peasants, who sold the objects they found to dealers.

Among the last Ottoman sultans, however, disinterest in antiquities was not absolute. Most exported antiquities came from classical sites or from those of more ancient civilizations; there was less interest in these at the Porte. Late in his reign, Sultan Abdulhamid II showed considerable interest in artifacts from the preceding six Ottoman centuries as well as in those from the entire Islamic period. In 1906 both of these came under the same protection that had been extended to more ancient antiquities since 1884. From 1908 the government housed them in their own wing of the Imperial Museum, indicating their raised status. Formerly, the Islamic materials had languished in a little-visited part of the museum.[16]

These developments were part of a cult of "Ottomania" sponsored by the sultan, who "focused in an unprecedented fashion on the creation myth of the Ottoman state." He attempted to create a cohesive Ottoman national identity, the existence of which seemed imperative if the empire was to transform itself into a nation, for new nations and nationalisms were rising all around it. Ultimately, his project failed, but it provided an important legacy for its successor. During World War I, the Ottoman Commission for Examination of Antiquities issued a report, stating in part that "every nation makes the necessary provisions for the preservation of its fine arts and monuments and thus preserves the endless virtues of its ancestors as a lesson in civilization for its descendants." Although time had run out for the old empire, these words would provide a challenge for the leaders of the soon-to-be-born republic.[17]

Informed Turks resented the selective pillaging of national treasures that had gone on under the empire and were determined to bring it to a halt. As early as 1920, when the republic was still surrounded by enemies and fighting against great odds, Mustafa Kemal found time to set up a department of antiquities. Halil Ethem Bey, who had replaced his brother at his death in 1910 (1910–1931), worked assiduously to close loopholes. When he learned that the French occupying forces in the Dardanelles and at Istanbul had carried out unauthorized excavations, he complained immediately to Charles Picard, director of the French School at Athens, warning that no further permissions to excavate could be granted until all the artifacts had been transferred to the Istanbul museum. Once this had been done, a new excavation permit for Teos arrived from Ankara. Halil Ethem could count on the support of the government of the republic, and this gave him unaccustomed influence with foreign archaeologists.[18]

Archaeological excavations carried more significance internationally than might be immediately apparent. Just as Sultan Abdul Hamid II used gifts of antiquities to gain the support of important European states, so European governments viewed archaeological excavations as important endeavors in the ongoing diplomatic competition in the Middle East. For the French, this competition, first with the British and then with the Germans, was the driving force for the advancement of excavations. Archaeologists were often the only representatives of European states in far-off corners of the region. Many of them were familiar with local customs, geography—they had maps—and languages, and they could bring officials at home up to date on recent developments in the area. David Hogarth, Leonard Woolley, T. E. Lawrence, and Gertrude Bell, archaeologists all, were recruited to work for Britain's Office of Military Intelligence, later renamed the Arab Bureau, in Cairo during World War I. Their French and German counterparts found similar employment. Archaeologists proved a great resource in peace and an even greater one in wartime.

French and German archaeologists maintained very close ties with the ministries overseeing their activities. Government funding made possible ambitious excavation programs in the Ottoman Empire. If ties in Britain were less formal, there was no lack of interest at Whitehall. The French government provided an annual budget for archaeology and would-be recipients had to apply in a timely manner each year to an oversight committee on excavations composed of officials, archaeologists, and museum curators for a grant or renewal of a grant. The committee could encourage excavations in areas considered of particular importance to the government, where they might further government policy. In September 1923 Picard took great pleasure in reporting to the Ministry of Public Instruction in Paris that his colleague, Professor Robert Demangel, would soon be working closely with museum authorities in Istanbul and that this would be good for French interests generally. Earlier, when the French proposed to establish a school of archaeology at Istanbul, the Ottoman minister concerned greeted the suggestion warmly, admitting that this would represent "a new intellectual bond between two peoples, of whom one has always considered the other its mentor." [19]

The Germans, too, rigorously pursued their national interests via the medium of archaeology. Kaiser Wilhelm II (1888–1918) proved a firm advocate, having participated in excavations in Germany and later on the island of Corfu. In Berlin, the archaeological establishment lobbied for large-scale, publicly supported excavations in Mesopotamia, reminding the public that it was a national duty to compete with the Americans, the British, and the French. In 1898 Minister of Culture Robert Bosse asked the Kaiser to use his upcoming trip to Istanbul to promote German excavations. The kaiser's well-documented visit to Baalbak that year, which led a French newspaper to accuse him of reveling in Wagnerian romantic historical scenarios, resulted in a German request to excavate the site and prompt approval from Ottoman authorities. The kaiser used funds placed at his disposal by the government to support the Baalbak work (1900–1904), which resulted in fifty-seven crates of antiquities being shipped to Germany. [20]

Sometimes the Germans pursued their interests too vigorously. In spite of Kaiser Wilhelm II's warm relations with Sultan Abdul Hamid II, repeated attempts to bypass lower-level officials by going directly to the Porte could prove counterproductive. In 1903 the German embassy asked the sultan to give the superb Mschatta gate, part of an Umayyad castle complex in Syria (now Jordan), to the kaiser. The sultan agreed, and in return the German ruler sent him a team of black thoroughbred horses. Although the sultan thought he had gotten the better of the exchange, Ottoman officials were furious, none more than Hamdi Bey. He began tightening restrictions on the Germans, denying them new excavation permits, sometimes refusing to allow them a share of antiquities from some of their sites in Iraq. The difficulties intensified when Halil Ethem became director of antiquities for he was a more committed nationalist than his brother and more resistant to foreign entreaties. These worsening relations emphasized the danger of trying to outmaneuver officials, who could frustrate foreign archaeologists in spite of apparent agreement at the top.[21]

Authorities of the republic did not lose sight of the continuing importance of such ventures in international diplomacy. In 1929 they approved establishment of a German archaeological institute in Istanbul, which they believed could strengthen Turkish-German ties. When they received similar requests from the French and the Americans, they approved these also on the same grounds.[22]

Yet the whole enterprise of foreign archaeology in the republic raised fundamental questions for the new government in Ankara. They knew of past excesses and violations by foreign expeditions, and they were determined to end the export of antiquities at all costs. Rightly or wrongly, many officials were suspicious of foreign excavators, concluding that they were merely treasure hunters. In their eyes every archaeologist was a potential looter. The republic tightened its control over excavations, relying on the Ottoman law of 1906 but closing all the loopholes. A Turkish commissioner was assigned to every excavation where work was in progress. Whereas Osman Hamdi Bey and Halil Ethem Bey had been prepared to give Western archaeologists some small share of what they had discovered, such generosity was anathema to the nationalists in Ankara. Their rigid policy brought complaints from foreign archaeologists and frequently from their governments as well, but officials remained determined.[23]

Compared to the European nations, the Americans arrived relatively late on the Turkish scene. They had excavated briefly at Assos (1881–1883), just south of Troy, and in the area of Baghdad, on the eastern margin of the then–Ottoman Empire. Having to rely solely on private funding, unlike their European competitors, they had faced a constant struggle to raise money and to maintain the interest of private contributors, who, of course, expected that their favorite museums would be suitably rewarded. The republic's stiffer regulations, which the Americans first encountered early in the 1920s, might have forced force them to withdraw altogether from Anatolian excavation. In what turned into a battle of wills, the Americans tested Turkish resolve.

## 2. THE SARDIS AFFAIR

As the new spirit of nationalism suffused the Middle East in the years immediately following World War I, tensions developed; wherever Westerners attempted to impose control, Middle Easterners resisted. One can observe these tensions in every sphere of activity, in business, in education, and especially in archaeology. This last, which has received relatively little attention from historians, proved one of the most contentious. Disputes over ancient sites and the antiquities they yielded went to the heart of the nationalist struggle; whoever controlled them obtained a useful tool for shaping the history and ideology of the nation. Following is the story of one such struggle, the course and resolution of which provides important clues to developments throughout the region during the interwar years.

In the aftermath of World War I, affairs in the territory of the former Ottoman Empire seemed chaotic—armed resistance in Damascus against French hegemony, in Iraq rural revolts against British control. Nowhere were political affairs more confused than in Anatolia, once the heartland of the empire. The victorious allies, France, Italy, and Greece, had territorial claims there, and Britain's troops occupied Istanbul.

The United States had few interests in the region. President Woodrow Wilson briefly considered a mandate in Armenia, but the Senate quickly rejected this suggestion. What remained were a few businesses, a number of missionary schools, some relief organizations, and, of course, the archaeological expeditions. American archaeologists had come to Anatolia late in the nineteenth century. They came from Princeton and Harvard Universities to expand their knowledge of the classical world that had once flourished along the shores of the eastern Aegean. One of their most successful ventures took place at Sardis, capital of Lydia, home of the legendary King Croesus.

The Ottoman government had invited Professor Howard Crosley Butler of Princeton University to excavate at Sardis in 1908. He enjoyed a good reputation with the authorities, having carried out earlier work suc-

**Figure 2.1.** Temple of Artemis, Sardis, with equipment abandoned by archaeologists in the foreground. Acropolis visible at top left. Photo by author.

cessfully in Palestine and Syria. With the backing of a number of wealthy individuals on the Sardis Committee, including J. P. Morgan and Cyrus McCormick, Butler undertook his first season there in spring 1910.

Fortune smiled, and over the next four seasons Butler discovered the remarkable Temple of Artemis and, perhaps more important, a stone bearing inscriptions in Lydian — until then undecipherable — and Aramaic, which provided the key to the ancient language as the Rosetta Stone had done for ancient Egyptian.[1]

Butler was never free, of course, from the entreaties of financial supporters on the Sardis Committee. Almost as soon as he arrived at the site, he began to receive inquiries from prominent backers in the United States, asking a familiar question: What will we receive from this? In Butler's case many contributors had close ties to the Metropolitan Museum of Art, and they were anxious that the museum acquire a substantial share of the antiquities he was unearthing.

In December 1911 Valentine Everitt Macy, a prominent New York entrepreneur and philanthropist and a trustee of the Metropolitan, wrote, urging Butler to get what he could out of Turkey in order to impress donors who, he said, were not interested in what was found but in what the museum would receive. Macy went on to suggest what Butler could do to avoid the Ottoman authorities. "Can you not follow the policy," he asked, "of having everyone who leaves Sardis, whether they are visitors or not, take some 'fragments' with them? I am afraid that if you wait until you leave, and should then attempt to take out several boxes of stuff, you might be held up."[2]

Actually, Halil Ethem Bey, longtime director of the Ottoman Museum in Istanbul, had been quite generous in the past, and Butler knew it was important not to antagonize him. The 1906 antiquities law accorded no rights to foreign expeditions to retain antiquities, but in practice they received a share. Under the law Halil Bey could have kept everything for his museum.

In these early years Butler favored keeping the Sardis antiquities together at Istanbul. He believed Americans should dig out of scientific interest, that donors should give out of idealism and generosity, not in return for acquisitions for their favorite museums.[3]

But Butler was ahead of his time, and arguments such as Macy's were more commonly voiced in museum boardrooms across the United States. Trustees, who were usually major donors, argued that the country had started relatively late to develop its museums, long after the Europeans had filled theirs with priceless treasures from around the world. Now it was the Americans' turn. Also, they believed that local populations cared little about the fate of these treasures, which would certainly be stolen for sale on the black market or destroyed through carelessness. American philanthropists, they claimed, were saving these treasures for humanity. Yet despite the appeals of Macy and others, most of what had been excavated over the years, 1910–1914, remained stored at Sardis when the Americans hurriedly departed on the eve of World War I.

Archaeology was an important issue among the victors. As soon as the war ended, a party of British and French officers was sent from Versailles to assess the condition of antiquities in the former Ottoman territories, soon to become mandates, and to recommend conservation measures. They made their report in February 1919. A year later, when Allied representatives sat down to draft the Treaty of Sevres, concluding peace with the Ottoman Empire, they did not forget the archaeologists, who had many contacts among officials. Thus, in article 421 of the treaty, the diplomats provided for the strict regulation of archaeological affairs; this called for abrogation of the 1906 law and a new measure, forbidding the Ottoman government from discriminating against archaeologists of a particular country, without good reason, and a guarantee that the finds from excavations would be shared. This latter requirement remained a sine qua non for most Western archaeologists; even the defeated Germans concurred. Halil Bey and his associates were especially stung by the proposed abrogation of the old law, under which they had treated foreign archaeologists rather well, they thought. But this article fit the exceedingly harsh tone of the treaty.[4]

The treaty encountered so much opposition that it became unenforceable. And as Turkish resistance to Sevres grew, the fragile unity of the Allies gave way to wrangling. The Italians and French rushed to avoid head-on collision with nationalist forces under Mustafa Kemal. Paris, already smarting from clashes with the Turks near Adana, abandoned most of its territorial claims in southeastern Anatolia to safeguard its mandate in neighboring Syria. Its withdrawal left Britain and Greece to deal with the nationalist tempest in western Anatolia.

Diplomats knew that the future of Anatolia awaited the outcome of the struggle between Greece and Turkey. The expansionist government of Greek Prime Minister Eleutherios Venizelos had sent its army to occupy Izmir and adjacent lands, including Sardis, in May 1919 at the invitation of the Allied leaders meeting at Versailles. Supported by British Prime Minister David Lloyd George, the Greek military advanced from the narrow plain bordering the Aegean to the Anatolian plateau, hoping to eliminate once and for all the challenge of Mustafa Kemal. Initial victories lured the army farther and farther from the coast until it neared the nationalist capital, Ankara, in the heart of Anatolia. In early September 1921, with their supply lines stretched perilously thin across the rugged countryside, the overconfident commanders ordered a general advance. The Turks met them with determined resistance on the banks of the Sakarya River, a scant fifty miles from their capital; the Greeks were thrown back in confusion. A long, dangerous retreat culminated in the chaotic evacuation of the Greek forces from Izmir in September 1922.

Amid this swirl of events, Butler and the Sardis Committee had to decide what to do with the prewar store of antiquities. Located only fifty miles inland from Izmir, Sardis had been on the front lines until the Greek army pushed deeper into Anatolia in June 1920. A young Arnold Toynbee, then a journalist, visited the site early in 1921 and reported considerable damage. Statues had been defaced, pottery smashed, but the important Lydian inscriptions had survived. Most of the damage had been the work of an unruly band of Circassians, who later went over to the Greeks.

Nevertheless, the damage was substantial, and these reports spurred demands for removing the remaining artifacts from danger. The Swedish consul, with the assistance of Halil Bey, had already removed some smaller, finer pieces to Izmir, and in 1921 with the aid of the Greek director of antiquities for Asia Minor the inscriptions followed.[5]

The Greeks wanted to house all the Sardis materials in a local museum, but the American consul insisted on keeping the inscriptions in trust for the Turkish government at the consulate. The Greek authorities consented; they hoped to avoid any disagreement that would discourage American archaeologists from returning as soon as possible and thus showing the world that the situation had returned to normal.[6]

Members of the Sardis Committee had their own plans. They began negotiating with the Greeks for permission to remove all remaining antiquities to New York. Perhaps alarmed by news of the depredations at Sardis, Butler now agreed, writing disingenuously to Stamos Papafrango, special Greek envoy in the United States, that the remaining artifacts were of little importance and would certainly not be coveted by any European museum. In fact, he added, it was probable they would not even have been removed to Istanbul.[7]

Former U.S. Minister to Greece Edward Capps (1920–1921), onetime Princeton professor and now head of the Sardis Committee, used his influence to obtain Greek permission for export. He pointed out that a large number of influential American Philhellenes, who had invested in Sardis, would be grateful to Athens if it issued an export permit. He requested that Prime Minister Demetrios Gounaris bypass his minister of public instruction and send an executive order directly to the governor general in Izmir. While these negotiations were under way, Butler received a letter of support from Cyrus McCormick, who had recently visited Sardis. Opening with a long, romantic description of his feelings as he surveyed the ancient site from its acropolis, he went on to say that he had many friends in Athens and that Butler should use his name if that would be useful.[8]

The negotiations dragged on into mid-1922 as the borders of the Greek enclave shrank ever closer to Izmir. T. L. Shear, Princeton professor of archaeology, who had replaced the aging Butler as field director, finally received permission as the Turkish forces closed in on the doomed city. U.S. Consul George Horton assisted Shear in overseeing the hurried loading of Lydian marbles aboard lighters and then onto an oceangoing vessel, waiting to carry them to New York.[9]

It remained Butler's task to raise money to pay shipping costs. Edward Robinson, director of the Metropolitan, convinced the trustees to authorize $2,000, but in return they expected that "all objects thus brought which are suitable for exposition in this museum, shall become its property." Butler found these terms unacceptable. He still planned to restore half the antiquities to Turkey when peace returned and thereby to receive its gratitude, which would benefit not only the Sardis Committee but also other American institutions hoping to work there.[10]

Robinson's demands put Butler in a difficult position. In desperation he wrote to Henry Osborne, whose brother served on the Metropolitan board, to see if he could soften the museum's stand. Osborne agreed to present the matter as soon as his brother returned from abroad, but even he cautioned Butler "not to be too generous with the Turks but to keep *all* you can for this country." Although Butler soon learned that the board's resolution had not required all materials remain with the Metropolitan, when the ship arrived in New York harbor the fifty-eight crates quickly found their way into storage at the museum.[11]

Not surprisingly, the board took renewed interest in the negotiations taking place at Lausanne to replace the defunct Treaty of Sevres. British and French delegates, along with American observers, tried to work out a satisfactory agreement with a determined Turkish delegation headed by Ismet Inönü, Kemal's second in command, who came with instructions to yield little. The board, out of touch with diplomatic realities, urged the State Department to ensure that article 421 of the former treaty, that governing archaeological expeditions, be included in any replacement. The Turks refused to consider granting any such privileges imposed from abroad, and the Allies, divided among themselves, had little leverage over the Kemalist regime.[12]

The authorities in Ankara made clear their determination to exercise full control over internal affairs, including archaeology. As the new government in Ankara took control, its officials insisted on the return of the Sardis antiquities. Throughout this affair Halil Bey came under increasing pressure from Ankara. As a survivor from the Ottoman regime, he found himself in an awkward position. He and his brother had for decades exercised a virtual monopoly over archaeology. Now officials of the republic were ordering him to resolve the problem in Turkey's favor.[13]

Thus Halil Bey made clear to U.S. officials, just as Butler had feared, that American archaeologists would not be welcome until the Sardis affair had been settled. This was not a meaningless threat for several American-sponsored groups waited for permission to excavate in Turkey. The University of Michigan had already prepared an expedition headed by Professor Francis Kelsey to dig at a site in central Anatolia (Antioch in Pisidia).

The crisis sidetracked his plans. Halil Bey told him plainly that approval awaited return of the Sardis materials.

Frustrated, Kelsey at first touted the benefits of gunboat diplomacy. In a December 1922 letter to Secretary of State Charles Evans Hughes, the professor urged a stronger U.S. military presence in the eastern Mediterranean, for the Turk, he thought, was unable "to contemplate anything except display of force." But through a combination of gentle prodding by U.S. High Commissioner Mark Bristol and Howland Shaw, U.S. consul at Istanbul, and friendly contacts with Turkish officials, Kelsey's views began to change.[14]

Bristol himself had undergone a considerable change of attitude since his appointment in 1919. He had arrived with a view of the Turks as unruly adolescents who had to be dealt with patiently but firmly; over time his respect for them grew, and he came to believe that they should be masters in their own house. Now he argued that Americans needed to understand both Turks and Muslims better, that there were too many inaccuracies presented to the public. He recommended that Kelsey approach the Turkish government directly rather than through the legation because that might hint at the old order, when foreign governments brought pressure on behalf of their citizens. Ankara was very sensitive on this point for the Turks were "suspicious of a political background to archaeology and historical work." The diplomats encouraged this work, which they considered an important indication of U.S. interest, but felt it might go forward more smoothly without their intervention.[15]

Gradually, Kelsey became drawn into seeking a solution to the impasse. He met with both Halil Bey and Adnan Bey, Ankara's representative in Istanbul. Writing to Professor David Robinson at Johns Hopkins University, Kelsey set forth his newly acquired philosophy. "The only way to deal with the Turks in this difficult time," he declared, "is by manifesting toward them a generous attitude with abundance of confidence both in their disposition to be fair and their willingness to cooperate." When all other suggestions had failed, Kelsey even agreed to accompany Halil Bey to New York to make a division of the Sardis cases in return for permission to excavate in Turkey.[16]

Unfortunately, members of the Sardis Committee, headed by the Philhellene, Capps, did not understand how much the situation in the Middle East had changed since before the war. They refused to return the antiquities despite protests from colleagues, Turkish officials, and their own government. Perhaps their response was not surprising given the fact that Western archaeologists and the institutions that supported them had rarely taken local views seriously. Prior to World War I, it was expected that Western expeditions would receive at a minimum half of whatever antiquities they discovered. Why else would the museums, universities, and governments of the West contribute to such expensive undertakings. Trustees wanted to fill their exhibition halls with treasures; for them, these were primarily business ventures. Yet what was beginning to happen in the early 1920s, wherever nationalist movements strengthened, was an increasing resistance to business as usual. This applied to every area of interaction, including, of course, archaeology. Western archaeologists, their financial supporters, and their governments often had difficulty adjusting to changed circumstances.

Thus the Sardis Committee, seemingly oblivious to changes under way in Turkey, wrote to William Buckler, former diplomat and now assistant director at Sardis, arguing that it could not afford the cost of returning the fifty-eight cases to Istanbul. Furthermore, the late Professor Butler (d. 1922) and Turkish officials, they claimed, had led them to expect a fair share of the antiquities and now to be forced to pay for their return would imply some guilt on their part. The committee wanted to keep everything (it would share the gold coins) and turn it over to the Metropolitan to be housed in a new Sardis gallery, which would be labeled a gift of the Turkish government. In return the committee would raise money to help the Turks ship the remaining antiquities from Sardis to Istanbul. Turning the issue on its head, the committee warned that if Ankara continued to act in this rigid manner it would discourage American archaeologists from choosing to work in Asia Minor in the future![17]

Buckler warned that such a letter would offend Halil Bey, as it would imply that he had in some way misled the Americans. The committee sent it anyway, following which Buckler refused any longer to represent its interests. Writing to Valentine Macy, Buckler complained that the members had to see "clearly the situation of 1924 — *NOT* as some of our compatriots do that of 1914." He confided to Admiral Bristol that "the Metropolitan people don't appear to grasp that in this delicate affair a blunder of theirs may injure U.S. interests in ways impossible to foresee." He hoped that the high commissioner could "save them — and their fellow-citizens, including [himself] from the consequences of their monumental ineptitude."[18]

Although Bristol had hoped to stay out of the delicate negotiations, telling the Turkish officials that this was not a diplomatic issue, he inevitably became deeply involved. In a series of interviews with Halil Bey, the museum director reported that he was very wrought up over the Sardis affair and the Metropolitan, "especially were his feelings hurt at the way that they did not answer his letters." Bristol wanted Halil Bey to understand that the U.S. government "could not control a private institution like the Sardis Committee or the Metropolitan Museum." It could only use its good offices to have the matter adjusted. He also argued that to restrict other Americans from digging because of what some of their countrymen had done seemed an unusual procedure.[19]

Meanwhile, Howland Shaw, who was on home leave, met with the Sardis Committee in New York and explained in detail the intricacies of the matter. He came away believing he had made little progress, but his straightforward delivery no doubt clarified the issue for those who had been poorly informed. Perhaps more important was a meeting between Buckler and J. P. Morgan Jr., in Venice, where Morgan was cruising the Mediterranean on his yacht, *Corsair*. Bristol and Shaw believed it was Morgan's intervention that led to a speedy resolution of the crisis.[20]

They may have been right. Morgan had considerable influence with his fellow trustees, not least because his family had loaned the Metropolitan many of its works of art. When he returned to New York in mid-May, he had been quite prepared to be, as he said, "severe" with the committee over the Sardis issue, but, he wrote, that had been unnecessary because the impasse was resolved a few days prior to his return. The two events were likely connected.[21]

Soon Bristol was able to announce an agreement, approved by the minister of public instruction, that all the Sardis materials, except the heaviest pieces, would be returned to Istanbul at the expense of the Turkish government, and there a division with the Americans would take place. Professor Kelsey promptly received his permit.

Macy wrote to Allen Dulles, director of the Office of Near Eastern Affairs at the State Department, to say that Halil Bey would be thoroughly disgusted at having gone to all the expense to return items of such little value. Then, apparently contradicting himself, he added, "American museums could use them more." Macy followed the antiquities back to Istanbul in July 1924, appearing in Halil Bey's office with a long list of what the Sardis Committee wanted. He had to settle for much less.[22]

Had he known of last-minute complications between Istanbul and Ankara, he might have considered himself fortunate to get anything at all. The minister of public instruction was having second thoughts about a division with the Americans. Believing that the committee would receive 50 percent of the Sardis materials, the minister reminded Halil Bey that this violated the law and that it set a bad precedent. Furthermore, as the antiquities were government property, the Grand National Assembly would have to approve the arrangement. Given these considerations, the minister ordered Halil Bey not to carry out the agreement.[23]

The museum director challenged this order. He replied that the Americans would receive one-eighth of the antiquities, not one-half as claimed, and furthermore that this did not constitute a precedent because the situation was unique, the committee having saved the Sardis materials from a war zone. Finally, he reminded the minister that the division had been approved both orally and in writing. If necessary let the Grand National Assembly decide. In any event, he had given his word, and if the government reneged, he would be obligated to resign. In the end Ankara relented, but Halil Bey's determined stand cannot have endeared him to officials in the new capital.[24]

All this, of course, went undetected by the New York gentlemen, who were by no means satisfied with the division. The committee expressed to Bristol its unhappiness with what had been allotted them in Istanbul. As a consequence, the Metropolitan had withdrawn its offer of a Sardis gallery. Had the Turks been more forthcoming, wrote Macy, "some Rockefeller money might even have been found for Sardis."[25]

In early 1926 Kelsey reported to Dulles that a committee member had asked him "bluntly" how he could get on with the Turks. And the following year Halil Bey wrote to Bristol of his astonishment when the committee had written him requesting almost everything from Sardis for themselves. Most of these items, he explained, had already been put on display and shown in catalogs as belonging to the museum. It was against Turkish law to part with any object so designated. There was no inherent right, he continued, on the part of the Sardis Committee to any part of the antiquities. "Please tell the committee," wrote the director, "that the case is closed."[26]

By the mid-1920s American views of the Turks were clearly in flux, and crises such as the Sardis affair helped to clarify American thinking. Bristol, who left his post in 1927, had shown himself a staunch advocate of improving relations with Ankara. He encouraged American archaeologists, and anyone else who was interested, to work in Turkey to expand the American presence there. He lobbied for establishment of an American school of archaeology in the former capital, and he urged Macy and his colleagues to use their influence to have the Senate ratify the Lausanne treaty.[27]

The State Department largely supported his efforts. Secretary Hughes argued for a new understanding of the Turks, explaining that Americans needed to abandon the language of the past and come to terms with the new spirit of nationalism in Turkey and elsewhere in the Middle East, which insisted on "freedom from outside control." Kelsey represented those American scholars with experience in the region, men such as Butler and Buckler, who had accepted the changes, concluding that the Golden Rule should guide relationships in future.[28]

But old sentiments about the "terrible Turk" lingered. One archaeologist wrote to Kelsey that the British and the Americans should cuff the Turkish ears properly. "Roosevelt and Curzon," he believed, "would make the right combination." Closer to home it seemed unlikely the members of the Sardis Committee could have been inspired to support passage of the Lausanne treaty, if they did not oppose it outright.[29]

Then, of course, there were the Turkophobes such as James Gerard, former U.S. ambassador to Germany (1913-1917). He represented the American Committee for the Independence of Armenia and published a long, vitriolic piece in late 1923, discussing in part the sad state of archaeological research in the Republic of Turkey. He claimed that "through Turkish ignorance, carelessness and even willful vandalism, the rapid destruction will continue of all traces of the great cities and superior civilizations, which flourished in the region before the long night of Turkish barbarism descended upon them. While scholars wait eagerly for the concessions to make researches, the evidences which they seek are destroyed through the reckless habits of a nomad and half savage race." Gerard's colleague, former U.S. Consul Horton, charged that the archaeologists praised the Turks only because they needed permission to work in Anatolia.[30]

Such attacks aided the antitreaty forces led by Senator William Borah (R-Idaho) to victory, but that did not close the door to American archaeologists. Kelsey continued to work in central Anatolia, and he was soon joined by an important expedition from James Breasted's Oriental Institute in Chicago, which quickly became the leading American representative in Turkey.

Nor did the Senate's action deflect Mustafa Kemal from his nationalist policies. By 1929 Halil Bey had been demoted, and complete control over archaeology was exercised by officials in Ankara, who retained almost everything foreign expeditions discovered. Occasionally as a mark of favor Ankara would allow export of some unexceptional piece, but this became rarer as the interwar years progressed. A visit to the galleries of leading American museums quickly reveals the impact of these policies. One often finds wondrous displays of objects from ancient Egypt, Iraq, and Iran but relatively little from Turkey. What exists in Western museums was usually obtained by expeditions before 1914.[31]

To those interested in U.S. foreign relations of the 1920s, a number of features of the Sardis affair will seem familiar—the encouragement of private interests to take the lead in negotiating with foreign officials, the close personal relationships between high-ranking American officials and prominent American citizens, among them. What may appear more surprising here was the apparent flexibility of American diplomats, who quickly recognized and adjusted to the new order in Turkey.

The Sardis incident was really a minor affair, and yet significant, for it typified what was happening throughout the region during the inter-war years. In Egypt, Iran, Iraq, and elsewhere, a series of crises developed relating to archaeological expeditions and antiquities. Many were more noteworthy than this one. But the Sardis pattern was remarkably similar to the others, which taken together provide an interesting and illuminating perspective on cultural relations during the period of transition between the world wars.

# 3. HEIRS OF THE HITTITES

Soon after the Sardis affair had been resolved, a new American player began to make tentative contacts with government officials in Ankara. This was James Breasted, whose Oriental Institute at the University of Chicago would become the most important American excavator in Turkey between the wars. Breasted was in some ways a visionary; his methods fit perfectly with the movement toward modernization and centralization that was taking place in the United States during the 1920s. He wanted to centralize American archaeology in the Middle East in his institute, which would become a kind of archaeological think tank. Backed by a liberal ten-year grant from the Rockefeller Foundation, Breasted sought ancient sites to excavate in all parts of the region. Before long he was sponsoring excavations in Palestine, Syria, Iraq, Iran, Egypt, and, of course, Turkey. He was a dynamo of energy and ambition, traveling constantly in the years 1919 to 1935 between Chicago, the Middle East, and European centers of power and learning. Somehow he found time to write several popular history texts on Egypt—his specialty—and the ancient world; he also served a term as president of the American Historical Association (1928). He and his son, Charles, who handled affairs in James's frequent absences, prided themselves on their straight-talking, no-nonsense business methods, an approach that worked well with Americans but often antagonized Europeans and especially Middle Easterners.

Breasted's demands quickly outgrew the supply of trained American archaeologists, for the discipline in the United States was still too young to provide all that he required. He turned to Europe, where expertise was plentiful but excavation money in short supply on the war-ravaged continent. The institute employed British, German, and Dutch archaeologists, many of whom returned to Chicago in the off-season to share their discoveries and to write up their reports.

For Turkey, Breasted obtained the services of a German, Hans Henning Von der Osten (1898–1960), who had served as an officer in World

War I and later traveled to the United States for study. Von der Osten understood the intricacies of working in the Middle East; he was, in contemporary parlance, a networker, who had grand ideas for his own and the institute's future in Turkey. He frequently ran afoul of Breasted, who considered him too independent, too difficult to control from afar, but Breasted tolerated him for six years (1927–1932), during which time he headed the excavation at Alişar, an important Hittite site in central Anatolia.

Von der Osten got on well with Turkish officials, better than he did with Breasted. Whether in sophisticated Istanbul or in the more frontier-like conditions of Ankara, he knew how to say or do just the right thing to ingratiate himself. In a book published in 1929, *Explorations in Asia Minor*, Von der Osten lavished praise on the new Turkey. He wrote of his admiration for the hardworking ministers, coping with difficult conditions, and of the friendly cooperation extended to foreign scholars. He called on visitors to come with open minds and to acknowledge and appreciate the distinct progress being made under Mustafa Kemal. Such kind words appealed to the nationalists, who often looked upon foreigners with suspicion.[1]

Having made an exploratory visit to Turkey in 1926, Von der Osten took his request for an excavation permit the following year directly to officials in Ankara, thinking, probably correctly, that they would be less suspicious if the request came from him than from the U.S. high commissioner in Istanbul. Given that such permits had to receive a host of signatures, both military and civilian, including members of the cabinet and ultimately that of the president himself, Von der Osten was pleased to receive approval in just nine working days. In the process, he reported, he had "sold" the director of antiquities, Mubareck Bey, on the Oriental Institute. He also made contacts with officers of the general staff through a former member of his regiment in Germany. He told Breasted of an incident with two minor officials who tried to sell him pilfered Hittite antiquities. He reported them to the director before setting off for Alişar.[2]

The first season proved long and expensive, continuing into the fall and running $5,000 over budget. This worried the cost-conscious Breasted, who let "the boys" know his displeasure when they joined him at Cairo in January. Still, the Turkish government had been relatively generous, giving them forty of two hundred boxes, containing many skeletons and pottery shards. This was a special favor, not to be repeated, despite Von der Osten's confident prediction that he would be able to secure half of future finds for the institute.[3]

In response to a request from the minister of public instruction, who was officially responsible for all excavations, the German agreed to mount an exhibition of the materials from Alişar at the ethnographic museum in Ankara. He and Erich Schmidt, a fellow German archaeologist and co-director for a brief period at the Turkish site, gave several lectures each day to top officials and the public. It was a great success, leading the local press to praise the work of the institute and especially of Von der Osten, whom the editor reported was studying Turkish and was known for his pro-Turkish sentiments.[4]

While Von der Osten was busy impressing Turkish officials, Breasted was making the rounds in Washington and writing letters to key diplomats to explain the objectives of the institute and to make certain that he would have their support should that become necessary. Breasted corresponded with U.S. Ambassador to Turkey Joseph Grew (served 1927–1932) shortly after his arrival at his new post, emphasizing that the institute was principally interested in salvaging and studying the evidence of past civilizations, not in securing works of art for American museums, but, he continued, "if incidentally such materials are given us they are, of course, very welcome." In May 1931 he had a meeting with Assistant Secretary of State William Castle and dined with Wallace Murray, head of the Near East Division of the State Department. Among the many issues discussed was the lack of a modern antiquities law in Turkey, which Breasted viewed as a shortcoming. The officials assured him of their interest in his work and stated that they were prepared for "real and effective intervention" in Ankara whenever he desired. Ambassador Grew, they continued, was very favorably impressed by the work of the institute, and on instructions from the department he would "make representations to the Turkish Government on this question." Indeed, Grew had recently reported that the institute's expedition and its members had "added considerably to America's prestige in Turkey" even though its leader was not an American citizen.[5]

Buoyed by this warm reception, Breasted fired off a letter to Von der Osten, ordering him to seek additional sites in Anatolia, keeping in mind "monumental returns for our collections." The institute, he confided, was now in a position to bring the influence of Washington to bear on the Gazi and the Turkish ministers on behalf of a reasonable and modernized antiquities law. Foreign expeditions could not go on indefinitely finding the Turks monuments without receiving anything in return.[6]

Breasted, of course, was not the only American archaeologist anxious to establish good relations with the diplomats. Three months after Breasted lunched with Murray, Ohio state senator Robert A. Taft wrote to President Hoover, seeking a letter of introduction to Ambassador Grew for Professor William Semple, who hoped to obtain a permit for the University of Cincinnati to excavate at Troy. In this age of relatively small government and intimate relations between officials and private citizens, such contacts were common. After all, the archaeologist carried the American flag to distant regions where there was no official U.S. representation; he was a chosen instrument, neither wholly public official nor private citizen but a mixture of both.[7]

Von der Osten had become involved in his own diplomatic maneuvers at the highest levels of the republic, proving that even foreigners could become instruments of American policy. This episode, which proved the high point of Von der Osten's career with the institute, came not at Alişar but in a series of events at Ankara. At the end of April 1930, he left New York on the SS *Europa* bound for Bremerhaven. After paying courtesy calls in Berlin to the leading archaeologists of the day, among them Walter Andrae, Ernst Herzfeld, and Julius Jordan, and examining recent finds from Assur in northern Iraq, he set out by train for Istanbul. There, too, he made the requisite rounds, calling on Halil Ethem, whose influence, although declining in the world of Turkish archaeology, could not be overlooked. By mid-May he was back in Ankara and soon meeting with several of Mustafa Kemal's closest advisors at their request. They questioned him closely about the work at Alişar and his experiences in Turkey, and two days later he received an invitation to dine with the president at his home in Çankaya. The invitation was both unexpected and unusual, for Von der Osten was being invited into the inner sanctum of the republic, a place where few Turks, let alone foreigners, could enter. The invitation revealed how intensely interested the president had become in matters of history and archaeology.[8]

Von der Osten has left a detailed account of the events of that long-ago evening, from the greeting by Tefik Bey, chief of the cabinet, at 7:00 P.M. to his departure sometime after 2:00 A.M. The president welcomed him cordially. With him were several university professors and one of his adopted daughters, Afet Hanum (Afet Inan), a teacher, who was becoming a leading advocate of the new historical thesis. After some preliminary talk, in the library, the Gazi began to expound almost uninterrupted for one and a half hours his ideas of early Turkish history and its importance in the development of peoples in the Mediterranean basin. Von der Osten was impressed with how much he knew, especially about recent archaeological work in Central Asia, but he thought that "many of his statements were erroneous, being based on impossible philological deductions." These ideas had obviously been confirmed by amateur linguists or those who wished to flatter him.[9]

When asked his opinion, Von der Osten very cautiously corrected a few mistaken ideas but generally argued that acceptance of such an extensive theory should "at least be corroborated in some instances by archaeological evidence." The others in the room became visibly uncomfortable at his frank responses, but the president seemed to accept them, as he made notes and asked him to suggest reading material. He finished by asking his visitor to read over a manuscript on the subject, probably "The Outline of Turkish History," and to make notes on it for him.[10]

By the time they adjourned to the dining room around 11:00 P.M., almost the entire cabinet had assembled. It was 2:00 A.M. when the president finally left the table. During the extended meal, the Gazi expressed great interest in the American way of life, and Von der Osten concluded from this and other statements that he wished to model the new Turkey on U.S. patterns, which he considered "a step higher up the ladder of development than those of Europe."[11]

Before the end of the evening the president asked if Von der Osten could undertake a small excavation near Ankara as he would like to see them at work, and the archaeologist agreed. When the president expressed interest in having more foreign expeditions in Turkey, his guest seized the opportunity to speak in favor of a change in the antiquities law to allow for some division of finds. The president again took notes, assuring him that he now intended to give much more attention to important cultural questions. Von der Osten came away from the evening much impressed with this "great man," whom he felt was a lonely modernizer far ahead of his associates in his vision for a new Turkey.[12]

The following day Von der Osten consulted with U.S. Chargé d'Affaires Jefferson Patterson regarding the request for a sample excavation. They agreed that Von der Osten would have to ignore his "strict orders" from Chicago to work only at Alişar that year, for it would be a serious mistake to turn down the president. He decided to excavate at Giaour Kalessi (Gavurkale), a small Hittite religious site approximately sixty kilometers southwest of Ankara, which he knew well from an earlier visit.[13]

Giaour Kalessi, a rocky outcrop rising some two hundred feet above the floor of a narrow, grassy valley, had rock-cut reliefs of Hittite deities and a later Phrygian burial chamber. It was reached by a dirt track all but impassable to vehicles after heavy rain. Von der Osten would have to hope for clear skies. Even then access over the hilly terrain would not be easy. Nevertheless, he managed to bring in his workers and equipment and on

**Figure 3.1.** Von der Osten greets Atatürk at Gavurkale (Giaour Kalessi), May 1930. Courtesy of the Oriental Institute of the University of Chicago.

May 23 they set to work, surrounded by flocks of grazing sheep, eyed suspiciously by guard dogs with spiked collars to protect them from wolves, watched by friendly, inquisitive shepherds.

One week later the president arrived with his entourage. For several hours he clambered over the rocks to get a good look at all the important features of the location, all the while asking historical and technical questions. Later he gave members of his staff who did not understand French a brief summary of the expedition's work. After tea he departed very pleased with the visit, despite what must have been a difficult journey. The following day the expedition members packed up and set off for Alişar via Ankara.[14]

Von der Osten felt a sense of relief at what he had accomplished. Perhaps this would put him momentarily ahead of the competition, especially the French and the Germans, who were always trying to gain advantages in Turkey. Both had established archaeological institutes in Istanbul, and Von der Osten would have welcomed a similar commitment from Breasted.

He was particularly concerned about the activities of the French—perhaps this was a carryover of suspicion from World War I—assuring Chicago that they had ambitious political aims in the country. As a precaution, Von der Osten had informed the British, French, and Germans that the Americans were interested in several sites in central Anatolia, especially Arslan Tepe near Malatya, where Erich Schmidt had already completed a survey. He hoped this announcement would serve as a guarantee against poaching, but he was to be disappointed. Professor Louis Delaporte, working through his ambassador, and reportedly using a copy of the Americans' own map, asked the Gazi for a permit for the site, which was granted. Von der Osten was furious, noting to Breasted that Delaporte had openly broken the international gentlemen's agreement to respect primary rights of either probed or discovered sites. He had little respect for the French, claiming that Delaporte was too old and inexperienced to be in the field and that he cut trenches through various levels without even recognizing them.[15]

Although some of these accusations may have been exaggerated, Breasted gladly took up the attack. He claimed to have encountered similar behavior from the French throughout the region, in Syria, Egypt, and Iran, and he took it upon himself to warn the State Department of "the kind of thing of which our French friends do not hesitate to be guilty in their scientific relations with other nations in the Near East." He went on to explain that their antagonistic attitude was not limited to politics, as at the recent disarmament conference in London, but extended "throughout the whole range of international relations."[16]

The loss of Arslan Tepe was the last straw, and despite Von der Osten's best efforts and the government's decision to make Breasted an honorary member of the Association for the Study of Turkish History, Breasted decided to end the excavation work at Alişar after the 1932 season and to withdraw completely from Turkey. The first decision did not come as a surprise to the German, who knew that Breasted expected major results there or the work would be halted. Breasted had earlier criticized the German's administration at Alişar as disastrous and had given him one final chance to prove himself. The second decision shocked Von der Osten, who had pictured himself heading another institute excavation somewhere else in Hittite country.[17]

Who can say how much Von der Osten's reputation as a heavy drinker influenced decision making in Chicago. Certainly he did not try to hide his taste for alcohol. He told students at Ankara University that he had had two donkeys at Alişar, one to carry water and the other to carry raki, the licorice-flavored spirits of Turkey. In an interview with an American official "he recommended late alcoholic evenings as the only way of getting the Turks to open up and of really knowing what is happening." This may explain in part why the Gazi, who had a similar appetite, found the German such good company.[18]

But above all, financial worries plagued Breasted in these early years of the Great Depression. Although he could still rely on Rockefeller support, funds from other donors were drying up; this was the same for archaeology everywhere. The accounts from Alişar were constantly in the red. Von der Osten had charged the cost of the work at Giaour Kalessi to the institute, without getting permission first from the director, who read about it in the newspaper. The following year he had assisted the government at a small excavation near Yozgat; this time, at least, he had received Breasted's grudging approval.[19]

The Turkish government, despite Von der Osten's good works, refused to share any antiquities with the Americans. In frustration, Breasted had written to Hamit Koşay, the new director of antiquities, to make the case one last time for a share of the ancient artifacts. They would, he claimed, "serve as a very desirable type of propaganda, reminding the Western world of the ancient background of civilization in Anatolia." This was all to no avail. Each tantalizing hint of a new, more generous antiquities law came to nothing. Turkey was the only nation in the region, aside from Greece, that did not share finds with expeditions, and Breasted decided to move the institute's operations to more promising lands.[20]

Breasted always found Von der Osten difficult to control. He thought he was all along preparing for his own future and using the institute to smooth his way. In August 1931 he wrote to Charles, "Without doubt Osten is playing his own private game. It would not surprise me to see him eventually taking a job with the Turks."[21]

The director knew his man. In 1935 Von der Osten was invited to teach at newly established Ankara University in its faculty of languages, history, and geography; here he continued until World War II, despite his lack of formal academic credentials. At the request of the Turkish Historical Society, he excavated the Roman baths and the Temple of Rome and Augustus in Ankara, where he supervised students from the university. After Atatürk died in 1938, Von der Osten's fortunes took a turn for the worse. When he became deeply involved in pro-Nazi activities, Turkish officials distanced themselves. During the war, President Ismet Inönü had him interned in the old hospital building next to the university, thereby showing his determination to keep Turkey neutral. After the war the irrepressible Von der Osten ended his days excavating happily in neighboring Iran.[22]

The Oriental Institute left Turkey at the very moment when many new developments in archaeology were under way there, some of which the institute itself had encouraged. It had, for example, contributed to the blossoming of interest in the Hittites, until this period a little-known empire that had ruled over much of Anatolia and the Fertile Crescent in the second millennium B.C.E. Its work at Alişar and Giaour Kalessi had received prominent coverage in the nationalist newspapers.

It was the Germans, of course, who deserved a full measure of credit for expanding knowledge of this ancient empire. Since 1906 they had excavated for long periods at Boğazköy, the Hittite capital in central Anatolia, an inspiring site built high above the plain on a terrace surrounding a number of immense rocky outcrops. After the first successful translation of the Hittite language in 1915, German scholars revealed much about this almost forgotten people.

All these investigations fed the nationalist belief that there had been a great civilization in Anatolia and that Westerners had unfairly ignored—or purposely suppressed—information about its contributions, pointing instead to the great debt owed to Egypt and especially to Greece and Rome. Expanding knowledge led to ever more extravagant claims, that the Hittites had been Turks, that other great civilizations developed from Turkish roots. Sometimes Westerners inadvertently contributed to these historical myths. In a 1926 radio address, for example, Professor Kelsey spoke of the people of central Anatolia whose ancestry probably went back to the time of the apostles or farther still to the people of Hittite times. In a booklet printed in 1928, an editor at the Oriental Institute wrote of connections between the Hittites and our own ancestry, concluding that "such exploration will carry us back along the trail of our own westward-moving ancestors."[23]

It should have come as no surprise when popularizers of such ideas made connections in a most straightforward and unscientific manner. The editor of the journal *Ankara* wrote, "The Hittite civilization . . . is nothing other than the civilization . . . of the Turks. . . . The Hittites are the brothers of the race of Sumerians. . . . The men who established themselves on the coast of the Aegean Sea and in the neighboring regions of the West are also of the same origins and the same race. . . . The objects found in the Egyptian tombs prove that Egyptian civilization came under the profound influence of Hittite civilization." Later the same editor praised the men of great culture who headed the republic and attached so much importance to archaeological excavations that "touch very closely to the history of our race." Something of a craze swept over Turkey during the

1930s, with banks and businesses taking Hittite or Sumerian names; and when it became mandatory to adopt a family name, some individual Turks followed suit.[24]

Although Turkish officials issued excavation permits to Europeans and Americans, they wanted well-trained archaeologists of their own to reveal the nation's past. Atatürk insisted on this after returning from a tour of inspection to Ephesus and Pergamon, where foreigners were busily at work. To make this a reality, the government began sending small numbers of students to Germany and France for training. One of the first, Remzi Oğuz Arik, studied at the Sorbonne from 1927 to 1931 on a government scholarship, returning to serve as commissioner at Professor Carl Blegen's excavation at Troy (University of Cincinnati, 1932–1938), then excavating for the Turkish Historical Society in Ankara and in 1935 beginning work at the Bronze Age/Hittite site of Alacahöyük. Two famous archaeologists, with long and successful careers, Ekrem Akurgal and Sedat Alp, studied in Germany (1932–1940), returning during the summers to Turkey to work at various sites. Akurgal claimed that he received a government scholarship because he was so well informed about the new historical thesis. While in Germany, Alp received a letter from Reçit Galip, minister of public instruction, urging him to study ancient history and archaeology; he did and became a leading Hittitologist.[25]

After 1935 the Turkish government began to make other arrangements, made possible in part by Hitler's rise to power in Germany. As the Nazis tightened restrictions on Jews and on those married to Jews, it became more difficult for them to work in the Third Reich. Atatürk took advantage of this situation to invite many Jewish scholars to teach in Turkey. Over twelve hundred of them came. Among those attracted to Ankara University were Hans Güterbock, a Hittitologist, and Benno Landsberger, a specialist in the ancient languages of Mesopotamia. They remained until the late 1940s, when they both went on to the Oriental Institute. Now, for the first time, Turkish students could receive advanced archaeological training at home.[26]

At the same time the program of the Republican People's Party, the sole political party, made a commitment to the study of Turkey's past. Importance was to be attached to collecting historical objects in order to enrich the nation's museums. For this purpose, it declared, "we shall undertake excavations, classify the works of antiquity, and preserve them where they stand, if necessary." In the spirit of this announcement, Turkish experts undertook their first major excavation, at Alacahöyük. Arik started the work and was soon joined by Hamit Koşay. After his training in Hungary

**Figure 3.2.** Hittite sphinx (and storks) at the city gate of Alacahöyük (c. 1930). Michael Ivanovich Rostovtzeff papers, Manuscripts and Archives, Yale University Library.

as an ethnographer, Koşay had worked his way up through the Ministry of Public Instruction, which had oversight of antiquities. He became director of antiquities in 1931, replacing Halil Ethem, who was given a seat in parliament. The new director worked hard and won the respect of this first generation of archaeologists.[27]

The excavation had considerable success, unearthing undisturbed tombs dating back to the Bronze Age (c. 2100 B.C.E) before the appearance of the Hittites. They had found one of the most valuable artistic treasures of ancient times, including fascinating works of gold, silver, and bronze. News of their discoveries sent shivers of excitement and pride through the nationalist ranks in Ankara.[28]

A high-level delegation was dispatched to Alacahöyük to congratulate the discoverers and to take possession of the sacred objects, which were carried immediately to Çankaya for Atatürk's careful inspection. They were then placed on public display. The discoveries aroused a passionate interest throughout Turkey, and Afet Inan organized a conference on the excavation to inspire the new Turk, the child of the republic. At Atatürk's suggestion the government ordered the restoration of two fifteenth-century buildings to make a suitable home in the capital for these and other ancient relics from throughout Turkey. The first section of the remarkable Museum of Anatolian Civilization opened in 1943.[29]

With rising interest, officials became concerned for the safety of archaeological sites. It would be necessary, they knew, to educate the public to their responsibilities. Addressing himself to the people's community centers established throughout the country, Hamit Koşay spoke of each individual as a voluntary guard for the national treasure. Atatürk explained that it was necessary that "the people themselves who were the real owners of the historical and national monuments become the protectors of antiquities." His daughter echoed these sentiments, adding that there was a moral obligation for citizens of the republic not to traffic in antiquities, "for that which is being sold is their own history, their own personality, and that is an unpardonable crime." Their protection must be considered by each man "a national duty."[30]

There was also concern that local authorities, without understanding, might destroy artistic masterworks in the name of urban reconstruction and progress. They could unthinkingly erase the evidence that the Turks had been highly civilized through the ages. By what right, challenged one Istanbul editor, did religious authorities demolish an ancient mosque, without first consulting the commission on historical monuments? Foreign museums, he acknowledged, would pay handsomely for what had survived the demolition, and all would be lost to Turkey.[31]

The director of antiquities found added reason to promote the study of archaeology. Turkish experts in this discipline would ensure that foreign scholars would not deceive them as they had in the past. Archaeology, he declared was as much a mission of the state "as the affairs of tobacco and fig." Atatürk agreed, urging then–Prime Minister Inönü to see that more students were trained in archaeology. The Ministry of Public Instruction regularly sent circulars to the schools providing guidelines on how to interest students in antiquities and encouraging teachers to organize field trips to local museums and archaeological sites. The syllabi for

Turkish schools encouraged such visits as part of the cultivation of a conscious link between schoolchildren and their ancient forebears.[32]

The culmination of Atatürk's campaign to instill confidence in the Turks and to gain respect for their accomplishments throughout history came in September 1937 at the second conference of the Turkish Historical Society in Istanbul. Ankara of the 1930s could offer no such grand venue as the Dolmabaçe Palace, the nineteenth-century residence of the Ottoman sultans on the European shore of the Bosphorus. Its grand hall with marble pillars and crystal chandeliers provided the perfect meeting place for what was to be an impressive international gathering. Unlike the first conference in 1932, leading scholars from Europe and the United States were expected to attend, and to encourage them, officials let it be known that the future of foreign expeditions in Turkey would be largely determined by how enthusiastically they supported the congress. The hope, of course, was that they might be convinced to endorse the historical thesis, which had become dogma to many in Turkey.[33]

Great effort went into preparations, and Von der Osten was drafted to assist the organizers. In honor of the conference, a special stamp was issued picturing the famous stag excavated at Alacahöyük. Atatürk took a close interest in all the arrangements, reading every paper, it was said. He attended a number of sessions and urged cabinet members, deputies, and other officials to do the same. Attached to the conference hall was a large historical exhibition showing different periods in Anatolian history. The popular display cases were filled with many artifacts on loan from museums in Europe and the United States. Large maps accompanied the displays, emphasizing Anatolia as the cradle of civilization. The displays remained open to the public for months and then were reassembled in Ankara.[34]

The distinguished foreign attendance pleased the government. Germany had by far the largest delegation, indicating both the extent of its excavation in Turkey and Turkey's strategic importance, perhaps, to the leaders of the Third Reich. Delegations came also from Britain, France, the nations of eastern and central Europe, the United States, and elsewhere.

Lest anyone mistake the central purpose of the conference, Afet Inan had been selected to open and close the gathering. She prefaced her remarks by praising the work of the Turkish Historical Society of which she was a founding member. She declared that it was not enough for Turks to understand that Anatolia had always been Turkish but that they must make the scientific world understand this also. One way to do this was to obtain the material for Turkish history by every path and every means. "In first place," she announced, "come archaeological excavations." [35]

Once the participants had gathered, there was little overt pressure on them to adopt publicly the official history; most of them praised the recent accomplishments of the Turks. None was more effusive than the Swiss anthropologist Eugene Pittard, Afet Inan's mentor at the University of Geneva, who made his remarks near the end of the formal proceedings and came close to a full endorsement of the historical thesis. As self-appointed spokesman for his colleagues, he acknowledged the debt to the Turks, declaring, "The Europeans who are here have come back to the land of their ancestors, and it is like a pilgrimage that we are making to your home my Turkish friends. It is for us an obligation, I will say even a pious duty, to thank you for having been our ancestors." [36]

Not every observer was so respectful. The American consul wrote to Carl Blegen, describing the congress as "a lot of hot air" at which, of course, "Homer was a Turk!" And yet despite the criticism, the historical thesis, or at least important elements of it, had taken root among the Turkish population, and foreign writers now approached the subject with more care and thoughtfulness than would have been true just a few years earlier.[37]

Just how effective the government's campaign had been could be seen decades later when the then–prime minister, Turgut Özal (1927–1993), published *Turkey in Europe* (1988) to justify his country's membership in the European Community. In those pages are resurrected many of the arguments of the historical thesis outlined above that he would have imbibed as a young student in the 1930s.[38]

It should be noted that although some of this was bad history, it was not merely chauvinistic. Atatürk talked about cultural unity among peoples. There was an emphasis on the contributions Turks had made over the ages to humanity and a call for future Turkish generations to renew this commitment. On the first page of the new official history, it was written that the aim for Turks should be to make great contributions to humanity, which would provide them an honored place in history. These were the values to be taught to schoolchildren.[39]

As the second congress came to a successful conclusion in Istanbul, far away in the southeast, in the sanjak of Alexandretta, or the Hatay as the Turks called it, long-simmering tensions were reaching a crisis point. Here came together conflicting ideas on the history of the region, the role of

Western expeditions, the linkages between politics and archaeology. The prize was not only territory but also some of the finest antiquities of the ancient world.

The sanjak, a strip of territory sixty miles from north to south and forty miles at its widest, lay in the extreme northeastern corner of the Mediterranean between the North Syrian Plain and Turkey's Çukarova Plain. It was a narrow coastal plain, backed by a range of rugged peaks up to seven thousand feet, on the eastern slopes of which lay the lower valley of the Orontes River, flowing through the historic city of Antioch. Both its chief port, Alexandretta (Iskanderun), and its capital, Antioch, had extensive economic links with nearby Aleppo in Syria.

Peoples of various cultures had met and interacted here for thousands of years, and the complex mix of the population reflected this. Turks, Arabs, Kurds, Armenians and Circassians, Muslims, Christians, and Jews inhabited this borderland, quite peacefully, it would seem, until the messages of competing nationalisms began to agitate the local population. Statistics are notoriously unreliable, but most observers agree that the Turks were the largest ethnic community (40 percent) in the sanjak but did not constitute a majority, nor were they unified initially in wanting to join the republic.[40]

Although the sanjak was part of the French mandate of Syria, Paris and Ankara had agreed that it would be allowed some administrative and economic, if not political, autonomy and that the rights of Turks would be protected. The nationalists considered its future carefully. In 1920 the Turkish assembly had included the Hatay as part of the republic, and the government claimed that a majority of the population was Turkish. As early as 1921 Atatürk told a delegation from Antioch that "a land that has been Turkish for four thousand years cannot live a prisoner in the hands of the enemy."[41]

The government in Ankara considered the Hatay traditionally Turkish, and the expansion of knowledge about the Hittites and their empire, which had extended well into northern Syria, fed Turkish irredentism. The term itself—Hatay—had been coined only recently to remind the Turks of the connection to the Hittites, their proud ancestors, according to the prevailing thesis. Any discovery of Hittite artifacts there seemed to confirm to Turkish nationalists that this land should be theirs. It provided an excellent example of using the past "to legitimize the present needs of the state."[42]

Long after the disappearance of the Hittites, when Rome and then Byzantium ruled, the area had prospered, and great temples and villas stood in Antioch, its suburb, Daphne, and the coastal city of Seleucia. The grand structures were gone, but some of the finest mosaic floors of the classical world remained. These, along with a few Hittite sites, drew many Western archaeologists to the sanjak after World War I.

They also came because the rules governing foreign archaeologists were certainly more generous than those in neighboring Turkey. Mandate authorities allowed a division of antiquities at the end of each season, with the provision that certain unique objects must go directly to the local museums and were not subject to division.

These end-of-season events were enormously important to foreign archaeologists, whose success in the field was often judged by the quality of antiquities brought home. One of the best accounts of a division comes from Agatha Christie's autobiography, *Come Tell Me How You Live*, in which she relates an experience in the late 1930s, when her husband, archaeologist Max Mallowan, was excavating near the Euphrates River in Syria:

> The burning moment of "The Division" is now drawing near. . . . It is left to Max to arrange everything found in two parts exactly as he pleases. . . . The real agony lies in making the two collections. . . . We all get called in to help. . . . "Now which of these two would you take? A or B?" Pause whilst I study the two. "I'd take B." "You would?" "B's evidently too strong." In the end we lose all sense of value. . . .
>
> At last the fateful day arrives. . . . Max is taking one last agonized look at the two shares spread out for display on long tables. . . . We lead him firmly away.
>
> All is over! The Division has taken place. M. and Madame Dunand [representatives of the antiquities service] have examined, handled, reflected. We have stood looking on in the usual agony. Then he flings a hand out . . . "Eh, bien, I will take this one." True to human nature, whichever half is chosen, we immediately wish it had been the other.[43]

Whether is was A or B, of course, mattered little to officials at home as long as the sponsoring museum received its fair share.

In the early postwar years American officials were anxious to maintain the open door in the Middle East, not only to guarantee access to oil, a subject that has been well documented, but also in every sphere of activity, including archaeological excavation. U. S. diplomats, for example, became concerned that the French were setting up a monopoly in their Syrian mandate when in January 1927 Dr. Ephraim Avigdor Speiser (1902–1965) was refused permission to dig at a site in northern Syria near the Iraqi border. The State Department urged Professor George A. Barton, head of the American Schools of Oriental Research, and Speiser to complain, which they did, with the assistance of Paul Knabenshue, the energetic American consul in Beirut. The French relented and gave Speiser the concession.[44]

Shortly thereafter a new director of antiquities, Henri Seyrig, was appointed. He served from 1929 to 1942 and exercised a firm command over archaeological affairs in the mandate. Known for his fairness, knowledge, and dedication, he was widely liked and respected. This was important, especially in the 1930s, when nationalism was on the rise in Iraq and Turkey and foreign excavators from many countries flocked to Syria.

Turkey's loss was Syria's gain. The Turks, of course, welcomed foreign expeditions — but on their own strict terms. President Walter Wright of Robert College, Istanbul, a friend of Hamit Koşay, reported to John Wilson, Breasted's successor as head of the Oriental Institute, a recent conversation with the director of antiquities. Koşay expressed a strong desire for the institute to return to Turkey and wondered why they had left Alişar. Wilson told Wright that the major reason was financial; however, he added, a contributing factor was the prohibition against exporting antiquities. "While it is perfectly true," he reported, "that we are looking for information rather than objects, we can get both in other countries and therefore have shifted our base for Hittite work into Syria."[45]

By the end of 1936 Western excavation was booming in Syria, especially in the sanjak. In addition to the Oriental Institute at Rihanie, Leonard Woolley, who had worked with Hogarth and Lawrence at Carchemish before World War I and later made the celebrated discoveries at Ur in Iraq in 1927, now represented the British Museum at Seleucia. It was rumored that Sir Flinders Petrie of Egypt fame and John Garstang, noted Hittitologist, who had originally sought the concession at Boğazköy that went instead to the Germans in 1906, were also coming.

Perhaps most important of all the expeditions was the Committee for the Excavation of Antioch and Vicinity (CEAV), a consortium of several institutions, including Princeton University, the Worcester (Mass.) Museum of Fine Arts, the Baltimore Museum of Fine Afts, Dumbarton Oaks, the Fogg Museum of Art, and the National Museums of France (the Louvre). Their principal objective was room-size mosaics of stunning beauty and artistry. To encourage Worcester's participation, the president of American University Beirut, Bayard Dodge, had written to the director there about the likelihood of excellent returns for his museum. As an

**Figure 3.3.** Oberlin students cleaning "The Hunt" in the entrance hall of the Worcester Museum of Art, 1978. Put in place in the late 1930s, the mosaic had come from the museum's share of the Antioch expedition. Courtesy Worcester Museum of Art.

added incentive, he wrote, "I feel certain that the presence of an expedition will start the peasants digging and bring in many objects for sale from the surrounding countryside."[46]

The archaeologists were well aware of the advantages the mandate offered. After an especially successful year, William Campbell of Wellesley College, site director for CEAV, wrote to the director of the Worcester Museum of Fine Arts congratulating him on the "rich haul" from Antioch and expressing his firm belief that that ancient city and its environs was the one remaining center of importance "from which objects of art can be secured for museums by excavation." In years that their share was substantial, members agreed to sell part of it to cover future excavation expenses.[47]

Unfortunately, this opportunity, too, might soon pass away. The Syrian nationalists had entered negotiations in Paris looking to end the mandate. What this would mean for foreign excavators, no one seemed to know. The curator of Oriental antiquities at the Louvre, René Dussaud, a noted archaeologist, who had organized the Syrian Antiquities Department after the war, feared the worst, and he shared his concern with the Americans. He hinted at calamity and urged Professor C. R. Morey, head of CEAV, John Wilson of the Oriental Institute, and others to seek the active intervention of the U.S. government to protect their interests. He assured Morey that the French government would welcome such intervention, presumably to strengthen its hand with the nationalists.[48]

Knowing that in France government officials and archaeologists worked closely together and that such an appeal probably had been sanctioned by the Quai d'Orsay, the American directors took Dussaud's warning seriously, quickly passing it on to the State Department. Morey cited all the standard arguments designed to elicit action in Washington. He explained to Secretary of State Cordell Hull that the funds necessary for foreign excavations were made available only on condition that institutions advancing money would receive a share of the objects found. For Baltimore and Worcester, this was a legal requirement of their charters. Should the law in Syria change, forbidding export of antiquities, the funds would stop, bringing an end to the progress of archaeology there as far as American scholarship was concerned. This would be a tragic loss as so much progress had recently been made in understanding the ancient civilizations of this "terra incognita." Furthermore, if the nationalists succeeded in denying export, others throughout the Middle East might soon follow suit. Antiquities installed in local Eastern museums, he added, were far less useful in disseminating information than objects installed in Europe and America, where they would also be better protected. Several months later Wallace Murray wrote to assure both Morey and Wilson that the French government was in favor of retaining the present antiquities regulations in Syria. The crisis seemed to have passed when the treaty talks fell apart. France remained in Syria until 1946.[49]

Paradoxically, the Oriental Institute was on the point of withdrawing completely from Syria in 1936. Seyrig could not understand this decision, he confided to U.S. Consul Theodore Marriner, for it would have a negative effect on American prestige in the region and, what might have been the director's real concern, would allow some other nation, presumably Germany, to take over from the institute.[50]

Spurred by the concerns of the diplomats and his own desire to reap the benefits of earlier efforts, Wilson sent a letter to John D. Rockefeller Jr. urgently seeking additional funds. He warned that the situation in the sanjak would soon change, closing the door to the export of antiquities, and "it is clear therefore that digging in North Syria must be done now." His appeal brought additional funds from Rockefeller that enabled the institute to continue its work there into the early years of the war.[51]

As political tensions in the sanjak mounted, archaeologists and diplomats became nervous. From Princeton, Donald Wilber, an expert on the region, cautioned Campbell against any public display of the antiquities that had been discovered. This, he claimed, would only arouse nationalist feelings. The new U.S. ambassador in Ankara, John Van Antwerp Mac-Murray (served 1936–1941), had similar concerns, reporting to the consul at Beirut that an article in the Turkish press had accused French and American archaeologists of taking Hittite treasures from the Hatay. In light of the strong possessive feeling Turks had cultivated for the Hittites and all their works, said MacMurray, it was possible this could lead to increased resentment. He wondered if there was any truth to the charge.[52]

Professor Philip Hitti, noted Lebanese American historian of the Middle East, visited the sanjak briefly. He reported that members of the Princeton excavation had been inundated with Arabic propaganda literature against the Turkification of the sanjak and cautioned Morey that they should keep their distance from local politics.[53]

Unfortunately, everything they did was political. Some saw them as treasure hunters; others believed they favored one side or the other in the increasingly vocal struggle for control of the sanjak. The casual observer might caution them to keep their distance, but this was well nigh impossible. And to make matters worse, the archaeologists did not always understand just how political their activities were. The records are full of sincere statements disclaiming any interest or desire to meddle in local affairs, and yet to do archaeology in the Middle East in those years, amid the swirl of nationalist movements and competing ideologies, was to enter the vortex.

Turkey claimed the Hatay as part of the "Hittite Biblical Kingdom of Anatolia." With its lofty mountains running north and south along the Mediterranean shore, the territory would serve as an ideal barrier to any force seeking to penetrate the great Çukarova Plain surrounding the city of Adana, an important grain-producing region of southeastern Turkey. Ankara might temporarily tolerate an autonomous Hatay but not its incorporation into an independent Syria. In practical terms, however, the region could not survive on its own, for it depended economically on neighboring regions in Turkey and Syria.

The Turkish campaign for the Hatay increased as Europe headed toward war. Turkish newspapers and books, which were widely available in the sanjak, promoted official policy. Ethnic Turks had relatives across the

**Figure 3.4.** Parade in Antioch (1938) celebrating the fifteenth anniversary of the establishment of the Republic of Turkey. The sanjak was still nominally part of the Syrian Mandate. Courtesy National Archives.

border; many of their children studied in universities there as well. Members of the Turkish Youth Sports Club and the People's House in Antioch, both of which received funding from Ankara, became advocates for annexation. The People's House was set up as a center to spread nationalist and secularist ideas through lectures, courses, and exhibitions. Within Turkey, the Society for the Independence of Hatay was secretly established by the government to oversee communications between Ankara and the People's House. Although Arab nationalist sentiment in the sanjak grew in response to the rise of nationalist fervor among the Turks, the Arabs had no outside support comparable to that of the Republic of Turkey.[54]

The die was cast in March 1938 at Geneva when the French promised the Turks a majority of twenty-two seats of a total of forty in the soon-to-be-elected assembly. Atatürk left nothing to chance, massing thirty thousand troops along the border with Syria. Despite his rapidly failing health, he made one last visit to Adana in late May to put pressure on France. On July 5, 1938, following signing of the Franco-Turkish friendship treaty, and with French agreement, Turkish troops entered the sanjak. On July 23, 1939, Turkey annexed the region, completing the boundaries of Atatürk's republic.[55]

The annexation led to a mass exodus into Syria of fifty thousand non-Turkish refugees, the largest number of whom were Armenians, who had originally fled from Cilicia. Such was the price Paris was prepared to pay to keep Ankara neutral in the coming conflict. The Syrians have never officially accepted the transfer of territory.[56]

How did the archaeologists fare during these fateful months when their fears were being realized? They were chiefly concerned about maintaining their excavation rights under the new regime. Early in 1938, just after the Geneva agreement, Bayard Dodge wrote to Campbell, urging him to get his valuable objects out of the sanjak without delay. Seyrig made the same recommendation. Dodge offered his campus as temporary storehouse for the antiquities. As news of the approaching Turkish occupation spread, near-panic seized much of the population. Campbell, following advice, called in Seyrig for a hurried division. Then, of course, he had "to get the stuff out." He agreed to exchange the Buffet Supper, a magnificent third-century Roman mosaic, now a prized possession of the Antioch Museum, because he did not have time to get it out of the ground.[57]

On receiving the latest news from Campbell, Morey turned again to Secretary Hull, requesting him to intervene with the French authorities on behalf of American archaeological interests in the sanjak. One month before annexation the French ambassador in Ankara informed his American counterpart that the Turkish government had agreed to recognize the validity of the archaeological concessions negotiated earlier with the French high commissioner.[58]

Before this agreement had been concluded, the excavators were exposed to a flood of local criticism from Turkish nationalists. A deputy in the Hatay parliament claimed that the expeditions had cheated the state and had taken away all the beautiful and worthwhile antiquities, leaving only inferior objects for the local museum. Other members agreed, with one arguing that if the expeditions continued, everything should be kept in the Hatay just as was done in Turkey.[59]

Campbell remained skeptical about what might happen in the territory. Leonard Woolley, he knew, had returned to Seleucia in 1939, but he was already looking for a new site as a precaution. Woolley and the Turkish government were not on the best of terms because of differences concerning his earlier work at Carchemish. He charged that the Turks did not take proper care of the monuments, that soldiers had used the reliefs of

Hittite gods for target practice; the Turks hinted of improper removal of antiquities and of encouragement given to Kurdish nationalists. Furthermore, after their victory over the British at Kut (Iraq) in 1915, the Turks had taken Woolley prisoner, along with many of his fellow soldiers. This wartime experience must have contributed to the general antagonism in their postwar relations.[60]

Campbell's worries were more immediate. He needed all his patience and powers of persuasion, it turned out, to bring the 1939 division to successful conclusion. Everything had started amicably enough when the new director of the Antioch Museum, Ruhi Tekardağ, had accepted group A, the government's half of the antiquities, leaving Campbell group B. Then annexation took place, and Campbell needed approval from Ankara to ship his share to Beirut. Permission did not arrive, and the American decided to visit responsible officials in the capital to expedite matters. Representatives in the Foreign Ministry and the minister of public instruction himself assured Campbell that the division would soon be approved. But clearly there was a problem, and he soon discovered the source. The director of antiquities, Hamit Koşay, adamantly opposed the settlement. Koşay, a staunch nationalist, had for years rejected the notion that any antiquities should leave the republic, regardless of circumstances, and he now offered a seemingly endless series of challenges to the validity of Campbell's concession and the recent division. Apparently, the Foreign Ministry, anxious to complete the friendship treaty with France and bring about the annexation of the Hatay, had accepted the concessions and had pressed the minister to agree. No one had thought to consult Koşay.[61]

The resourceful Campbell contacted the American, British, and French embassies to get them to increase pressure on the Foreign Ministry. Later that same day he renewed his sparring with Koşay, who became angry and stormed out of his own office, saying that nothing could be decided until he had seen the antiquities himself. Campbell followed him into the street and announced that he would stay in Ankara until Koşay was ready to travel to Antioch.[62]

The following day the director of antiquities, obviously under great pressure from the Foreign Ministry and his nominal superior, the minister of public instruction, changed his tone and told the American he would leave that evening for Antioch to make the supplementary division. Remzi Arik joined them for the long train journey across the plateau, through the mountains, and down into the plain beyond. Relations among the three of them became quite amiable as the hours passed, and after a few days of sightseeing together in Antioch, the Turkish officials approved the original division with only one change. Then they wired Ankara for the export permit. By the time they left for Ankara on August 28 it had still not arrived, but the U.S. embassy kept up its efforts, and despite other more urgent matters associated with the outbreak of war in Europe, President İnönü and the Council of Ministers signed the necessary papers.[63]

With considerable effort made more difficult by the recent confiscation of all private vehicles and the rationing of gasoline in the mandate, Campbell finally got the antiquities to American University Beirut, then promptly embarked for the United States. This would be the last shipment of mosaics from the Hatay to grace American museums. It was mid-September 1939.[64]

Atatürk would surely have approved of Koşay's determined stand, which had characterized government policy since the beginning of the republic. The Gazi had died just ten months earlier, throwing the country into a national period of mourning. He had willed much of his estate to further the archaeological work of the Turkish Historical Society, which he had founded. His body was temporarily laid to rest in a grave at Ankara's Ethnological Museum, where Koşay had once served as director. A splendid mausoleum was being prepared as a final resting place. It took fifteen years to complete.

Atatürk's passing elicited countless valedictories praising various aspects of his epic career; among these, many emphasized his contribution to Turkish nationalism through devotion to history and archaeology. According to one of Turkey's leading archaeologists, Tahsin Özgüç, who as a student at Ankara University in the late 1930s was taught by Güterbock, Von der Osten, Remzi Arik, and Afet Inan and attended the second Turkish historical congress and saw Atatürk, "The importance that Atatürk has accorded to archaeology does not come solely from the interest that he had in science, but also from his nationalist sentiments. These facts make it difficult to separate Atatürk from archaeology in Turkey." He gave it a permanent place alongside history.[65]

# 4. EGYPT AWAKENING

Even those who are generally unfamiliar with the ancient history of the Middle East and of wondrous sites at Boğazköy, Ur, or Persepolis will quickly recognize pictures of the wonders of the Nile Valley—the Pyramids, the Sphinx, the treasures of Tutankhamun. Along with the classical sites of Greece and Rome and those in Palestine and Israel associated with the Bible, there are in the West no better known antiquities than those of Pharaonic Egypt. Its history captures the imagination of the general public, beginning with schoolchildren, who study the art and engineering of the Pyramids, the refined and somewhat macabre processes of mummification, the hieroglyphs of gods and goddesses that still decorate the tombs of pharaohs, nobles, and priests throughout the valley. A seemingly endless series of televised documentaries intrigues viewers and lures hundreds of thousands of them as tourists each year, contributing billions of dollars to Egypt's less than robust economy.

Americans and Europeans see links to ancient Egypt in the Bible, but beyond that lies a fascination with the power, splendor, and refinement of that ancient civilization made manifest in numerous Hollywood films. Throughout the twentieth century, look-alikes have sprouted from coast to coast in the United States, none more famous perhaps than the Luxor Casino in Las Vegas, another tourist magnet.

This interest on the part of Westerners is not new; it goes back to the beginnings of Egyptology in the early years of the nineteenth century, when the young Napoleon came seeking glory in the East in the footsteps of another young conqueror, Alexander the Great. For three years, from 1799 to 1802, the French ruled Egypt, but Napoleon found little glory there and soon returned to Paris and an empire. Nevertheless, he left an important legacy in the published work of the scientists who accompanied him. They worked with determination to recover the history of ancient Egypt, which the West had largely forgotten and locally had become the subject of countless myths. The results of their efforts, appearing in the

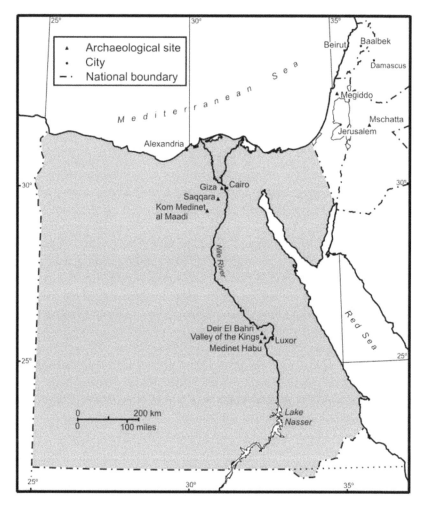

Egypt

multivolume *Description de l'Égypte* between the years 1809 and 1828 fueled a wave of Egyptomania; Jean-François Champollion's deciphering of the Rosetta Stone, which unlocked the secrets of hieroglyphics, furthered the fascination. Thereafter, the interest of scholars and adventurous laypeople rarely flagged. One need only consult the long list of nineteenth-century publications to confirm the place of ancient Egypt in Western literature. The wealthy made the obligatory journey up the Nile on well-appointed sailing vessels (*dahabiyyas*) in much the same way that eighteenth-century English gentlemen and their ladies had toured romantic Italy. Then, too, there were the treasure hunters, who came seeking fame and fortune. They tore apart ancient mounds and left their graffiti in burial chambers and temples from the Delta to the cataracts of the Nile and beyond. Much of what they unearthed was destroyed or disfigured in the process; what survived they shipped home to fill the museums of Europe and later those of America as well. In their haste and ignorance they unintentionally destroyed much of the historical record. Further, they helped to create a market for Egyptian antiquities, encouraging local peasants (*fellahin*) and dealers to expand their treasure hunting.

At first Europeans gave little attention to Arab or Islamic art, which they did not consider part of their own imagined past. According to the historian Donald Reid, its motifs "evoked an 'Oriental other,' variously hostile or alluringly exotic." By the end of the nineteenth century, the Comité de Conservation des Monuments de l'Art Arabe and the Museum of Arab Art had been established, but they remained poor relations of the Antiquities Service and the Egyptian Museum, which focused on the Pharaonic period.[1]

In the early years authorities were powerless to stop the depredations. Under Muhammad Ali (1805–1848), the first laws to control excavations were introduced, but little changed. The ruler himself, like his nominal Ottoman overlord, used gifts of antiquities to foreign rulers and their representatives in Cairo to gain leverage on various foreign policy matters. In 1858 Auguste Mariette, a Frenchman, became director of antiquities in Egypt. Khedive Said, whose close friend, Ferdinand de Lesseps, another Frenchman, was digging the Suez Canal, appointed Mariette to the new post. He and his successors, Gaston Maspero (1881–1886, 1899–1914), Pierre Lacau (1914–1936), and Étienne Drioton (1936–1952), headed the Egyptian Antiquities Service for almost a century. The Anglo-French treaty of 1904 formally recognized the continuing dominance of France in the cultural life of Egypt despite Britain's political control.

Mariette and those who followed him did what they could to protect Egypt's vast store of antiquities and to balance claims of foreign excavators with the increasing demands of local nationalists to keep them in Egypt. Constantly underfunded and undermanned, the Service des Antiquités seemed to be fighting an unequal battle to protect the ancient monuments. An excerpt from the British annual report for 1906 captures the frustration of the task:

> At Luxor thieves broke into a tomb and tried to remove wall paintings decorating the chamber. They only succeeded in destroying the fine

plaster work. . . . Whole sections of the cemetery at Saqqara had been destroyed in similar fashion. . . . Much of the destruction has resulted from the zeal of foreign scholars or their agents who in seeking to purchase antiquities for their museums from Egyptian dealers have used known tombs as models of what they wanted. The purveyors without hesitation attacked those same tombs that were used as models. . . . The attention drawn to these monuments by the studies of European and American archaeologists has contributed unintentionally to the destruction of the most valuable ones.[2]

A bizarre case in 1911 saw the accusers become the accused. Agents of the Antiquities Service arrested three residents of a village near the Pyramids whom they found prowling around the monuments at daybreak. Through the testimony of the dealers of antiquities and others from the village, however, charges were soon brought against the arresting officials themselves, who were brought to trial and given harsh sentences. This alarmed and enraged Maspero and his superiors in the Ministry of Public Works, and on appeal the convictions were overturned. This case prompted the director to seek passage of a new, stronger antiquities law, something he had lobbied for since his return to Egypt in 1899. Although this became law in 1912, a significant loophole remained. Because of capitulatory treaties, Europeans could not be bound by these new, tighter restrictions, and it was often these individuals, rather than the peasants, who had carried out some of the worst depredations on ancient monuments.[3]

Added to this came the attacks of the *fellahin* in search of *sebbagh*, or fertile soil, in the ancient mounds. In digging and carrying away this material, often without permission, historical evidence of walls and buildings was destroyed and small antiquities removed for illicit sale. These "mining" operations proliferated during World War I when Egyptian farmers faced demands for increased production to feed Allied troops. The government of Egypt took steps to end the persistent practice, but in March 1934 the University of Michigan archaeologist Enoch Peterson reported constant digging by the *sebbakhin* at Kom Medinet al Maadi. The following year at another site he complained that a small railway line had been constructed through the middle of the ancient mound to reach gravel deposits on the other side.[4]

Illicit digging continued to be a problem in the interwar years, and only gradually were the authorities able to impose a measure of control. A greater challenge, however, came in the form of foreign expeditions representing museums and universities in Europe and the United States. These groups often enjoyed strong support from their governments and their diplomatic representatives in Cairo, and it was difficult for the director of antiquities to exercise firm control over them. Although Maspero wished to limit concessions to those representing bona fide scholarly institutions, sometimes he was pressed to favor individuals who had strong political and diplomatic support. Such was the case in 1902 when Lord Cromer, the real ruler of Egypt at the time, urged him to grant a concession at Giza to a member of Britain's Parliament, which was, according to one archaeologist, "a mere looting operation." Gradually, these personal concessions became the exception, and by 1918 only Lord Carnarvon's grant in the Valley of the Kings at Luxor remained.[5]

Egypt had for many years followed a fifty-fifty policy regarding the division of antiquities at the end of each excavation season. Under this arrangement the collection in the Egyptian Museum grew immensely, becoming the finest in the world. So, too, did the collections in foreign museums. In 1912, for example, the American Clarence Fisher discovered the decorated tomb of Akhet-mery-nesuwt, and Henry Clay Frick, formerly Andrew Carnegie's partner in steelmaking, bought it from the Egyptian government (at that time under British control) and sent it as a gift to the Boston Museum of Fine Arts at his expense. Foreign archaeologists and their supporters at home expected to receive fine artifacts as rewards for their investments of expertise and money, and they were seldom disappointed.[6]

Maspero could be very generous to foreign excavators as long as he was assured the antiquities would go to public museums, not to private collections. George Reisner, director of the joint Boston Museum of Fine Arts–Harvard University expedition, reported ecstatically on the division of 1908 that he had received "the greatest lot of masterpieces that ever went out of Egypt at one time. . . . [A]ny one of the six best pieces would be a considerable addition to any museum in the world. . . . We have received the lion's share." And again in 1912 he wrote, "We *have received everything of value*. . . . I have never had such a favorable division."[7]

Sometimes such largesse led to crisis, especially years later when nationalists discovered just how much of Egypt's past had found its way abroad. The Germans, for example, received the famous head of Queen Nefertiti in a division just prior to World War I, and they gave it pride of place in Berlin. Years later, no one could explain how the foreigners had obtained this fine example of Pharaonic craftsmanship. Many stories, all of them involving an element of German chicanery, were circulated, yet despite several attempts to reclaim the treasure, it remained in the German capital.

One need only tour the impressive Egyptian galleries of the Louvre, the British Museum, the Metropolitan Museum of Art, the Boston Museum of Fine Arts, and many lesser institutions to view superb pieces, most of which were acquired either by excavation or by purchase prior to 1918. This was indeed the great age of collection building.

Not to be overlooked, however, is how much was lost or damaged in transit at that time. The shipment of antiquities to the West was a hazardous undertaking. Packing was sometimes careless, and there were many reports of broken pottery and cracked or shattered carvings. A painted inner room of the chapel of Akhet-mery-nesuwt was practically destroyed by water when a fire broke out in the ship's hold. In November 1915 a German submarine torpedoed the *Arabic*, sending the Metropolitan's shipment of antiquities to the bottom of the Atlantic. This catastrophe led to an abrupt cessation of such traffic until the end of the war.[8]

The interwar period, 1919–1939, brought a gradual end to the relatively free and easy days of archaeological excavation. Although many Western archaeologists, who had left in 1914 and returned after the war, expected conditions to remain as they had been earlier, they soon discovered they would have to face more controls; if they could not adjust, then they would have to do their digging elsewhere. The history of these years is one of a gradual increase in restrictions on archaeological excavation.

James Breasted (1865–1935) had interests throughout the region, but he was by training an Egyptologist. He began his fieldwork in Egypt in 1894, during his honeymoon, having recently completed his doctoral program in Germany under the renowned scholar Adolf Erman. Over the next four decades Breasted returned repeatedly to Egypt, but perhaps his most important visit came just after World War I when Egypt was experiencing a revolution. Breasted had been teaching at the University of Chicago since 1895, and in 1918 he came up with the idea of undertaking a survey of the state of antiquities in the Middle East, using the occasion to search out possible sites for future archaeological work. Always with American museums in mind, he could use the trip also to purchase the best of the antiquities that had accumulated with dealers during the war. John D. Rockefeller Jr., who had a long-standing interest in Chicago and in Breasted, agreed to finance the expedition. The Egyptologist set out in August 1919.

Arriving in London only to discover that finding passage to Egypt would take time, he used the six-week hiatus to meet with prominent British intellectuals and politicians, men such as H. G. Wells; Lord Carnarvon; Viscount Allenby, high commissioner of Egypt (1919–1925); former Prime Minister Arthur Balfour; and Lord Curzon, the British foreign secretary. The latter three offered to help smooth his way as he traveled through a Middle East still recovering from wartime disruptions. Breasted arrived in Egypt on November 1 after an absence of twelve years and only a few months after Britain had put down an uprising against its continued occupation.

Although accorded little respect by Westerners, the nationalist movement had grown powerful by the end of World War I. It had a charismatic leader in Saʿd Zaghlul, who elicited deep affection from the Egyptian masses. Early in his career he had risen through the establishment to serve as minister of public instruction (1906) and minister of justice (1910), but in 1912 he joined the opposition and became its outspoken leader in the legislative assembly.

Two factors had led Egyptians to believe that they would gain their independence after the war. First, Egypt had contributed vast supplies of food to the Allied war effort, so much, in fact, that famine appeared in the countryside. Second, they came to believe President Wilson's rhetoric about self-determination. Saʿd Zaghlul sent the American president a letter at the end of 1918 praising his ideals, and leaders of the Wafd Party wrote in January 1919 welcoming him to Paris. What disappointment in April, therefore, when the British refused to allow the nationalist delegation to present its case at Versailles, and Wilson publicly supported continued British control over Egypt. Saʿd Zaghlul's subsequent exile to Malta triggered the revolution, which—Breasted's observations notwithstanding—proved very destructive in the countryside, where the population had suffered more than in the cities.

In contrast to his intense interest in Pharaonic Egypt, Breasted showed little understanding of or patience with its modern successor. Like most of his fellow archaeologists, he gave little support to the idea of Egyptian independence. The civilized world, meaning the West, had an obligation to keep order there and throughout the region. "God save Egypt from the Egyptians," he wrote to his wife. On only his second day in the country he was prepared to give an assessment of the political situation, which was more complex than he knew. The country people were quite ready to settle down under British authority, he concluded, but "the little tarbushed effendis in Cairo and Alexandria" were still making trouble. He cautioned his family in Chicago not to be at all anxious for his safety for any trouble in the Egyptian capital would be confined to certain quarters, "just as was the negro rioting in Chicago." The authorities, he assured them, were almost hoping for a confrontation to show the rioters the mailed fist.[9]

Throughout these disturbances and after, Breasted remained in close contact with British officials, exchanging observations on the domestic situation. He and his colleagues were especially concerned lest Britain too soon abandon its dominant position. Clarence Fisher, who was excavating for the University of Pennsylvania at the time of the revolution, wrote to his director, George Gordon (1910–1928), in Philadelphia to warn of the consequences of Egyptian autonomy. "It will mean," he predicted, "that our chances of receiving a square deal in the future are slim. No native officials would treat our expedition with the fairness and courtesy which has always been accorded by the British."[10]

Breasted, of course, had similar concerns and stated his belief boldly to Dwight Morrow, a confidant of Calvin Coolidge, explaining that "no monument is safe in the Orient. . . . The only monument that is safe for science is the one that has been removed from the Orient." Breasted never really changed his mind, but he learned to be more cautious in expressing his opinions.[11]

Breasted received a long reassuring letter from a friend at the British residency, who wrote condescendingly of any thought of Egyptian independence at that time. As any father with an "unruly son," the British had determined that the Egyptians had not shown themselves worthy of greater freedom. Now the nurse would have to watch over him and keep a firm hold, "kick and struggle as he may" until "the little legs are stronger." The nationalist leader Saʿd Zaghlul and his associates had refused to cooperate, so they were being sent into exile for a second time. This official expected everything to quiet down now that the tail had lost its head. He assured Breasted that whatever happened in the long run, provisions would be put in place for protecting the antiquities administration.[12]

What, of course, concerned them all was the Milner Mission report, which was based on Lord Milner's official inspection visit to the country in 1919 following the revolution. It recommended to Prime Minister Lloyd George that Egypt be given autonomy but with several areas being reserved for Britain, including defense, communications, the Sudan, and foreign interests. Under this scheme, the administration of antiquities would come more firmly within Egyptian control.

No Egyptian political party, certainly not the Wafd, headed by Saʿd Zaghlul, could accept such limits of sovereignty. Negotiations collapsed, leading to Britain's unilateral declaration of Egyptian independence in 1922. This solution pleased no one, but it seemed the best that could be done in the short term. Despite its refusal to accept formally the limited autonomy offered by London, the Wafd participated in the first parliamentary elections in fall 1923. Given the strong public support for Saʻd Zaghlul, the party won an overwhelming victory, with its leader becoming prime minister in January 1924.

Amid these tense political developments came Howard Carter's remarkable discovery of Tutankhamun's tomb in the Valley of the Kings, with rooms full of wonderful funerary objects the likes of which no one had seen since ancient times. The discovery served as a lightning rod, attracting the various forces struggling for power in contemporary Egypt. Among many nationalists it fostered renewed pride in the glories of the Pharaonic past, whose ancient power and splendor they hoped to resurrect. The site and its contents became a battleground, hotly fought over for several years and revealing all the antagonisms that existed between the nationalists and their opponents. It was a memorable struggle and must have seemed to Carter a cruel trick of fate that he should have discovered this remarkable treasure at the very moment that the Wafd came to dominate Egyptian politics.

Carter had spent a lifetime excavating in Egypt. At one time he had served as an inspector for the Antiquities Service, but an unfortunate incident at Saqqara in 1905, involving a scuffle between some inebriated Frenchmen and Carter's Egyptian guards, led to his resignation. Thereafter, he had worked for Lord Carnarvon, who by the early postwar years was the only individual still holding a concession to excavate in Egypt. For all his years of experience, Carter was not a trained archaeologist, and some of his colleagues questioned his methods, but he was determined and usually prepared to seek the assistance of those more knowledgeable when necessary.

To supplement his income, Carter had served for years as a middleman, purchasing antiquities on a 15 percent commission for museums and individuals in Europe and the United States. He enjoyed a good reputation, and his services were regularly recommended to any institution seeking to expand its collection of Egyptian antiquities. Thus in 1920 Henry W. Kent, secretary of the Metropolitan Museum of Art, wrote to Frederic A. Whiting, director of the Cleveland Museum of Art, to extol Carter's virtues: "He is acknowledged to be the most skillful trader with the natives, he is a gentleman." Carter proved a good salesman in his own right, urging Whiting to "think of what educative value, importance, not to speak of the public pleasure, a really fine piece renders to both the collection and instruction." He cautioned that now was the time to buy both because competition for purchases was becoming more intense and Egypt was becoming more restrictive as to what could leave the country.

He left Whiting in no doubt that should Cleveland not find the money to make the purchase, he could easily sell this particularly fine piece elsewhere. Whiting bought this and a number of other pieces for the museum's collection.[13]

Lord Carnarvon, too, expected to sell antiquities abroad to pay for excavation costs in Egypt. Meeting with Edward Robinson, director of the Metropolitan, in February 1921, he sought assurances that the museum would continue to buy from him. Robinson avoided a formal commitment, which might lay the museum open to charges of assisting in the smuggling of valuable antiquities, but gave his opinion that the Metropolitan would purchase material presented to it either in New York or in Europe as it had in the past. Robinson wrote excitedly to Albert Lythgoe, the museum's curator of Egyptian art, of a wonderful cache of Eighteenth Dynasty (1550–1292 B.C.E.) jewelry in a dealer's hands about which Carnarvon had told him. According to Robinson, "If we succeed in getting the whole lot it will place our jewelry collection in the very first rank, as Cairo has nothing to correspond with it."[14]

The purchase of antiquities from dealers or directly from the *fellahin* had long been common practice in Egypt, and few Egyptologists had not made or encouraged such acquisitions from time to time. In the postwar years, however, there was a small but growing opposition to the trade, the argument being that it encouraged illicit digging and the destruction of monuments everywhere. George Reisner and the Frenchman Pierre Lacau, Egypt's director of antiquities (1914–1936), were two prominent opponents of the practice.[15]

While doing business on the side, Carter patiently continued his excavations and finally on November 4, 1922, his years of perseverance paid off when his workers uncovered the sealed entrance to the tomb of the Eighteenth Dynasty pharaoh, Tutankhamun (c. 1355 B.C.E.). He sent an urgent and enthusiastic message, summoning Lord Carnarvon from the Winter Palace Hotel in Luxor; soon all Egypt and then Europe and America were abuzz with reports of the wonderful discovery.

Carter spent the next several months carefully removing treasures from the tomb to his nearby laboratory. Fellow archaeologists and other specialists, several on loan from the Metropolitan's own excavation in the valley, assisted him in this difficult yet exhilarating task. It would take several years to empty the tomb and transport its precious and fragile contents to Cairo.

For Carter, however, this crowning achievement after a lifetime of hard work brought more troubles than rewards. Carnarvon unwisely made an

**Figure 4.1.** Lord Carnarvon (left), Lady Herbert (his daughter), and Howard Carter at the entrance to the tomb of Tutankhamun in the Valley of the Kings (c. 1922). Courtesy University of Pennsylvania Museum, Philadelphia.

agreement with the *London Times* that granted the newspaper exclusive rights to information concerning the tomb. This raised the hackles of the foreign press, whose correspondents flocked to Luxor. Even more upset was the Egyptian press, which rejected the idea of restrictions being placed on them by foreigners, keeping them from access to what rightfully belonged to Egypt.

From the beginning, also, there was disagreement over ownership of the contents of the tomb. The Egyptian government and Lacau as its representative argued that the tomb had been found intact and that therefore according to the terms of the concession all of the treasure belonged to the government. Carter and Carnarvon claimed that in fact there had been an ancient break-in and the tomb had been resealed. Technically, it was not intact. Therefore, the contents should be subject to a division.

Adding to Carter's problems were a group of Egyptologists, including Breasted, Alan Gardiner, Lythgoe, and Percy Newberry, who took it upon themselves to chastise Lacau and through him the Egyptian government for what they termed the unfair treatment of the discoverer. The larger issue for them concerned the future of foreign archaeological expeditions in Egypt. They also hoped to obtain part of Carnarvon's expected share of the Tutankhamun treasure for their own institutions.

In the midst of all the controversy surrounding the tomb, even the experienced Breasted could occasionally be overwhelmed by the grandeur of the discovery. Writing to the Rockefellers, Breasted conveyed to them in his beautifully descriptive prose what he had seen and felt that day as he stood in the tomb. Here he describes the nested shrines:

> Between the first and second was a broader space occupied by a heavy frame of gold-covered wood which supported the beautiful pall of black linen, studded with golden rosettes, like a dark night sky spangled with stars. At my second visit we opened the doors of the third and fourth shrines and beheld the massive stone sarcophagus within. I forgot the evidences all about me of the trouble, hurry, and confusion which had once surrounded the king with noise, dust, and wrangling. For the first time I stood in the silence of the tomb and felt the majesty of the dead Pharaoh's presence.[16]

Such quiet moments were rare for him. Always full of enterprise, Breasted had already conceived a scheme to turn the discovery to his advantage. He arranged to bring a party of Americans, wealthy philanthropists, up the Nile on a chartered steamer so that they could be present at the opening of Tutankhamun's sarcophagus. Presumably, he would be rewarded for providing them this unique experience. His one concern was that Carter might do something to ruin these plans.[17]

Carter's temperament was not suited to the controversy that developed with the Egyptian authorities, for he could be obstinate and did not like to be contradicted. These characteristics might have contributed to his success as an excavator, but they did not serve him well in the difficult negotiations over control of the tomb that dragged on for two years.[18]

Lacau, Maspero's successor as director of the Antiquities Service, staked out the government's position. Lacau had earlier served as head of the French Institute of Oriental Archaeology of Cairo, and he enjoyed a solid scholarly reputation. When he finally took up his new position in 1918, however, it became apparent that he would be less flexible than his predecessor on the issue of dividing antiquities with foreign expeditions. He believed that there should be no automatic right for excavators to claim 50 percent of their discoveries at the end of a season but rather that the Egyptian Museum should take all objects necessary for its collec-

**Figure 4.2.** Foreign tourists at Luxor in the 1920s, showing the Avenue of Sphinxes near Luxor Temple. Courtesy National Archives.

tion. This might be more or less than 50 percent. In no case should such objects find their way into private collections. Furthermore, Lacau believed that concessions should go only to major foreign institutions, which had the resources to build up sizable collections and to attract the public in large numbers. He had in mind the Louvre, the British Museum, and the Metropolitan and the Boston Museum of Fine Arts in the United States. Thus smaller museums such as the Toledo (Ohio) Museum of Art need not apply. He was anxious that antiquities go to established centers of Egyptology, where they would be studied, and not lost in such isolated outposts as Bucharest, Tokyo, or Sydney.[19]

Today this might seem an enlightened approach, but he angered many at the time. Such views were anathema to the archaeologists, who had worked under the more liberal regime of Gaston Maspero. They accused Lacau of pandering to Egyptian politicians to save his office or of favoring French interests over those of the Americans or the British. Breasted often seemed to take the lead in opposing the director of antiquities, and therefore his involvement on Carter's behalf seemed less than judicious.

Lacau was in an unenviable position, caught between the demands of

**Figure 4.3.** Foreign tourists with a guide at Luxor Temple, 1920s. Courtesy National Archives.

Egyptian nationalists, who came to power early in February 1924 and saw the Tutankhamun controversy as a metaphor for the independence struggle, and the foreign archaeologists, who stressed the noble, scientific nature of their work, which no civilized nation should oppose. The nationalists found that they could maneuver quite effectively in an area of interest such as archaeology, where they were not restricted by Britain's reserved powers. The British on their part hesitated to challenge Egyptian decisions in such a peripheral area, where they had little to gain and where the French had historically taken the lead.

After a series of minor clashes with Egyptian authorities, Carter's final break came in February 1924 when the minister of public works, who had responsibility for antiquities, ordered that any visitors to the tomb must first obtain permission from his office. Carter had planned to give the wives of those assisting him a private tour of the site, and when the new order arrived, he flew into a rage. After consulting with his archaeologist colleagues, he determined unilaterally to close the tomb until further notice, sending a letter of his intentions to the prime minister. Sa'd Zaghlul answered Carter politely but firmly, reminding him that it was not his property to close. Furthermore, he could not understand how Carter could abandon such important research — important not only to Egypt but to the whole world as well — over such a trifling issue. On February 23 the government rescinded Lord Carnarvon's concession and sent a delegation to take control of the tomb and its contents. Carter was devastated. He left Egypt for London and in April traveled to the United States for an extensive speaking tour.[20]

Even Breasted's elder son, Charles, played his part in this affair and did nothing to bring credit to his father. Before coming out to Egypt, he had made an agreement with Victor Lawson, publisher of the *Chicago Daily News* and the *Christian Science Monitor* to ignore the monopoly of the *Times* and to file stories on the continuing Tutankhamun saga under an assumed name. Breasted senior knew of these arrangements and seemed to encourage them as part of his son's "finding himself." He made him privy to a great deal of inside information that was unavailable to other correspondents. What was even more troubling about this project was the perspective and tone the young Breasted presented in his articles and in his letters to his editor in Chicago. They appear often to have reflected his father's views as well.

Writing on February 24, 1924, the day after the seizure of the tomb, for example, Charles Breasted referred to the crisis as "only another evidence of Near Eastern bravado, of the decline of occidental prestige, and of the intoxicating effect of sudden freedom and independence upon an ignorant, decadent, mongrel people, totally unfit for self-rule." To further this image, he wrote that "the Egyptian masses maintain an extraordinary, fanatical state of autointoxication" as they waited for Sa'd Zaghlul's train to pass on its way to Luxor. There was, he claimed, no scientific or patriotic interest in the discovery, only a desire to make money, either individually by selling antiquities to dealers or by having the government sell the treasure and put the money into the treasury. All of this, he argued, was being abetted by the French to spite the British.[21]

Spurred by such incidents as Breasted reported, one angry citizen wrote to Secretary of State Hughes, decrying the "sissy-like foreign policy" of which people of a superior nation like the United States were getting tired. Pushed around by "Japs" in the Pacific and angered by abandonment of the Armenians and increasing disorder in Mexico and Haiti and now the fiasco in Egypt, the troubled writer argued that "superior peoples of this earth" needed to take control.[22]

While Carter was away in the United States, Herbert Winlock, director of the Metropolitan expedition in Egypt, took on the unenviable task of handling the dispute. At one point he wrote to Carter to inquire about a wooden head of Tutankhamun found in the archaeologist's storeroom in the Valley of the Kings. Its discovery, he reported, had made a bad impression because there was no explanation of how it came to be there. The Egyptian officials thought the worst, and they informed the prime minister immediately of their discovery. Carter did not return until December 15, 1924.[23]

During the ten months that the Wafd held power, January to November 1924, the nationalist press argued repeatedly the government's case for absolute control over all sites and ownership of all antiquities. One editor claimed that Carter had lorded it over weak ministers, opening and closing the tomb as he wished, as if it were the tomb of his father rather than that of Pharaoh, but now the strong Zaghlul ministry would control him. Another cited the need to train Egyptians to study their own antiquities and not just stand around as onlookers. A great state and a rising nation could not leave "this great work to be monopolized by foreigners."[24]

Egypt's hope for rebirth was set in stone in the work of the nationalist sculptor Mahmud Mukhtar, whose celebrated statue, "The Awakening of Egypt," was first erected in front of the railroad station and later moved to the entrance of Cairo University. It showed a young woman raising her head covering, one hand—a link between ancient and modern Egypt—resting on the sphinx at her feet, which was about to rise. Mukhtar also completed an impressive statue of Sa'd Zaghlul, which was erected on the Corniche in Alexandria. Here, the Wafd leader assumed the typical pose of Pharaoh, standing with one foot forward and fists clenched to hold the symbols of his authority. In both cases, the connection between ancient and modern in the mind of the sculptor was unambiguous.[25]

During the interwar years, Pharaonic Egypt was often personified as a woman; this became a common representation in cartoons, prints, and paintings of the period. One prominent women's magazine, *Al-Nahda al-Nisa'iyya* (The Women's Awakening), which began publication in 1921, featured a photograph of Mukhtar's "Awakening" on its cover for more than a decade. Female nationalists reminded their countrymen that Pharaonic women had enjoyed rights far in advance of those in surrounding countries during Egypt's period of ancient glory. They cited this evidence to support their calls "for women's progress together with national revival."[26]

The Tutankhamun discovery intensified the wave of nationalism sweeping Egypt. Although historians have debated the extent of influence of the so-called Pharaonist movement in early-twentieth-century Egypt,

**Figure 4.4.** Model of Saʿd Zaghlul from which Mahmud Mukhtar sculpted his monumental statue of the nationalist leader that stands on the Corniche in Alexandria. Photo by author.

evidence shows that focus on the Pharaonic past reached a high point in the 1920s and then continued at a reduced tempo in subsequent decades.

Throughout the interwar period, according to one recent scholar, "the dominant territorial nationalist orientation inspired by a Pharaonic past . . . was never seriously shaken in the curriculum." The Ministry of Education urged teachers to take their students on visits to important historical sites. School texts emphasized the glories of ancient Egypt, which preceded "by thousands of years other nations in the domain of progress and civilization," and called upon students to renew the successes of their ancestors.[27]

Writers, many of whom made pilgrimages to Luxor and the Valley of the Kings, reported being filled with pride at witnessing the remarkable accomplishments of their ancestors. They contrasted the glory of the past with the depressing state of contemporary Egypt, but they were optimistic that under the leadership of Saʿd Zaghlul Egypt could regain its ancient luster. In one poem Ahmad Shawqi imagined "the Pharaoh rising from the tomb only to be shocked by the lowly state of his country under foreign domination." In another, "Pharaoh's Pride," he spoke of the influence of ancient Egypt on Greece and Rome, and while commending Lord Carnarvon for discovering the tomb, he emphasized that "our ancestors belong to us," and no one should take them or their belongings from Egyptians. Otherwise it would have been better to have left them buried in the earth. He urged his countrymen to visit the tomb and pay their respects to the king. A visit to the monuments at Aswan inspired Abbas Mahmud al-Aqqad (1889–1964), a native of that city, to write poems praising ancient Egyptian civilization. Salama Musa, an important nationalist, wrote in his autobiography that studying in Britain had alerted him to "the greatness of Egyptian civilization in Pharaonic times and the use a study of its history could have for stimulating national pride" in the struggle against the British. "Egypt today is the Egypt of the Pharaohs," he remarked. "Do not expect Egypt to change her Pharaonic identity." For Musa, a Coptic Christian, the emphasis on the legacy of Pharaonic Egypt could provide a common bond among all Egyptian nationalists, regardless of religious affiliation.[28]

Certainly the most influential of the "Pharaonic" group of intellectuals was Muhammad Husayn Haykal, editor of the influential newspaper *Al-Siyasa*, who wrote of his overwhelming sense of excitement after his visit to Luxor in 1922. In a series of articles he referred to "humanity at its highest perfection." Many Islamic and Christian rituals relating to marriage and burial, he believed, could be traced back to the practices of ancient Egypt. Just as Europeans had become stronger through knowledge of their Greek and Roman origins, so Egyptians must study their ties to Pharaonic Egypt as a way of strengthening their determination to build a strong nation. Knowing what Egypt had accomplished in the past, he was filled with hope for the future.[29]

Sa'd Zaghlul was alive to the possibilities for the nationalist cause created by the recent discovery; he saw at once how one could make the connection between antiquity and the present. He sent a high-level delegation to the reopening of the tomb in March 1924. Only illness kept him from attending in person. "The delegation was welcomed at railroad stations wherever it stopped by crowds clamoring for the complete independence of Egypt and the Sudan." Just as the tomb and its treasure had been reclaimed from Carter and Carnarvon, so Egypt could be freed from Britain's grasp.[30]

After Sa'd Zaghlul, who had charted a more independent course for Egypt and reportedly referred to other Arab states as "an assemblage of zeros," had resigned in November 1924 in the face of a British ultimatum, there was a gradual shift away from the emphasis on the ancient past, but it continued to be an important theme in the work of many prominent figures. Ahmad Hussain, founder of Young Egypt, a right-wing nationalist movement, had a conversion experience at Luxor during a scouting trip to Upper Egypt in 1928. When he saw the unparalleled grandeur of ancient Egypt, he concluded that "if Egypt had once been great it could be so again." That same year, at the dedication of Mukhtar's statue of Sa'd Zaghlul, Prime Minister Mustafa al-Nahhas reminded his audience of ancient Egypt's eternal greatness as the "cradle of human civilization, the source of human wisdom."[31]

Mainstream writers such as Naguib Mahfouz, Taha Hussain, and Taw-fiq al-Hakim referred in their work to the glories of Pharaonic Egypt. Mahfouz's early works (1939–1944) were based on the history of ancient Egypt. The young Sayyid Qutb, then a literary critic, praised his *Thebes at War* (1944), which became a set text in Egyptian schools. Al-Hakim made repeated references in his *Return of the Spirit* (1933) to the continuing importance of the Pharaonic period. In one famous exchange a French archaeologist lectures a British official on the continuity between past and present, saying, "You don't imagine . . . that these thousands of years that are Egypt's past have vanished like a dream and left no trace in these descendants. . . . They claim this nation has been dead for centuries, but they have not seen its mighty heart reaching toward the sky from the sands of Giza." Hussain, who would later become minister of education, wrote that "the new Egypt will not come into being except from the ancient, eternal Egypt. . . . [W]e do not wish, nor are we able, to break the link between ourselves and our forefathers."[32]

After Sa'd Zaghlul's death in 1927 a lengthy debate ensued concerning the design of his tomb. Should it be Pharaonic or Arab/Islamic? Following heated debate among political elites, the Pharaonic style won the day. One scholar has pointed out, however, that most of the buildings in this style were constructed between 1925 and 1930. It became less common in the 1930s as leaders, even those who had once strongly embraced Pharaonism, increasingly emphasized the Arab and Muslim roots of modern Egypt, which fit better with the understanding of new political forces, deeply rooted in the Egyptian masses. They emphasized that the revival of interest in Egypt's ancient civilization did not mean the triumph over its Islamic heritage, which was paramount.[33]

It was not only the discovery of Tutankhamun's tomb that contributed to the glorification of the past but also awareness of developments in Turkey that served as a model for Egypt. Just as Turkish nationalists were praising the ancient Hittites and their links to the modern state, so Egyptians could establish links to Pharaonic Egypt with equal confidence. In *Al-Balagh*, a major Wafd newspaper, an Egyptian nationalist detailed the differences between Turkey and Egypt. In the former, leaders had abandoned the history books written by foreigners, which had made Turks feel ashamed of their past. They had rewritten history, creating a Turkey with a glorious past of which all citizens could be proud. So what if critics claimed that much of this was made up? Were not all historians affected as much by their emotions as by their knowledge? In Egypt, they were still turning to the European history books, which weakened self-confidence. They needed to follow the Turks with histories full of examples extolling the glories of Egypt's past. As a result Egyptians would be able to lay claim to many of the same firsts as the Turks.[34]

Fortunately for the nationalists, archaeology was a peripheral area where they could make large claims against foreigners and their governments without much risk. Thus the British government did what it could to distance itself from the Tutankhamun affair in the belief, no doubt, that there were more important issues to address. The nationalists pushed for more control, knowing that they would face little determined opposition. Although archaeologists stressed the importance of their work to Anglo-Egyptian affairs and officials privately agreed, in public they were cautious not to challenge nationalist demands.[35]

George A. Reisner (1867–1942), one of the most prominent and successful American Egyptologists, applauded British caution, for he understood that these were perilous times for foreigners in Egypt, especially for archaeologists. Reisner first came to Egypt in the 1890s and spent the rest of his life there, excavating in the Sudan, Upper Egypt, and, most successfully, at Giza. There in 1925 he made his greatest discovery, the secondary burial of Queen Hetepheres, mother of Khufu (c. 2650 B.C.E.), builder of the Great Pyramid.

Reisner introduced a scrupulously thorough system of excavation; no detail was overlooked, and photography played a larger part than ever before. In another innovation, Reisner trained his most promising Egyptian workers to perform duties usually reserved for Westerners. They kept the daily diaries of his excavations, took the photographs, and often arranged the transportation of antiquities to Cairo from the site. Given his own formal training in Germany, he disparaged the work of amateurs, who lacked the credentials he thought essential for excavation. Thus Carter and Carnarvon came in for considerable criticism in his correspondence with the Boston Museum of Fine Arts, which along with Harvard University sponsored his work at Giza. Writing to the museum director in November 1922 only a few weeks after the discovery of Tutankhamun's tomb, Reisner let loose a barrage of criticisms of Carter and Carnarvon. He accused them of "booming the find," that is, exaggerating its importance and value, thus drawing the unwelcome attention of the nationalists to archaeological matters generally. He added with much foresight that "this tomb will probably cause no end of trouble for all concerned." He claimed that Lord Carnarvon spent 10,000 pounds a year purchasing antiquities for his private collection (most of which the Metropolitan purchased after his death) and thus encouraged "thieves and illicit excavators," causing untold destruction of historical material.[36]

Later Reisner explained that he had not spoken to Carter since he learned in 1917 that he was involved in the antiquities trade, adding that neither Carter nor Carnarvon should ever have been granted an excavation permit. He also blamed Breasted, Gardiner, and others of his colleagues for supporting Carter in a hopeless confrontation with the Egyptian government and therefore making everything more difficult. He had kept his distance from the affair, and thus his expedition was, he thought, in a fairly strong position.[37]

Reisner had a good deal of sympathy for his friend Lacau, who had a difficult job to perform. They communicated frequently for Lacau trusted Reisner, whose letters are full of favorable references to his work as director of antiquities.

Reisner's comments on Egyptian politicians in general and on the Wafd in particular were highly critical. He had little use for the idea of an Egyptian parliament, especially one controlled by the Wafd. He declared that most of the ministers in Saʿd Zaghlul's government were unenlightened, "intensely anti-foreign, and determined to insult and humiliate all foreign officials." He took much comfort from the thought that King Fuad (1922–1936) might get the upper hand. The king, being amenable to diplomatic pressure on questions concerning foreigners, could be kept in control, "while a parliament of political leaders would be as tractable as a loose pig." The king, moreover, had a great interest in archaeology.[38]

Reisner cast a troubled glance across the Mediterranean to events in Turkey, where the nationalist victories over the Greeks had stirred local political circles. He recommended that the European powers should do their best to keep Mustafa Kemal out of Istanbul and thereby help to quiet the nationalist clamor in Cairo as well.[39]

Reisner was less intensely political than his fellow American, Breasted. He wanted to be left alone to carry on his excavations, and anyone who threatened the status quo, whether Egyptian or foreigner, came in for criticism. Although he related well to his Egyptian workers, who idolized him, one can easily exaggerate the importance of that relationship. His approach to them was paternalistic. There is no record of his having strongly supported throughout his long career the development of a body of Egyptian archaeologists. His men remained firmly under his direction, with little opportunity to introduce initiatives of their own.

His letters are full of unkind, today we might even say racist, remarks about Egyptians in general and the political class in particular. "The nationalists are merely demanding the expulsion of the British from Egypt, that is, the removal of all civilized control over their [the nationalists'] former right to plunder the mass of the people." "The native brutality of a half-civilized people is still alive in the hearts of the Egyptians," he claimed. "[They are] still a half-savage race. . . . The lust of blood and plunder is part of the constitution of every man and woman. . . . SELF GOVERNMENT CAN NEVER BE ANYTHING BUT A FARCE." Although Reisner and Breasted almost always found themselves on opposite sides of the important archaeological issues of the day, they shared to a remarkable degree an Orientalist perspective of Egyptians.[40]

Whereas Reisner wisely stood aloof from the Carter controversy, the American minister J. Morton Howell had little choice but to get involved, for the State Department had requested that he try to work out a compromise between Carter and the Egyptian government. American archaeologists, Breasted and Lythgoe, were indirectly responsible for this directive; they had urged this action in letters and visits to Washington. They were concerned that should the dispute drag on, for Carter had initiated a legal case against the government, the atmosphere would be poisoned for all of them.

Howell had been in Cairo since June 1921. A political appointee from Ohio, he was none too skilled in diplomacy, but he seemed pleased with what he considered the positive change in Egypt under Saʿd Zaghlul, whom he characterized as astute, capable, and by far the strongest and most effective Egyptian leader of the day.[41]

In March 1924 Howell, accompanied by Breasted, met several times with the minister of public works, Murqus Hanna. Breasted actually initiated the talks when he told Howell that he had received intelligence that British Prime Minister Ramsey McDonald wanted the Carter affair resolved as soon as possible. The ensuing negotiations began promisingly, and the U.S. minister told Washington that he thought a solution was in sight. Despite his optimism, they quickly bogged down, and he had to report his failure. When Breasted set sail for home early in April, Howell urged his superiors to talk with him while he was in Washington in order to gather information from him that could be useful in the future in supporting American interests in Egypt.[42]

Breasted planned his trip carefully, advising his good friend, George Hale, director of the National Research Council, that he would be in Washington in time to attend the dedication of the new Academy of Science building. He asked Hale to include an invitation to the new Egyptian minister in Washington to whom Breasted would give a tour of the new home of organized science in America. He hoped to dazzle him into writing a favorable report to Cairo on the academy, which had been so concerned for the state of scientific work in the Nile Valley.[43]

Breasted had excellent connections in the new Coolidge administration, not only with Secretary of State Hughes but also with Dwight Morrow, whom Breasted claimed would be "the most influential man in the new administration." Morrow, Breasted informed his wife, had a great interest in archaeology, and he would not hesitate to seek his help at the White House. In a letter to his son Charles he had revealed that he had perhaps as much influence in the White House as he would have had if his late friend Teddy Roosevelt had been president.[44]

By the beginning of 1925, Breasted even fancied that he might receive appointment as American minister to Egypt. He had support from Vice President Charles Dawes, but the resignation of Hughes temporarily thwarted this project. Although he desired a Cairo appointment for himself, he looked with disfavor on his son's suggestion that he, too, might seek a diplomatic career. Breasted reminded Charles of various embassy secretaries they had encountered over the years who were doing rather meaningless tasks. "Except in times of great stress," he argued, "playing around in the European capitals as a diplomat is simply to give your life to being a social figure-head. . . . [Y]ou have far more in you than such a career could ever call out." In the end, neither of them became diplomats.[45]

Breasted did use his influence to press the French government to change its antiquities policy in Egypt and in other parts of the Middle East. Not only did he oppose Lacau's policies, but he resented French refusal to allow him to export a shipment of antiquities from Beirut on the basis of "the alleged value of the collection to the people of Syria." Breasted ridiculed this argument: as far as he was concerned, "orientals" had neglected and destroyed their monuments for centuries. The real reason he thought was French jealously and refusal to allow America to build up its collections as France had done generations earlier. He rarely missed an opportunity to criticize them. In October 1924 he wrote asking Morrow to intervene with Secretary Hughes to support American scientists in the Middle East. He meant, of course, "our endeavors to bring its ancient monuments to America for the enrichment of our museum collections."[46]

Breasted unburdened himself to Hale on the perfidy of the French and the need for the State Department to advise Paris that Lacau's policies were harmful to American scientific interests in Egypt. The French seemed to be everywhere in the region. In Turkey, they absconded with a site Breasted had unofficially claimed for his Oriental Institute. In Syria, they were the mandatory power and raised objections to Breasted exporting Phoenician antiquities at the same time that they were exporting them from their own sites. This disagreement dragged on for several years, with Breasted eventually losing. In Iran, the French had a monopoly over archaeological excavation, and after 1930 a Frenchman served as director of antiquities there. And, of course, in Egypt they had considerable influence, extending back to the early years of the previous century.[47]

Breasted was determined to overcome what he termed French obstructionism. On the advice of Oscar Straus, former U.S. ambassador at Istanbul, Breasted wrote directly to U.S. Ambassador Myron T. Herrick in Paris, informing him of the problems caused by French officials in the Middle East. He recommended that Herrick remind the French government of all that Americans, both public and private, had done and were doing for France. It was Rockefeller funds, after all, that had paid both for the Phoenician antiquities in Syria and the extermination of tuberculosis in France itself. His battle with the French continued through the 1920s and 1930s right up to his death in 1935, but he won only a few skirmishes. Breasted had little faith in French archaeological methods, and his views tended to be stereotypical, perhaps a legacy of his years in imperial Germany during the 1890s.[48]

The Carter affair finally reached a settlement on January 13, 1925. Carter had an audience with the king the following day. According to the new concession, Carnarvon's heirs—Lord Carnarvon had died of a virulent infection in April 1923, launching stories of the curse of King Tut—gave up any claims against the Egyptian government and any rights to antiquities from the tomb. Carter reported the return of the tomb to his charge on January 25 with "great pomp" just a little less than a year after he had defied the Wafd government and closed the tomb.[49]

Lacau did not attend the ceremony. According to Carter, "It would seem that he was ashamed to show his face." This unkind remark showed Carter's unforgiving nature toward the individual, who according to Reisner and the French ambassador, had been more responsible than anyone else for getting Carter back into the Valley of the Kings. And yet Carter had gained some perspective from his travels, privately admitting that as a result of stress and bad advice he had done and said many foolish things, which he deeply regretted. Now he looked forward to completing the challenging work of preparing the contents of the tomb for shipment to Cairo.[50]

King Fuad traveled to the site at the end of the year and declared himself well pleased with the work that had been done. So, too, did the Egyptian ministers, who were invited to the museum in early January 1926, with Carter and Lacau present. When the curtain was drawn back, they let out a collective "gasp of pleasure" to see such beauty as the gold mask and solid gold coffin of Tutankhamun.[51]

Years later King Faruq (1936–1952), who had inherited his father's interest in antiquities, facilitated the return to Egypt without publicity of a number of artifacts from the tomb that had been found among Carter's possessions after his death on March 2, 1939. Although a kindly explanation assumed that he probably got them from Lord Carnarvon or took them on account, one Foreign Office official concluded that Carter had stolen the objects from the tomb and went on to point to the moral of the story: "We are so accustomed to adopting the 'holier than thou' attitude towards Egyptians generally . . . that it is indeed a shock to find that a British Egyptologist can, on occasion, behave as a crook." Officials worried that given too much notoriety this incident would play into the hands of Selim Hassan, an Egyptian archaeologist then facing corruption charges himself. Faruq, who had tried to bring Hassan to trial, wanted no such reprieve for him and thus made possible the quiet return of the pilfered objects.[52]

To the extent that the Carter affair brought attention to archaeology generally, it served as a catalyst for the movement to tighten Egyptian control over foreign expeditions. The movement predated Carter's discovery, but it had sputtered until this controversy arose.

Soon after accepting the post of director, Lacau determined that the rules of divisions must change in the interest of maintaining Egypt's rights. The Frenchman took seriously his responsibilities as an Egyptian official, much to the horror and disgust of many Western archaeologists. One of Breasted's early postwar letters from England contained a pointed attack on the director as a hopeless administrator and idealistic dreamer. He believed in Egypt for the Egyptians, said Breasted, which meant he would abandon the old policy of fair divisions and "swamp the Cairo Museum" with monuments it could not possibly install or administer. "He forgets that the number of educated Egyptians who can appreciate such things is an insignificant handful," while in the West "our birthright and inheritance from the past" could be a wonderful educational influence.[53]

In April 1920 the Metropolitan expedition was already experiencing Lacau's new policy of keeping all major pieces for the Cairo Museum. The following year the expedition decided to postpone the division until 1922 because Lacau wanted so much of what they had already discovered at Deir El Bahri that they might get to keep more if the pot were larger. Whereas Lacau stressed the importance of "pure science," Herbert Winlock championed "practical science," meaning a guaranteed share of the antiquities. Why else, he asked, would anyone put up the large sums required for a season of excavation? Legally, the Metropolitan's board could only spend funds entrusted to them that would benefit the museum, that is, result in acquisitions.[54]

In December 1921 P. M. Tottenham, undersecretary of state in the Ministry of Public Works, and Lacau wrote a response to the Milner Commission report, which had included some unflattering conclusions about the Antiquities Service. The commission's suggestion that the Egyptology Committee, which oversaw archaeological activities, should become an international body was, they said, totally out of step with the actual political circumstances in the country. Regarding divisions, everything found should remain in Egypt "as evidence of its greatness and civilization." Excavators should be working to expand the frontiers of science, and, they argued, scientists could easily come to Cairo to study the materials. This was soon followed by a circular from the Ministry of Public Works, indicating that 1922–1923 would be the last year of fifty-fifty divisions. The Egyptian government's determination stiffened with the Tutankhamun discovery.[55]

The expectation of an impending change in the division laws sent foreign archaeologists scurrying to their own governments for support. The French were in an unusual position. Although Breasted assumed a great French conspiracy in Egypt and throughout the Middle East, he would have been surprised to learn that the government in Paris had little influence over Lacau. Annually, the director visited the relevant ministries in the French capital to discuss archaeological affairs in Egypt, but he considered himself first and foremost an Egyptian official. When, during one of these meetings, Lacau decried the growing British influence in Cairo, the Foreign Ministry officials said that they could do little about this except to urge him to do all he could to maintain French cultural influence there.[56]

Lacau had disagreements with his fellow Frenchmen in Egypt. Georges Foucart, his successor as director of the French Institute (1914–1928), disagreed with Lacau about almost everything. Foucart had predicted that once Egypt became independent many opportunities for scientific and cultural influence would open for France, but this did not happen. Foucart lamented the lack of government funds to support an active program of expeditions, leading to the withdrawal of French archaeologists, who often were replaced by Americans. He disliked the newly proposed policy on divisions, writing that the office occupied by Lacau had traditionally been thought of at Paris as an "annex to our national system," but this was no longer the case. His reports, like those of his friend Reisner, were as much about politics and diplomacy as they were about archaeology and science. He lamented the general decline under Saʿd Zaghlul, whose own partisans in the Wafd had put so much strain on him that he was chronically ill.[57]

As Foucart rightly observed, it was the Americans whose influence grew most rapidly during the interwar years. They always seemed to have more money than the Europeans. Hence by the early 1920s seven out of eight foreign expeditions in Egypt were sponsored by American institutions. This was, of course, the reason American archaeologists often took the lead in opposing changes in the laws relating to their activities. The archaeologists had exceptional connections and often bypassed the minister resident in Cairo to take their arguments directly to officials in Washington. Museum directors became frustrated with Lacau's attempts to tighten the laws governing divisions, just at the time that they were competing to build up their Egyptian collections with the acquisition of remarkable pieces. It was difficult to purchase such works and difficult to keep them if they were unearthed in legitimate excavations.[58]

In 1923 George Gordon, director of the University Museum at the University of Pennsylvania, tried to purchase a wonderful limestone head from a dealer and send it through Egyptian customs. Lacau refused to clear it. Gordon toyed with the idea of sending it via the diplomatic pouch — if the legation would agree — but in the end the impatient owner reclaimed the head, which disappeared without a trace.[59]

Gordon drafted a long memorandum that set out his thinking on the antiquities question:

Modern civilized communities recognize the fact that the materials on which the history of civilization is based are common property and not the exclusive property of any geographical or political division. . . . We do not admit the justice of any pretense that the past history of the human race is the monopoly of any one country or people or nation. . . . The materials upon which the reconstruction of ancient history is based are the common inheritance of human society and especially of those communities that have done most to promote learning and that are at present responsible for the progress of the world and the preservation of knowledge.[60]

Lacau, not one to be easily cowed by such extravagant claims, replied that governments have absolute rights to change their internal laws, without foreign interference, and that Egypt was actually assisting the work of science by keeping collections together. The country was only acting in accordance with the conclusions of the recent International Academic Union meeting in Brussels (1922), which claimed that the important historic or artistic pieces in the mandate states should be kept together in a local museum to facilitate their protection, study, and representation of the nation's past. He was certain that the U.S. government would adopt a similar policy if it were a question of American antiquities.[61]

Lacau became the bête noire of many American archaeologists and their sponsors. The Metropolitan took the lead in opposing the proposed changes; and former Secretary of State Elihu Root brought his fellow trustees' strong resolution directly to Secretary of State Hughes in Washington. Following the meeting, Hughes informed the members that he had instructed Minister Howell to bring the matter informally to the attention of the Egyptian government to secure a favorable modification of the provisions.[62]

Breasted saw that the issues of Tutankhamun's tomb and the newly proposed division law were intertwined. It was jingoism, and he thought nothing could stop Lacau, who would forever occupy a special niche in the history of Middle Eastern archaeology as "the most destructive influence that ever beset the scientific efforts of the West in the East."[63]

Despite Breasted's apparent resignation, he was far from accepting the proposed changes. In early March 1924 he had a meeting with Saʿd Zaghlul, whom he found, much to his surprise, to be a keen and intelligent old man. He went on to meetings with a series of ministers and officials, concluding that this would show them that "we men of science have no horns, hoofs and a barbed tail." He hoped that these encounters might help to head off Lacau's revisions.[64]

It was in Washington, however, that Breasted and his associates were most effective. They urged the State Department to resist the proposed changes, and when the department expressed its concern to the Egyptians, they relented, saying that there would be no changes for the upcoming season (1923–1924) but making no promises for the future. Edward Robinson, director of the Metropolitan, thanked Secretary of State Hughes for this satisfactory result.[65]

American institutions were under no illusions that this was anything more than a temporary reprieve. Thus they decided to make a supreme effort to extend the digging season and intensify their efforts in the expectation that this might be the last fifty-fifty season. The Egyptian Exploration Society, which had been in the field since the 1880s and regularly raised funds from various American museums, which shared in the results of their excavations, used this tense situation to raise larger than usual sums for the 1923–1924 season.[66]

Lacau had told some of his confidants that in practice he intended to change very little. Although Egypt would have the right to keep everything, he would only exercise that right if pieces of novel or outstanding character were involved that had no equal in the Cairo Museum collection. Otherwise, expeditions might actually get more than they had previously. What concerned the archaeologists, however, was implementation of the new policy if removed from Lacau's hands. Who could guarantee how Egyptian officials in the future might interpret the new and apparently tighter restrictions?[67]

The American archaeologists returned to the charge the following year, with Lythgoe writing to Robinson to complain of the threat that hung over them from Lacau. He asked the director to go back to the State Department to get them to complain once again to the Egyptians and the French to see what could be done to "put an end" to Lacau or at least to get him to stop his objectionable activities. Lythgoe followed this up with a personal visit to Washington to brief officials.[68]

In Cairo, Breasted and several like-minded archaeologists sent Lacau a letter warning that his policies "must inevitably lead to the destruction of scientific work in Egypt." They followed this with a letter to Prime Minister Zaghlul, appealing to him not to regard his country as the sole possessor of all antiquities but rather as trustee over them. They added, "We censure Monsieur Lacau, who has a double function in Egypt, for having been a *bad adviser* of the Egyptian government." They hoped to appeal to the prime minister's concern over Egypt's international image while at the same time raise questions about Lacau's "double function" as Egyptian official and French appointee. Despite these efforts, the Zaghlul government decided to go ahead with the proposed changes, insisting, as had Lacau, that changed language would not affect the divisions in practice.[69]

Lacau wrote a statesmanlike letter to the Metropolitan, trying to dissuade them from stopping their excavation work for the 1925 season. He argued that the museum's publications were surely more important than their display cases, and he urged them to raise money for their work that would come without restrictions. Egypt, he promised, would keep only what it needed to deepen its collection in Cairo with examples of objects that it did not yet possess.[70]

The archaeologists wanted more assurances, and they tried to convince Britain to declare archaeology a "foreign interest," thus excluding it from Egyptian control. Breasted carried this message to a meeting with Secretary of State Frank B. Kellogg in May 1925, who agreed to send a letter to London supporting such a move. Elihu Root weighed in again with arguments that would have pleased his former chief, Theodore Roosevelt. He railed against Britain and France and their mistreatment of selfless American explorers in Egypt, a situation that must surely be taken seriously by Washington, for "neglect of such things tends to destroy a country's prestige and to impair the respect which its citizens everywhere receive." Secretary of State Kellogg and Allen Dulles, head of the Office of Near Eastern Affairs, received his views sympathetically.[71]

As a result of this activity, the American minister in Egypt was urged to consult with his British and French colleagues with a view to drafting a joint note to the Egyptian government for restoration of the fifty-fifty division. But Howell, moved to some degree by his growing antipathy to Breasted, urged caution. Diplomats take a dim view of those who go over their heads, keeping them all the while in the dark about proposed projects. Reisner contributed to Howell's suspicions, telling the minister that many of the same American institutions that were complaining vociferously about the new law in Egypt "worked happily under exactly the same conditions in Palestine." This led Reisner to conclude that they had a special hostility to the Egyptian Antiquities Service.[72]

Lacau had his hands full with other Egyptian officials, who were reluctant to guarantee in writing what he had promised to foreign institutions. Chief among these was Dr. Abdul Hamid Bedawi Pasha, head of the Contentieux de l'État, a part of the permanent bureaucracy responsible for giving legal advice to government ministers. He had received an advanced law degree in France, and the British referred to him as "a highly intelligent man, with a subtle lawyer's mind." A determined nationalist, he had a critical say in when and in what form the government's assurances should be given. Only the minister of public works could override his decisions, and he, a political appointee, seemed reluctant to do so.[73]

Eventually, Howell and his colleagues presented three separate notes to the Egyptian Foreign Ministry, asking for a clarification of the antiquities law. The elections of May 22, 1926, gave victory to the Wafd Party, and although the British barred Sa'd Zaghlul's return to power, the change in government would likely make such an official statement much harder to obtain. Bedawi Pasha must have tried to drag out the affair until the new government took office, but Howell, suddenly energized, used his contacts at the palace to press Ziwar Pasha, the outgoing prime minister, to issue the letter. On May 26 the Egyptian Foreign Ministry issued an aide-mémoire that gave assurances that divisions would continue, albeit with some restrictions. The new prime minister, Adly Pasha, and his foreign minister, Sarwat Pasha, accepted this as a fait accompli, even though many members of their party opposed *any* export of antiquities.[74]

An assessment to this point shows that the Egyptian nationalists had been remarkably successful in imposing control over Western archaeologists. Although the greatest discovery of the interwar years had led to a series of clashes with foreign Egyptologists, their supporting institutions and even their governments, the entire treasure of Tutankhamun remained in Egypt. Moreover, the Egyptians set the rules under which Howard Carter had been allowed to complete his technical work in the Valley of the Kings. On the question of divisions, an issue of major importance to the great museums in Europe and America, Lacau had given little away. The fifty-fifty division had become only a memory.

# 5. HOUSING EGYPT'S TREASURES

Since his first postwar visit to Egypt in 1919, James Breasted had returned every year and always with an impressive list of projects to complete. Spending time in Cairo was obligatory, if distasteful. He preferred the quiet of Upper Egypt, especially Luxor, whose slower pace of life allowed him time to visit the nearby monuments regularly. Here, he could oversee the work of his epigraphic survey team, catch up on his voluminous correspondence, and entertain the constant stream of guests, archaeologists, dignitaries, officials, friends, and friends of friends. After the new Chicago House, with its spacious grounds and lovely gardens, opened on the eastern bank of the Nile, Luxor became even more alluring for the sixty-something Egyptologist. He disliked the crowded, noisy streets of the bustling capital, from which he could escape only briefly in the gardens of Shepheard's Hotel in the Ezbekiyeh quarter. He decried many of the changes that had taken place since his early visits in the calmer, quieter days of Lord Cromer. But Cairo was the center of power, and to accomplish his goals he had to meet with important leaders to seek their understanding and support. He became a well-known figure among both the foreign and the Egyptian elites.

It was there in fall 1924, while the joint crises over Tutankhamun and the new antiquities law moved toward resolution, that Breasted brought forth a new project, perhaps his grandest, which quickly rekindled all the old antagonisms. The project, to build a state-of-the-art museum and archaeological institute in Cairo, using a $10 million grant from John D. Rockefeller Jr., was at least in part an American response to the frustrations of the recent past and the growing assertiveness of Egyptian nationalism.

The idea began with Breasted, a man of broad vision, and evolved out of his experiences in Egypt in the early postwar years. He knew that the Egyptian Museum had become overcrowded as thousands of antiquities flowed into its storerooms and that the small staff was unable to give ade-

**Figure 5.1.** Street scene in front of Shepheard's Hotel, Ezbekiyeh quarter, Cairo. Breasted stayed here when in Cairo. Courtesy National Archives.

quate attention to the newly arriving materials. Antiquities from earlier periods, especially from the time of Auguste Mariette, had never been properly identified by the excavator, and now there was little chance that many of these objects would be put on display in the increasingly cluttered showrooms. Items were often poorly labeled, and the amateur needed a guide to lead the way through the maze. There was no climate control to slow deterioration, and there were often rumors of leaks in the roof and flooding in the basement, which were said to have damaged some of the irreplaceable antiquities in storage. Critics often exaggerated the extent of damage, and Lacau and other officials of the Antiquities Service challenged them, but the rumors persisted. The service struggled on, then as now, with a slim budget, antiquities not being a priority of governments with more fundamental demands to meet. Thus a new museum and research institute, thought Breasted, would resolve many of these worsening problems.[1]

There was a second issue here as well, and this was equally important to Breasted. As one expatriate editor reported, the Egyptian government was beginning to send small numbers of students abroad to study archaeology who on their return would expect to replace foreigners in the antiquities department. "If they do not get these posts," the editor continued, "they will make themselves heard on the subject and if they do get them, the result almost certainly will be to the detriment of Egyptology." An institute under proper direction could guide a new generation and prepare students for their responsibilities in a systematic and scientific fashion, thereby delaying the strident demands of nationalist politics. Breasted had this much in mind as he drafted his proposal. He wrote to his friend, George Hale, that "the result will be disastrous unless we can hold them off for another generation."[2]

Breasted sent his proposal to Rockefeller at the beginning of October 1924. Although he made a strong case for building the museum complex in Cairo, Rockefeller had reservations about the project. He explained to his trusted adviser, Raymond D. Fosdick, that if preservation of antiquities were the prime factor, perhaps they could convince the Egyptian government to sell all of its collection, "including the things from the tomb of Tutankhamun," to pay the national debt. The antiquities thus purchased could then be placed in a museum—assuredly in the West—where they could be cared for and made available to scholars. If, however, the decision was made to go ahead with a building project in Cairo, the "donor," as he was referred to, worried about who in the Egyptian government could be trusted to carry out such an enterprise. Rockefeller's concerns must have deepened when he received a letter from his friend Cyrus McCormick, who had just returned from Egypt. McCormick cautioned him to go slowly for the situation there was fragile and without Sa'd Zaghlul's approval the museum project could be overturned in the future. Rockefeller asked Breasted to visit him so they could discuss the matter in detail. At those face-to-face meetings, the director persuaded Rockefeller and his advisers that this project, a gift to the people of Egypt, should be supported.[3]

They laid their plans carefully; the proposal went through several drafts before final signature in October 1925. Breasted, Fosdick, V. Everitt Macy (of Sardis fame), Welles Bosworth, the architect-in-waiting, and an engineer toured museum buildings throughout the United States to gain inspiration for their Cairo plans. With the final plan agreed, Rockefeller designated Breasted, Fosdick, and Macy trustees for the project.[4]

The proposal called for the building of a new, modern museum with sufficient display area for many of those antiquities currently hidden away in basement storerooms. Alongside the museum would be an institute where Egyptologists would study the ancient materials and incidentally teach their scientific skills to young Egyptian apprentices. The complex would be located on the banks of the Nile on the site where the Qasr-el-Nil barracks presently stood. This was not far from the present museum and at the very heart of downtown Cairo.

The Rockefeller gift, approximately $10 million, would pay for construction and leave a sizable endowment to cover operating expenses for the complex far into the future. This would be administered by an Egyptian archaeological foundation. To guarantee that all would run efficiently, an Egyptian museum commission would have oversight of the entire complex for thirty-three years. The foundation would be composed of two members each from Egypt, France, Great Britain, and the United States, and its members would also serve on the commission. Although control over the museum would end after the initial period, control over the endowment and the institute might go on indefinitely.[5]

The Egyptians had no part in planning the project and did not even learn of its existence for many months. The British Foreign Office, however, had been informed almost immediately. At first they approached the new issue cautiously, trying to stay in the background to avoid upsetting the Americans, the French, or the Egyptians. On February 18, 1925, an official minuted that the Egyptians would probably object that they should be masters in their own house and then added, "Of course they are not, but who will persuade them?" He went on to decry the obstructionism of Lacau, who frustrated every attempt to remedy the sad state of affairs of Egypt's antiquities. In their heart of hearts they could not be averse to the passing of French control over archaeology in Egypt. Breasted could not have agreed more. If the issue were resolved solely in the interests of science, without reference to politics, he argued, any impartial judge would decide that continued French control was preposterous.[6]

Breasted chose not to inform the French director until the last possible moment, even though the proposal would have considerable impact on his position. When questioned by Lythgoe in April, Breasted responded, "Oh, he [Lacau] knows nothing about it, but will undoubtedly jump at it!" How could Breasted have arrived at such a conclusion, given his earlier brushes with the Frenchman? Perhaps he really did not believe what he told Lythgoe. More likely he thought that the director would become irrelevant once the Egyptians learned the details of the proposal, including the handsome gift from Rockefeller. Surely, he might have argued, the project was more important than the interests of any individual.[7]

Having received Rockefeller's approval, Breasted turned next to Great Britain, which still exercised substantial power in Cairo, despite the 1922 unilateral declaration of Egyptian independence. The British controlled Egypt's defenses, its communications, including the Suez Canal, the Sudan, and the so-called foreign interests, referring largely to the affairs of the minority Greek and Italian communities located chiefly in Alexandria. Furthermore, Breasted expected the British forces to abandon their old barracks in the heart of Cairo, as they had earlier promised, to make room for the new museum complex.

Before traveling to London in June, Breasted sought support at the State Department, and in a series of meetings on the project, officials, including Secretary of State Kellogg, agreed to assist him in every way possible. Hale, who had met with them earlier on Breasted's behalf, reported that he had been surprised at how well informed they were and how anxious to support American interests in a direct and emphatic manner. This represented a remarkable change from the prewar years, an expression of growing American activism internationally.[8]

Breasted also wrote to Sir Frederick Kenyon, director of the British Museum, to explain the project and to seek his help. He envisioned a combination of British political power and American money that could save the marvelous heritage of Egypt. This was a view he would return to repeatedly throughout the negotiations. He lamented the prospect of passing this heritage into the hands of "indifferent native officials seeking only a well-paid job and having no intention whatever of doing any work." If the project succeeded Western scientific control in Egypt would be continued for another generation and, most important, "it may be possible in some manner at least to prepare a new generation of Oriental archaeologists of Egyptian blood to equip them for carrying their new responsibilities very much more successfully and intelligently thirty years from now than is possible at present."[9]

Breasted arrived in London on June 12. He felt comfortable moving in familiar places within the top echelon of British officials. He received a friendly reception, reminding him of his successes there just six years earlier. The American ambassador, Alanson B. Houghton, made clear to Foreign Minister Austen Chamberlain that the State Department was very interested in the purpose of Breasted's mission, which it supported. Breasted enjoyed a private meeting with Chamberlain and Lord Balfour, now president of the British Academy and lord president of the council, and he was able to explain to them the details of the proposal. He spoke again enthusiastically of an Anglo-American cultural condominium in the Middle East, stretching from Cairo to Jerusalem, Babylon, and Nineveh, "which have been recovered from Mohammedan rule . . . by a great Christian Nation [Great Britain]." Such cooperation would have far-reaching consequences among all English-speaking peoples. Chamberlain responded warmly, indicating that America and England had come closer together in the outlying regions of the British Empire than anywhere else.[10]

Breasted met several times with John Murray, chief of the Egyptian affairs section at the Foreign Office, who was very friendly. Murray helped to arrange a meeting with Sir George Lloyd, who was replacing Lord Allenby as high commissioner for Egypt. Breasted hoped to convince him to commit to evacuation of the barracks in Cairo, but Lloyd insisted that he wanted first to see the situation on the ground. Although the Foreign Office favored Breasted's project, approving the proposed Egyptian Museum Commission, it would not press the high commissioner for an immediate answer. Breasted could only hope that the barracks issue would soon be resolved in his favor.[11]

One of the most important outcomes of the extended stay was a change of priorities for the American archaeologist. When he wrote to Bosworth in May, he listed three difficulties standing in the way, the barracks, adjustment of relations with the French, and "the obstacles which will undoubtedly be raised by the Egyptians." In this letter he indicated that he might have to visit Paris during the summer to discuss the project with the French Foreign Office or the Ministry of Public Instruction. Indeed, British officials in Cairo had recommended this course of action. All this changed as a result of his talks in London, where Murray and others convinced him that he "need not consult the French until after the project had been arranged with the king [Fuad] and his ministers." This was perhaps not surprising advice given the overall direction of British foreign policy in this period, when London was fleeing French fears about its security, turning its back on Europe, and embracing once again a splendid isolation. Breasted had long criticized French policy and French officials in the Middle East, and he had never had much success in his relations with them. He welcomed the opportunity not to go to Paris that summer, writing in his diary, "If I can escape it, I shall not see the French at all." It would be better to present them with a fait accompli as the British recommended.[12]

Murray promised that Lord Lloyd would have an answer about the barracks by early winter, and he asked Breasted not to approach King Fuad before then. Breasted heard from the high commissioner in late November, but the news was not good. He reported he could not evacuate the barracks because of the increasingly tense situation in the region. An uprising

in Syria against the mandate authorities followed by the French bombard-
ment of Damascus with much loss of life had put British forces on the
alert in Cairo. A withdrawal under these circumstances would embarrass
the British; hence the transfer of the barracks could not take place.[13]

Rockefeller insisted to Breasted that that was where the museum had
to be located, and as the disagreement intensified, the donor shrank from
the thought of adverse publicity, urging Breasted to remember that the
purpose of the project was to render service and promote goodwill, and
if these two objectives could not be attained it might be better to abandon the project. Eventually, after much persuasion, Breasted was able to
reconcile Rockefeller to the loss of this much-favored spot, substituting
land on Gezira, the island in the Nile just across from downtown.[14]

During these months spent in Egypt waiting for Lloyd's response,
Breasted's initial concern about Egyptian reactions seems to have lessened
as well. He confided to his wife, Frances, that once "we get by the British,
the Egyptians are not going to cause us much trouble." The "bait" of a
new museum and a rich endowment would be too much for grasping politicians to resist. This was a surprising conclusion from one who reputedly
knew Egypt so well. He clearly did not appreciate how much conditions
had altered there since the war, even though the controversies over Tutankhamun and the law of divisions indicated how sensitive such issues had
become. Old ways of thinking change slowly if at all, and many of those
who had worked in Egypt in the prewar period, men such as Breasted,
Carter, and Lythgoe, had difficulty making necessary adjustments.[15]

Against his better judgment Breasted had to rely on Howell to arrange
an audience for him with the king. He said he had been warned by the
State Department "not to use this pompous and stupid old country doctor, from Ohio, a small town product," but he had no choice for diplomacy
required such an official introduction. He did not reveal anything of his
plans to the minister, however, keeping him completely in the dark until
just two days before the project became public knowledge.[16]

Finally came the day when Breasted could present the proposal to the
king. In preparation, the Rockefeller trustees had printed a handsome
booklet, magnificently bound in red Moroccan leather and with beautiful
sketches of the artist's conception of opening day for the new complex,
with royal barges carrying dignitaries along the Nile to the foot of the
monumental stairway leading up to the museum. Buildings were shown
festooned with banners and flags. Other sketches revealed the exact floor
plans of the new structures. No expense had been spared in putting this
attractive package together, "and with this ammunition" he expected "to

**Figure 5.2.** Drawing from a presentation book for King Fuad, showing artist's conception of the proposed Cairo Museum seen from mid-Nile as it might appear at its dedication. Courtesy of Rockefeller Archives Center.

intoxicate the king," boasting that "if that doesn't get a vain and self-conscious Oriental, nothing else will." [17]

To Breasted's amazement the king barely looked at the materials or the personal letter from Rockefeller, in which he explained that as it had taken the United States thirty years to produce a generation of archaeologists, this plan would allow Egypt the same length of time. Fuad ridiculed the plan as visionary and impossible and complained about American interference. Who can know what lay behind this royal outburst? Surely the failure to have consulted any Egyptian about the proposal during the year of preparation must have rankled, especially for this king who was intensely interested in Egypt's antiquities. Breasted interpreted the king's response as a sign of vanity and loss of pride, knowing that Egypt could not take care of its own ancient heritage. The American's attempt to end the audience triggered a remarkable change of tone, with Fuad expressing some appreciation for the Rockefeller offer and indicating that it would be sent to the prime minister for consideration. [18]

Breasted came away believing that he would have to place full reliance on the British, whom, he thought, would be able to make the project a reality. He turned immediately to Lord Lloyd, who in separate meetings with the king and the prime minister, Ziwar Pasha, stressed the importance of such an opportunity that should not be allowed to fail. They both agreed to support it. Breasted had convinced himself that informed Egyptians generally would want this great plan, and he toyed with the idea of using the press to publicize the proposal so that public opinion there and abroad could force the hand of Egyptian officials.[19]

But even he soon had to admit that modifications would be necessary if the project were to be acceptable to Ziwar Pasha's government. He suggested a number of these, including appointing an Egyptian minister to head the museum commission. Breasted and Chauncey Belknap, a member of Fosdick's law firm who had been loaned to assist the negotiations in Cairo, sought approval to share responsibility for control of the museum complex between Egypt and the international commission, but Rockefeller rejected this. Next they suggested that the purpose of the commission be changed so that instead of administering the museum, it would only monitor the actions of the Egyptian government and if in agreement with those actions would advance funds from the endowment to support the complex. Belknap, they decided, should carry this amended proposal directly to New York.[20]

Along with his own report, Belknap carried a letter from Bosworth, who also had been helping out in Cairo. In it he observed that a basic problem in gaining Egyptian acceptance might have been the lack of preparation and their belief that they were being asked to act too quickly in such an important matter on which they had too little time to reflect. This seemed a sensible observation from one with relatively little experience in Egypt.

Breasted had hoped that everything could be kept out of the public arena until all the details had been worked out, but news of the project leaked, forcing him quickly to release some details to the Egyptian press on February 14. Rockefeller was furious that he had not first been consulted but later apologized for having hastily rebuked Breasted.

Over the ensuing eight weeks the museum project became the subject of attention both within Egypt and abroad. Breasted had done his best to convince the local press that the gift represented a selfless act of philanthropy. He did not spell out the conditions attached to it. A February 15 editorial in the leading *Al-Ahram* praised the gift as a sign of the nobility of character of Americans and as an indication of the respect other countries should show toward Egypt, "the mother of civilization." The Unionist Party paper, *Al-Ittihad*, took a more cautious approach, arguing that the offer needed to be studied and discussed but certainly not dismissed out of hand as some Wafd publications had recommended.[21]

On February 24 a prominent lawyer, Muhammad Lotfy Gomaa, used the pages of *Al-Ahram* to criticize the proposal, referring to Rockefeller as "the American Haroun," referring to Haroun al-Rashid, the early Abbasid caliph famous for his untold wealth. Gomaa rejected the idea that Egypt needed a tutor to show it how to take care of the "great wealth inherited from the forefathers." Never would Egypt mortgage its antiquities for a whole generation. Perhaps these new friends from the West would help the Egyptians to reclaim "all the monuments and antiquities that fill the museums of London, New York, Paris and Berlin." He, for one, would never part with his share of Egypt's heritage. Charles Breasted responded in predictable fashion that the letter contained all the typical things "a narrow-minded Gyppie would say."[22]

Some Egyptian officials, too, made public their opposition. Ismail Sirri Pasha, minister of public works, whose portfolio included the Antiquities Service, opposed the gift, saying that Egypt did not need alms and that he would never allow the Antiquities Service to come under the control of such a committee as Rockefeller proposed.[23]

Breasted also had to respond to private criticisms, none more eloquent than that from Cecil Firth, longtime British employee of the Antiquities Service and close friend of Lacau and Reisner. Firth claimed that all the secrecy associated with the project had naturally led to rumors of intrigue. What the country needed most, he believed, was not a great museum and institute but rather a training facility to prepare the Egyptians for working with antiquities. He wondered whether the great foreign museums would accept such a proposal, which if carried into effect would virtually guarantee that Egyptian masterpieces remained in Cairo. Finally, he claimed that Breasted had given far too little recognition to the work of the service and especially to Lacau, who had accomplished a good deal under very difficult circumstances. In this regard, he concluded that the destructive part of Breasted's work had concealed the constructive part.[24]

Breasted replied immediately, disclaiming that he was seeking international control of the antiquities but rather the proper housing of Egypt's treasures. While praising Lacau as a scholar, he argued that he was not a good administrator. He dangled before Firth the possibility that with all his experience, training, and ability, he might choose to participate in "the erection of such a great plant as we have in mind."[25]

Firth wrote again several weeks later, after the proposal (but not the details) had become generally known. He said he was pleased that now his chief [Lacau] also knew of the project. He repeated some of the rumors that were rife, concerning conditions attached to the gift, among them that the international board would take control of the service, that one-half of all antiquities found would go to Europe and America, that the board would have the final say in all divisions, that one quarter of the Tutankhamun treasure would go to the Metropolitan Museum of Art and the same amount to the British Museum. All this indicated the extent of misinformation Breasted had to overcome. Building on his earlier letter, Firth made several suggestions, calling most urgently for an agreement among all foreign museums not to purchase illicitly excavated antiquities from dealers, for they and their agents, he noted, were more active than ever before.[26]

Nothing in the project appealed to fellow American archaeologist George Reisner, a longtime critic of Breasted. Writing confidentially to the director of the Boston Museum of Fine Arts, which sponsored his expedition, Reisner complained that Breasted "was to be made dictator of antiquities in Egypt." Having learned earlier than most about the project, he had informed Lacau. This fact, and Reisner's suggestion that the funds would be better spent training Egyptian archaeologists, suggests that he had been in contact with his neighbor, Cecil Firth. Reisner championed the cause of the French director and indeed of the long line of French directors who had built Egypt's collection into the finest in the world. His communications were also filled with rumors of designs to destroy the service and to pillage sites, which had been withheld from excavation. All this for Breasted's aggrandizement, he declared.[27]

Reisner discussed the project with Howell, when the American minister visited him at his camp at Giza. Later the diplomat refused Breasted's request to speak in favor of the proposal to the French minister, reporting to the State Department instead that the entire French community opposed it. Breasted undiplomatically admitted to Howell that officials at the department had known of the project for at least a year; apparently they had chosen not to share the information with their representative in Cairo.[28]

The French minister in Cairo, H. Gaillard, urged his government to be very careful not to express an opinion on the project, for they did not want to offend the Americans and certainly not Mr. Rockefeller, one must presume, who had given large sums to postwar France to restore several medieval buildings and to improve the health of the nation. In any case, Gaillard assured Paris, the project would fail because no Egyptian government would be able to give over to foreigners such important controls.[29]

**Figure 5.3.** Pierre Lacau (white beard) and King Fuad and his entourage leaving Meydum Pyramid, Fayoum, early 1930s. Courtesy of University of Pennsylvania Museum, Philadelphia.

Lacau, of course, had no such hesitation. He interpreted the project as an attempt to destroy the service and to remove him from his position, and he actively lobbied the king against it. In a letter to Gaillard he summarized the arguments he had given Fuad, stressing that he did this not for French interests but "solely from a practical and scientific point of view."[30]

The American press also weighed in on the issue. There were sensible pieces such as the one in the *New York World*, which acknowledged that the Egyptians had every reason to be suspicious of such a generous gift but concluded that Rockefeller's conditions were so reasonable their continued opposition was difficult to understand. And there were unreasonable ones, such as two letters from Amos Q. Pipp in the *New York Sun* addressed to King Fuad. The first claimed that controls were necessary to ensure that the $10 million would not be turned over to a lot of camel drivers or cigarette makers or used to stock the Nile with speckled trout. The second doubted whether anybody else would give that much for "the whole country including the Pyramids." They revealed at best a lack of understanding of the Egyptian position and at worst a brazen effrontery.[31]

Even presumed allies had complaints. Lythgoe of the Metropolitan charged that Breasted had promised not to introduce the museum project until the problem of the divisions had been resolved, but he had gone ahead regardless, confusing the State Department, which thought the two issues were joined, and stirring up nationalist opposition in Cairo. All this for Breasted's glory.[32]

This criticism might have weakened the determination of a lesser man, but James Breasted seemed remarkably unaffected. He concluded that this was the price one had to pay for furthering the enlightened mission of America and American civilization. In a letter to Mrs. Rockefeller he emphasized how important it was to make such efforts "to save these people from themselves." Whatever the result, "the whole transaction has created in the Near East a new impression of the real strength and greatness of America—that new America which Mr. Rockefeller is doing so much to make a beacon of hope to all peoples." Every country had its share of bigots into which class he put men like Ismail Sirri Pasha. At root the problem was Egyptian vanity, the dominant characteristic. One could get the Egyptians to accept even the most disagreeable dose if it were properly sugar-coated; they wanted only the semblance of power and authority. "How different from the sturdy self-respect of the Anglo-Saxon, proud of his independence and resentful of intrusion upon it." To neutralize Lacau, Breasted wrote again to the American ambassador to France, Myron T. Herrick, asking him to intercede with the French government to press the director of the Antiquities Service to stop obstructing the museum enterprise.[33]

While the museum project awaited a final decision, Breasted continued to carry out his duties as director of the Oriental Institute. In late March he wrote to Rockefeller from Megiddo, or Armageddon, in Palestine, where the American philanthropist's generosity was supporting another institute excavation. In this letter he showed his remarkable ability to relate the ancient world to contemporary times to draw in the reader, especially one steeped in the Old Testament. Breasted first recalled his own boyhood on the Illinois prairie, where he and his peers would struggle every Sunday over biblical names such as Rehoboam and Shishak, pharaoh of Egypt. Imagine his wonder, therefore, to find a fragment of a stele that this very same Shishak had erected to commemorate his long-ago conquest of Jerusalem.[34]

Breasted went on to recount the remarkable find of the feet of a golden calf, dating from approximately 1800 B.C.E., in the hands of a dealer in

Jerusalem. This had such great historical significance that Breasted sought permission to purchase it with money Rockefeller had earlier donated for another purpose. Such was the enterprise of the amazing Dr. Breasted.[35]

Returning to Cairo in early April, he was still confident that the project would succeed, writing to Winlock that "the horse is up to the trough and he may drink before we sail." It was not to be. In a meeting with the prime minister, Ziwar Pasha told Breasted that the conditions set by Rockefeller could not be accepted by the cabinet, and so the American reluctantly withdrew the offer. Although the two sides had drawn closer together, there remained an unbridgeable gap. Ostensibly it was demands for foreign control over the hiring and compensation of museum personnel and making a Westerner the real head of the commission that led to the stalemate. As one recent author sums it up so effectively, however, "the seed of the project's failure was contained within its very conception. The plan, presented as a national museum complex, was a circumvention of the sovereign rights of the people for whom it was to be built." The Cairo museum had become such an important symbol to Egyptian nationalists, in part because of Breasted's continual emphasis, that it had to be put beyond the possibility of foreign control.[36]

Breasted departed Egypt soon after his meeting with Ziwar Pasha, but over the next several months he kept alive the hope that a compromise could be reached. Fosdick wrote to him in September, reminding him that as long as the government persisted in its demands for control over the proposed museum commission "in matters of personnel and policy" there could be no project. Breasted's response makes it clear that he only dimly perceived the real issue for many Egyptians. He talked of changing the makeup of the commission to include an additional Egyptian representative and perhaps a German as well. He made a more important point when he wrote that they needed to spell out in the contract their plans for training young Egyptian scientists, an oversight pointed out by the ever-vigilant Bedawi Pasha.[37]

Well into the new year Breasted remained hopeful, but the longer the time that elapsed, the more his confidence waned. He began to understand why Egypt had rejected the initial offer. In March 1927 he told Fosdick that the terms would have to be changed for the Egyptian government could not put Europeans in control and survive nationalist sentiment. Breasted added that he should have understood this before. Two months later, in his final report on the project, he went further, admitting that even with all his experience in the region he had not fully realized the amount of patient effort necessary to reach such an important agreement with an "oriental" government. "We ourselves," he wrote, "have learned that we cannot lay down before the Egyptians a contract signed by ourselves and merely point a finger to the dotted line."[38]

These were important admissions, but they came too late. On the Egyptian side there was much suspicion, which had festered over the previous year, and now also the Wafd, decidedly more opposed to such foreign schemes, was about to resume power. As for the donor, Rockefeller was unlikely, despite his continuing admiration for Breasted, to consent to the less stringent conditions Breasted now advocated. Even Breasted gradually lost interest as he turned his attention toward new challenges farther east, especially in Iraq and Iran.[39]

In subsequent years Breasted was able to reestablish reasonably good relations with Lacau, remarking after his visit to Chicago House in Luxor that the director "had been so cordial and seemingly so sincere that the old amicable relations disturbed by the Tutankhamun negotiations and completely destroyed by the Cairo Museum affair seemed really to have been restored and to no small extent by a statue of Tutankhamun!" The director of antiquities had just awarded a seventeen-foot-high quartzite statue of the young pharaoh, a duplicate, to Chicago. (It has impressed visitors to the Oriental Institute, as Breasted knew it would, ever since its installation in September 1934.)[40]

Breasted might forgive the Egyptians and even the Frenchman but not those Americans who, he believed, had worked to sabotage the project from the beginning. He was well aware of Reisner's opposition and took the opportunity in a letter to Lucy Aldrich, whose brother was a prominent trustee of the Boston Museum of Fine Arts, to criticize his fellow archaeologist. Reisner, he argued, had opposed the project from "petty motives," and he wanted her brother to know this. According to the director, Reisner was a fine archaeologist, perhaps the best in Egypt, but he had for too long focused on the sequence of changes in a few neighboring mounds; he had no broad vision of the whole process that carried man from savagery to civilization, which fascinated Breasted.[41]

Breasted's attitude toward the American minister in Cairo hardened beyond reconciliation. He had no respect for the minister, and his letters and reports were filled with criticisms. Howell had not supported the project, and his actions had weakened the American position. Furthermore, according to Breasted, Howell had antagonized Lord Lloyd by challenging British authority in a number of petty, public incidents, thereby becoming something of a hero to the radical nationalists. The high commissioner remarked to Breasted, "It is peculiarly painful to me, that the

**Figure 5.4.** James Henry Breasted and George A. Reisner at the Continental Hotel, Cairo, November 15, 1935, just three weeks before Breasted's death. Courtesy of the Oriental Institute of the University of Chicago.

French and Austrian ministers must step forward in defense of Great Britain in Egypt, against the attack of the American representative."[42]

Breasted decided that the situation had deteriorated so badly that some action would have to be started in Washington, seeking Howell's recall. Breasted urged his son to move cautiously for he did not want his own name associated in any way with this, even recommending that his son destroy the letter. His caution was motivated by the fact that Vice President Charles Dawes and Dwight Morrow and others had moved to have Breasted appointed U.S. minister at Cairo. He did not want them to think that he acted out of a desire for personal advantage. Breasted told Charles to explain everything to Fosdick, who would know how to proceed. To his relief he received news in early May 1927 while homeward bound that Howell had resigned. To what extent his intervention had succeeded remained unclear.[43]

As Rockefeller's interest in Cairo was receding, that for Jerusalem was on the rise. During his brief visit to Palestine in March 1926, Breasted had reported on the need for a museum there as well. Although reluctant at first to become involved in another museum project, the philanthropist gradually became convinced of the benefits of such an undertaking. Palestine, too, presented a very different situation, for there the British had full control over such matters. During a brief visit in April 1927, Breasted easily worked out arrangements with Lord Plumer, high commissioner for the mandate. According to the terms, Rockefeller would donate $2 million for the project and its endowment. The conditions were so generous compared to those extended earlier to Egypt that Fosdick cautioned against making the gift letter public "because . . . if the Egyptian project should ever be revived, the contents of this letter might prove embarrassing." Fosdick admitted finding it easier to deal with the British than with other races. One wonders whether the more lenient terms were the result of this factor or whether the Rockefeller group had learned a salutary lesson from the failure in Egypt. Perhaps it was a mixture of both. The new museum opened to the public in January 1938.[44]

As the Jerusalem project indicated, the failure at Cairo had done nothing to weaken the ties between Rockefeller and Breasted. In fact, in 1929 they spent several months together, touring the Middle East, including Egypt, Palestine, and Syria. At Cairo Breasted had an unpleasantness with the new U.S. minister, Franklin Mott Gunther, a career diplomat. He did not invite the Breasteds to a luncheon in honor of Rockefeller and later tried to keep the director waiting in his anteroom while he discussed the museum project with Rockefeller alone. He should have known better; Rockefeller insisted that Breasted join them. Wherever they traveled Breasted acted as guide, presenting slide shows and talks for the party. Rockefeller had asked the director not to talk business during the trip, but the whole experience indirectly furthered Breasted's plans by increasing Rockefeller's enthusiasm for the study of antiquity. The American tycoon wrote to his children, praising Breasted, with whom it was a privilege to be associated in learning of the development of history and the progress of civilization. Breasted was, he wrote, "perhaps the greatest living archaeologist."[45]

Rockefeller's comments on the native inhabitants, both Arabs and Turks, were much less generous; among them he found filth, squalor, and poverty. "The men of both races," he told the children, "seem to have great facility in standing, sitting or lying in the sun and doing nothing." This was an observation worthy, perhaps, of Mark Twain's *Innocents Abroad*.[46]

Years later, Charles Breasted had occasion to write to the elderly Rockefeller to share with him his thoughts upon learning of the riots

**Figure 5.5.** Lantern slide from the Rockefeller visit to Egypt in 1929. Shown are (right to left) David Rockefeller, Dr. James Henry Breasted, Murray Dyer (David Rockefeller's English tutor), Mary Todhunter Clark, Robert W. Gumbel (John D. Rockefeller Jr.'s secretary), John D. Rockefeller Jr. Breasted is lecturing to the group at the Ramesseum, Luxor. Courtesy Rockefeller Archives Center.

and destruction in Cairo that presaged the 1952 Egyptian revolution. He wrote, "When the holocaust befell Cairo recently, I resisted the impulse to write you, to express my profound sense of gratitude that there was no Rockefeller museum there to be pillaged and destroyed." Whether such an institution would have come under attack on Black Saturday, as it is known, is a fine question.[47]

Events of the 1920s, the rancorous Tutankhamun affair followed closely by heated debate over the Rockefeller museum proposal, had evoked strong nationalist objections, even among those not particularly interested in the monuments and antiquities of Pharaonic Egypt. They complained of decades of being robbed by foreigners, and nothing rankled more than knowing that the showpieces in many Western museums had lain for millennia in Egypt's soil. Just as the Greek government periodically sought restitution of the Elgin Marbles on display in the British Museum, so, too, did various Egyptian ministries seek return of the head of Nefertiti, a prized possession of the Berlin Museum, which many Egyptians believed the Germans had smuggled out of their country. The government refused to allow Germans to excavate there until the issue had been resolved.[48]

In October 1929 Lacau was sent to Berlin to negotiate with the Germans for the return of the bust. This made other Western institutions nervous, and Kenyon of the British Museum kept a close eye on the discussions. An official at the Foreign Office noted that it would be an awkward precedent for Britain if the Germans decided to return the head. Fortunately for them, the negotiations failed, and Lacau came back to Cairo empty-handed.[49]

The French director would face more serious disappointments as the decade came to an end. Not only had many foreign archaeologists criticized his administration of the Antiquities Service, but so, too, had many Egyptians—but for different reasons. The latter looked forward to the day when the service would be staffed entirely by Egyptians, a prospect that concerned many foreigners. In February 1928 the minister of public works, Uthman Muharram Pasha, a stalwart of the Wafd Party, intervened directly in service affairs, forbidding export of any antiquities without his personal approval. His action threatened to make the matter of divisions impossibly cumbersome. Under this pressure and in declining health, Lacau thought seriously of resigning. That rumor sent officials in Paris scrambling to find a suitable replacement.[50]

The French government and the national museum, the Louvre, had traditionally worked closely with the archaeologists in Egypt, including those at the French Institute in Cairo. They contributed money for expeditions, but this was more difficult to justify when fewer antiquities were being shipped to Paris. The Metropolitan and other such institutions faced similar problems. This development led George Reisner to declare that the days of museum funding for antiquities was passing and to recommend to Harvard University that it establish an endowment to carry on the important archaeological work there, without any expectation of receiving antiquities in return. This seemed to him the only feasible approach as the Antiquities Service became more "Egyptianized." The French still hoped to maintain the status quo.[51]

Lacau came out of this crisis in a stronger position, for he had the support of the king. In May 1929 the service was transferred from the Ministry of Public Works to the Ministry of Public Instruction. This was a reflection of the recent dispute but also a recognition of the important cultural contribution of the work of the Antiquities Service. Similar changes were being made in other Middle Eastern states. Not that the new overseer necessarily proved more efficient than the old; archaeologists still complained of long delays in having divisions approved when necessary papers became misplaced or lost within the bureaucracy.

Lacau also sat on the Comité de Conservation des Monuments de l'Art Arabe, where he exercised considerable influence. Though the Egyptians had a sizable majority on the committee, Lacau and the few European members often had their way. When Ali Baghat, conservator of the Museum of Arab Art, died in 1924, leaving the post open, a brief contest ensued between those who wanted another Egyptian and those who sought a European expert for the job. At a meeting in March 1926 Lacau and Harry Farnall, a British official, argued that there was no competent Egyptian available and that it would take time to train young Egyptians for the post. Abdul Hamid Sulayman Pasha countered that they should give the position to an Egyptian and then find European specialists to assist him. The committee sided with Lacau and offered the position to Gaston Wiet, whom the French government had recommended. Looking to the future, the committee gave him a three-year contract, during which time he was to begin preparing young Egyptians to head the museum. Wiet was still at his post twenty-five years later on the eve of the revolution.[52]

As the 1930s proceeded, concern over Lacau's retirement rose. Officials at the Quai d'Orsay realized that he was worn out after fourteen years of skirmishing with local nationalists and Western archaeologists, not to mention trying to frustrate the continuous attempts to dig illegally in all parts of the country. At the end of 1932 Lacau admitted to the king that he would like to go. At first the French government could find no Frenchman of sufficient stature to replace him. He had by now earned the grudging respect of many in Cairo, and they would have to find someone who could deal diplomatically with Egyptian nationalists. Given recent developments in Egypt, this might be France's last opportunity to nominate a director. Officials in Paris did not want an American or an Englishman and certainly not an Egyptian, although Lacau made it clear he would not object to the latter.[53]

Most Western archaeologists and their sponsors in Europe and the United States wanted to put off the terrible day when Europeans would no longer manage the affairs of the Antiquities Service. Some of those who had earlier harshly criticized the Frenchman now advised their colleagues to support him to avoid undermining his authority and thereby hastening the day when "an Egyptian, however inexperienced and unsuitable for such a post," would be appointed. Throughout the interwar period they argued that Egyptians were incapable of taking on such responsibility and directing archaeological matters fairly, efficiently, and skillfully. Disparaging comments such as Breasted's were the rule, not the exception. Even Reisner, who had cooperated closely with Lacau and the service, lamented the fact that eventually it would be Egyptianized. What is, of course, remarkable is how little Westerners had done to train young Egyptians to take over this important legacy. Only a handful went abroad to study between the wars. Of these the best known were Selim Hassan, Sami Gabra, and Mahmud Hamza, all of whom traveled to western Europe on Egyptian government scholarships in 1923 when they were in their thirties.[54]

The sins of the Westerners were not only those of omission. Whenever the Egyptians proposed to establish a school in Cairo to train young students, Westerners did what they could to frustrate their efforts. In the words of one leading scholar, "In the half century before 1922 Western archaeological interests in the Antiquities Service forced three indigenous Egyptological schools in succession to close by refusing to employ their graduates." The achievement of limited independence for Egypt in 1922 followed by Carter's phenomenal discovery led to "a permanent—if rather limited—commitment to Egyptology on the part of the upper-class Egyptians who now ran the government." In August 1923 the government decreed the founding of a school and named Ahmad Kamal, a member of the first generation of Egyptologists, its director. He died the same day. He had been frustrated throughout his career, but his students of the second generation, Hassan, Gabra, and Hamza, would have more success, helping to train a third generation, which would take full control after the 1952 revolution. Even in the 1920s Westerners did not passively accept the new school. George Foucart, director of the French Institute, saw the move as an anti-European strategy and did what he could to kill it, including lobbying several Egyptian ministers. This time the attempt failed.[55]

The contest to replace Lacau began in earnest in 1935, once it became certain that the director would leave the following year. Immediately, Egyptian nationalists began a campaign to secure the post for Selim Hassan, who had recently received his doctorate from the University of Vienna at age forty-one. Three years earlier the French minister had indicated that Hassan was "jockeying for the post." Now he had been considerably strengthened both with an advanced degree and with considerable experience overseeing his own excavations at Giza.[56]

At first the press campaign did not mention Hassan by name, citing rather a host of arguments supporting the appointment of an Egyptian. *Al-Balagh* took the lead, espousing the reasonable argument that to select an Egyptian "will be an act of justice rendered to Egyptians who may be devoted to the study of Egyptology to the end of serving the history of their country and cleansing it of the accusation which was made against them that they were disinterested in the history of the monuments of their own country." The editor went on to acknowledge the earlier contributions of the French but concluded that the time for change had come at last. Three days later the editor took a more strongly nationalist position, arguing that "the fact that a candidate is an Egyptian is at least as important as the qualities possessed by candidates." Another editor, recalling, perhaps, the blighted career of Ahmad Kamal, remarked that he hoped "the time has passed when an Egyptian must be treated unjustly in his country because he is an Egyptian." *Al-Ahram* urged Prime Minister Ali Maher Pasha to make a just decision, which could be welcomed by Egypt for its children.[57]

In the middle of this campaign, France made known its nominee, offering Étienne Drioton (1889–1961) as Lacau's replacement. Drioton, a canon in the Roman Catholic Church, had served as a conservator at the Louvre for many years. He had taught Selim Hassan briefly there in the early 1920s. From the Western perspective he appeared an ideal choice. Western archaeologists and officials, who rarely agreed on anything, were unified in their support. British High Commissioner Sir Miles Lampson had told the Foreign Office that no Egyptian was capable of replacing Lacau. Pierre Jogruet, new director of the French Institute, thought that his friend, Lacau, had been far too indulgent to the Egyptians and that consequently the French had suffered humiliations at the hands of the nationalists. He hoped Drioton would be firmer with them. Jogruet must have had in mind the recent accusation that he had been lax in overseeing an excavation run by his institute from which valuable papyri had disappeared. He had good reason to take the offensive. He, too, agreed that the Egyptians did not have the skills to direct Egypt's antiquities and thought it wrong to flatter their vanity. Even Reisner had earlier reported that Selim Hassan was inexperienced and that he had done his excavating with the assistance of workmen trained by European expeditions and with the advice of Western archaeologists, including himself. Yet despite his lack of qualifications, the American believed that Hassan would eventually become director general of antiquities. What drove this, he believed, was the suspicion and hatred of the foreigner among the Egyptian ruling class.[58]

Once the Egyptian press learned that Drioton's name had been put forward, its editors began to question his qualifications and praise those of Hassan. *Al-Balagh* found the Egyptian clearly better qualified, having published more and spent more time excavating. When word leaked that an assistant director would also be appointed—an obvious attempt to pacify the nationalists—the editor decried such a transparent stratagem. A letter to the paper signed simply, "An Archaeologist," argued that this was the most important position in the Egyptian administration for protecting the ancient history of the country. This was clearly an issue of patriotism. The editor followed with one of the broadest claims to date— that Egyptian scholars were in a better position to understand the history of Egypt because they knew better than foreigners the traditions of the country, which were, after all, carried down from antiquity. They could understand, in other words, things that foreign scholars could not. *Al-Siyasa* added a similar argument, stating that public posts belonged to nationals of a country; this was the pattern all over the world. Even if inferior to a foreign candidate, the Egyptian should be appointed providing "his designation is not contrary to the interests of the service."[59]

Countering this campaign for Selim Hassan was the fact that the ailing King Fuad supported Drioton. There were those who believed that the monarch was unlikely ever to champion one of his subjects over a European expert. Fuad, who had been raised in exile with his father in Italy, spoke Arabic imperfectly and never understood the people over whom he reigned. They in turn showed little enthusiasm for him. With his great interest in antiquities, Fuad was unlikely to support the Egyptian candidate, who was, furthermore, the darling of the opposition. The king died on April 28, 1936, in the middle of an election campaign, which the Wafd won overwhelmingly. The formal designation of Lacau's successor awaited installation of the new ministry under Fuad's son, the sixteen-year-old Faruq. It was rumored that no one in the outgoing cabinet wished to take responsibility for filling the post vacated by Lacau.[60]

The new ministry of Nahhas Pasha also hesitated to announce its decision. On June 8, almost a month after the change of government, the French minister met with the prime minister to complain bitterly about the delay in naming Drioton, which, he said, only contributed to the frenzy in the press. He reminded Nahhas Pasha that Selim Hassan was in no way the equal of the Frenchman. Imagine, he continued, an archaeologist who did not know Greek and Latin. If he had been faced with the Rosetta Stone, he never would have dreamed of using that trilingual document "to pull out the explanation of hieroglyphics." According to the minister, only Hassan's candor of ignorance could compare with the indisputable mastery of his competitor. Nahhas Pasha only partially escaped this

dilemma when he announced that Drioton would become the new director and that Hassan would occupy the new position of assistant director,
with the expectation that he would eventually succeed to the top post.[61]

It is difficult to explain the ministry's decision. It would soon pursue
a policy of Egyptianizing many other positions in the government, why
not the post of director of antiquities as well? Perhaps it had to do with
a desire not to antagonize the French while Egypt was in the middle of
difficult treaty negotiations with Great Britain. It might also have been
true, as the French claimed, that Selim Hassan had little respect among
his Egyptian colleagues. Whatever the reasons, the decision angered the
nationalist press, which saw the appointment as a national humiliation.
One editor lamented the fact that French colonialism was alive and well,
concluding that as far as understanding their ancient history, Egyptians
would remain children compared to foreigners.[62]

From the perspective of foreign archaeologists and their supporters,
the ensuing three years saw a continuous series of attempts by Hassan to
take de facto control of the Antiquities Service. He was angry that he had
lost a decade of his career because the Europeans had shut him out of the
field, forcing him to work as a schoolteacher. They complained that he
tried to push Drioton aside, worked to have European, especially French,
officials dismissed, and tried to ingratiate himself with the palace. All the
while, they charged, he carried on a campaign of self-aggrandizement,
which belied the fact that he lacked the expertise of a real Egyptologist.
Jogruet, who had had differences with Hassan—on one occasion he had
nearly thrown him out of the institute—urged Drioton to be less self-
effacing for his own good.[63]

It is difficult to determine how accurate were the complaints lodged
against the new assistant director. One must bear in mind that many Westerners, influenced by the dominant Orientalist perspective, often disparaged the qualifications and accomplishments of Egyptians. The American
minister admitted as much when he wrote at the time of the appointment
that "considering the extreme degree of jealousy which exists professionally among archaeologists of all nationalities, it is not a matter for surprise
that foreign archaeologists should be inclined to speak disparagingly of
the work of Dr. Selim Hassan." A former keeper of Egyptian antiquities at
the British Museum has acknowledged that many Western archaeologists
did not want to allow Egyptians into positions of power.[64]

George Reisner, well known for his independent assessments, enter-
tained Hassan on several occasions at his Giza camp, where they discussed
Hassan's forthcoming book in a very friendly manner. Reisner's family

**Figure 5.6.** Division 1937 at Harvard Camp, standing left to right: Mahmoud Said, Abd es Salam Effendi, Selim Bey Hassan, George Reisner, Étienne Drioton, Evelyn Perkins, chauffeur, looking east toward Khafre Pyramid. Harvard University–Boston Museum of Fine Arts Expedition. Photograph by Mohammedani Ibrahim c 1937 Museum of Fine Arts, Boston.

and assistants attended a farewell party given by Hassan for one of his protégés who was leaving to study at the Louvre. Certainly, the newspapers gave him a good deal of favorable coverage, with front-page stories featuring photographs of his ongoing work at the Pyramids.[65]

From most other quarters reports remained strongly critical. The French embassy reported that Hassan had burned his bridges with Faruq, trying too hard to impress the young king. The monarch chose Drioton to accompany him on his frequent visits to ancient sites, where the director served as his tutor. They enjoyed a cordial and perfectly trusting relationship, said the minister. Ambrose Lansing of the Metropolitan told the American minister that changes were taking place too quickly in Egyptianizing the service and that Egyptians lacked the tradition of service and respect for the monuments. "It would be a great pity," he concluded, "if through undue haste this nation should lose the prestige which years of devoted work on the part of outsiders have brought it." American officials cautioned against any formal complaint regarding matters in the service, for this might only make matters worse, they believed. Since the signing of the Anglo-Egyptian Treaty (August 6, 1936) guaranteeing more domestic control to Cairo and an end to the capitulations, the government looked upon such foreign protests with a jaundiced eye.[66]

Both the British and the French opposed Hassan. An official at the Foreign Office referred to him as "an ignorant rogue" and urged some intervention to ease him out of his position. Miles Lampson claimed that the assistant director was threatening to blackmail government ministers if he were dismissed by releasing information about their dalliances with young women. There were additional charges of theft and corruption against him. Ultimately, Faruq was responsible for Hassan's dismissal from the service in July 1939, although he was unable to have him brought to trial as he had wished.[67]

Ironically, the king, whose name has become synonymous with corruption and neglect of duty, received accolades for his part in "saving" the Antiquities Service. The French praised his devotion to Egyptology, citing as proof his marvelous collection of antiquities. They welcomed his determination to seek the collaboration of foreigners far into the future, which was in complete contradiction, they pointed out, to "the xenophobic campaign" actually taking place in the press to stir up public opinion. The British agreed with the French official who explained that there was still no qualified Egyptian to replace Drioton or other Europeans in the service. The Americans cautioned against any complaint that might weaken the French director and lead to his replacement by an Egyptian.[68]

Retaining a French director, however, was by the mid-1930s little more than a symbol of a bygone era. Little by little the government was able to impose more rigorous conditions on excavators, such as a law that all antiquities found had to be seen and cataloged by service officials immediately rather than at the end of the excavating season. Like his predecessor, Drioton worked diligently to ensure that Western archaeologists abided by these rules. He routinely sent letters, reminding foreign institutions that they would have to return antiquities they had on loan for study or lose their concessions. He urged foreign museums and universities not to buy any Egyptian antiquities without first verifying their source, so that once the merchants saw there was no market, the vandalism of monuments in Egypt would be checked. If they did not cooperate, he warned, they could be assured that the Antiquities Service would be less liberal with them in the future. Given the many conflicting demands on him, he had to be, according to one account, a clever diplomat.[69]

For all their optimism about the young king, the Westerners had linked their cause to a fading power. Faruq's popularity declined sharply through World War II, reaching its nadir in the disastrous 1948 campaign against the Zionists. The rout of Egyptian forces in the Sinai provided the cata- lyst for plots by disillusioned young army officers, culminating in the July Revolution of 1952. Faruq was in no position to assist Western archae- ologists, and, indeed, little excavating took place in Egypt during the two decades that followed the outbreak of war in September 1939. George Reisner died at Giza in 1942. The Metropolitan Museum of Art refused to excavate under the new, more stringent guidelines. The Egyptian Ex- ploration Society had given up its concession in 1936. The University of Chicago did not dig again in Egypt after it ended its excavations at Medinet Habu. When John Wilson, now director of the Oriental Insti- tute, returned to Egypt briefly in February 1946, he had many complaints about the state of Egyptology. He found only "hate, distrust, political chi- canery and bureaucratic ineffectiveness." At the service he found Drioton checkmated by his new Egyptian assistant and the Selim Hassan case still "a bed of hot coals." "Could the West salvage," he wondered, "a little of what the Egyptians ably assisted by the Director-General [Drioton] are wrecking?" Wilson happily departed Egypt through the Sinai with hardly a backward glance.[70]

Selim Hassan's reputation was resurrected after the revolution, but by then he was no longer in his prime, unprepared to take an active part in administering Egypt's Antiquities Service. Drioton had been on home leave when the revolution began, and he did not return. Mustafa Amer, an Egyptian, was appointed director, ending a century of French adminis- tration. The street outside the Egyptian Museum was renamed for Selim Hassan and his statue graced the garden. Many years after his death in 1961, the *Annales* of the service dedicated two volumes in his memory; the editor reminded readers of his long and successful career as an Egyptolo- gist and of the fact that he had trained many brilliant Egyptian scholars and excavators. At last the long transformation was complete.[71]

# 6. FRANCE'S CLOSED DOOR

After World War I nationalists in one country after another took action to limit what they considered the "theft" of their heritage by foreign archaeologists. Ensuing negotiations lasted many years, often drawing in European and American diplomats, called upon to support their compatriots, whom, they argued, worked under difficult circumstances, selflessly serving science and humanity. The story of another such effort, that to end the French archaeological monopoly in Iran in the 1920s, involved a familiar cast of archaeologists, diplomats, and nationalists and typified developments unfolding at approximately the same time throughout much of the region.

This affair began in August 1900 at Paris where Muzaffar-ed-Din Shah (1896–1907) signed a concession allowing French archaeologists "the exclusive and perpetual right to make excavations in all parts of the empire." By the terms of the concession, all artifacts from Susa, ancient capital of Elam and later a center of Achaemenid power in southwestern Iran, would become the property of the French government, without any remuneration to the Persian treasury. Elsewhere in the shah's realm, gold and silver objects would remain the property of France, but Tehran would be paid their value by weight. All other artifacts would be divided equally by the two governments. The shah undertook to facilitate the work of French archaeologists in the various provinces and to protect them as necessary, and they were to be exempt from all customs charges.[1]

This seemed a generous concession but not surprising to those familiar with the closing decades of Qajar rule in Iran. Beginning with Nasir ed-Din Shah (1848–1896) in 1873, monarchs of the Qajar dynasty (1794–1925) developed a passion for European travel. Muzaffar ed-Din Shah continued this tradition, traveling three times to Europe between 1900 and 1905. These extended journeys, with large retinues, cost vast sums, and in part to raise money for such personal extravagances, the Qajars encumbered the resources of Iran through contracting foreign loans or granting broad

Iran

concessions to foreigners. This was the background of the archaeological convention of 1900.

French archaeologists had been busy at Susa since the early 1880s and had amassed thousands of objects. The most recent agreement combined a number of earlier royal *firmans* (decrees) and conventions and a few adjustments based on experience. Jacques de Morgan had come from Egypt to serve as the first director of the French Archaeological Mission at Susa (1897–1908), followed by Roland de Mecquenem (1908–1938).

Early in the new century, the expedition, financed by the French government, built a "château" at a cost of 300,000 francs (then, U.S. $60,000) to house the archaeologists and their servants, supplies, and artifacts. It was an impressive structure that towered above the countryside. With its high walls, towers, and massive gate, it could easily be mistaken for the fortress of some local magnate were it not for the French tricolor flying from the highest point. When the château was built conditions in Khuzistan were unpredictable; tribal skirmishes frequently forced the archaeologists to withdraw to the safety of their stronghold, fastening the solid gates behind them. As late as March 1923 they complained of being held like hostages at Susa by tribes in revolt. In fact, three members of the expedition were taken hostage then, and the government in Tehran rushed to resolve the issue to avert a possible crisis with France. In November of that year Sheikh Khazal, chief of the local Arab tribes, resided there several weeks to escape the cholera at Mohammerah (now Khorramshahr) and to organize the region for the coming contest with the central government. The stronghold served many other purposes over the years, a center for British soldiers in World War I, a residence for Iranian officers in the tribal campaigns of the 1920s, a dormitory for American railroad engineers in the early 1930s. All this, of course, when the French archaeologists were not in residence, which was most of the year.[2]

On the hot, humid plains around Susa the digging season was short. Archaeologists usually arrived in mid-January and stopped their work by early April. After shipping artifacts to the Louvre, by barge down the Karun River system to its juncture with the Shatt al-Arab and from there by ship, the archaeologists soon followed, arriving home in time to enjoy the mild temperatures of late spring in France.

Although they enjoyed a monopoly in all of Iran, the French concentrated their efforts at Susa, and they were richly rewarded. The Iranian rooms in the Louvre were filled with the wondrous treasures from those years. More impressive than the objects of gold and silver were the colorful walls of enameled brick, showing the archers and foot soldiers of Darius I (521–486 B.C.E.). The French did well from their decades-long excavation.

And yet the monopoly came under increasing challenge elsewhere in Iran. The French lacked the resources to engage in excavations throughout the realm, thus opening the way for clandestine digging on public lands and open excavations on private property. De Mecquenem noted that all the hills surrounding the shrine of Abdul Azim outside Tehran had been dug up in the search for antiquities. French ministers complained repeatedly to the Foreign Ministry about these violations of their monopoly but with little success. In 1916 the foreign minister, Vosuq ad-Dauleh, denied that the convention of 1900 applied to private property, on which owners enjoyed an absolute right to excavate. French diplomats cited many cases of Iranian nationals conspiring with foreigners to export antiquities; and these frequently turned up for sale in Paris, not far from

**Figure 6.1.** "Château" at Susa built by the French archaeological mission in Iran at the beginning of the twentieth century, July 2003. Photo by author.

the ornate halls of the Musée du Louvre. The practice was impossible to stop, said the French minister, because certain officials were profiting from the arrangement, and successive Iranian governments, which generally did not approve of the French monopoly, delayed responding to French complaints for months or even years.[3]

The greatest threat to French rights came with the rise of Iranian nationalism and the outbreak of the Constitutional Revolution in 1906. Iranian patriots quickly challenged the actions of the later Qajars, who had pawned the nation's resources to satisfy their personal desires. Rumors were rife concerning the vast wealth the French had extracted from Susa. One newspaper reported—probably with considerable exaggeration—the sale of a statue from Susa that had brought 5 million pounds at a time when Muhammad Ali Shah (1907–1909) could not borrow 10,000 tomans from England or Russia. All this pointed up the foolishness of the Qajars and reinforced opposition to the French monopoly. This was just one of the hated capitulations or unequal treaties to which Iran had been subjected in the declining years of the feeble Qajar dynasty, and which became prime targets for Iranian nationalists.[4]

Opposition to the convention of 1900, however, went deeper than mere rejectionism, for many prominent Iranians had become convinced that the past held a special significance for the "new" Iran they hoped to create. Influenced in part by the writings of Western Orientalists, such as Henry Rawlinson and Edward G. Browne, these men came to believe that the history of the Iranian nation extended unbroken into the past for thousands of years. The glories of the ancients, especially of the Achaemenid and Sasanian dynasties, which arose out of peoples on the Iranian plateau, could serve as inspiration for a people too long subjected to the uninspired rule of the corrupt Qajars. As one newspaper reported, recent discoveries near Tehran might lead to the information that "fifty thousand years ago Persia existed and was ruled by an independent government." Resurrecting and reconstructing this history of the nation was too important a task to be left in the hands of foreigners, who seemed interested only in filling museums in their far-off Western capitals.[5]

Iranians, however, were more than passive receivers of Western scholarship. One recent scholar has argued that "Iran" and its corresponding territory was no nineteenth-century innovation but that such a concept "had old roots and simply found a new application and context in nationalism." Long before the advent of the Pahlavi dynasty (1925–1979), and even before the Constitutional Revolution of 1906, intellectuals such as Fath'Ali Akhundzadeh (1812–1878) and Mirza Agha Khan Kirmani (1855–1898), to name but two of the most prominent, had written in praise of pre-Islamic Iran. They argued that the glory of ancient Iran had ended with the invasion of the Arab tribes. "All the despicable habits and customs of the Persians," wrote Kirmani, "are either the legacy and testament of the Arab nation or the fruit and influence of the invasions." They presented the earlier period as a time when Iranians had been free and had chosen their rulers, whereas the Arab conquest ushered in a time of despotic rule. Their conclusions might bear little relationship to historical fact, but what was important was creating a new identity for Iranians; increasingly this meant turning elements and rulers of the earlier period into icons of the new nationalism. One goal of such writers was to undermine the reigning dynasty by comparing it unfavorably with its glorious predecessors and holding it responsible for the nation's shameful decline.[6]

Although at first these ideas did not reach much beyond the elite because of a dearth of national institutions and a restricted press, the coming of the Constitutional Revolution saw the development of national institutions and a vibrant press—247 journals were founded between 1906 and 1912—which together helped "to universalize Persianist ideals in the name of Iranian nationalism." Even the staff of a journal such as *Azarbayjan*, published in Tabriz in Azeri Turkish, "could take pride in the (mythologized) glories of ancient Iran." By the end of World War I, after repeated attacks on the old regime for its inability to defend the sacred homeland, many middle-class Iranians, having been exposed to a stream of nationalistic plays, poems, and press articles endorsed the need for change.[7]

The fervor of nationalism also spread within the military, which was being reorganized under the watchful eye of Riza Khan, minister of war and later prime minister. The army became an ideal environment in which to instruct officers and their troops in the virtues of the new nationalism. In 1923 one military man, Riza Kalantari, wrote to the press praising the reforming efforts of Riza Khan; then he continued in a typically florid style to give thanks to both ancient and modern Iran and the eternal "deeds of the fathers in keeping the nation alive." How widespread this propagandizing had become can be glimpsed from an encounter in Shiraz at the close of the 1920s. The commanding general there reminded a visiting British writer that for three thousand years his people had been "lords of Persia." Now, to overcome the ill effects of foreign intimidation during the nineteenth century, the military authorities had to encourage a certain arrogance among their charges to make them realize that they were heirs to a mighty past. After his successful coup in 1921, Riza Khan had sent the following message to reassure the military: "Gentlemen! Our dear homeland stands in urgent need of its brave sons. . . . Be alert and diligent: the dust of Ardashir is watching over you." Throughout his political career, the founder of the Pahlavi dynasty encouraged patriotism and national progress by conjuring images of ancient glory in his speeches to the troops.[8]

As more Iranians imbibed this new spirit, it became increasingly clear that the French monopoly could not last. Henri Massé, French epigrapher and linguist, visiting Tehran in 1923, reported that "the Persians, very proud of their past, are not at all disinterested in the question of excavations which they consider as national." He might have added that Muhammad Ali Foroughi (Zoka al-Mulk), a leading political figure of the time, had already written (1901) and revised (1917) a nationalist history of Iran incorporating Western methodology and that he served as president of the newly formed Society for the Preservation of the National Heritage.[9]

Even to those less intellectually inclined, the sad state of Iranian antiquities caused genuine alarm. When Riza Khan, then serving as minister of war, escorted Ahmad Shah (1909–1924), last of the Qajars, to his ship at Bushehr in 1922, he visited Takht-i Jamshid (Persepolis) en route, and the deplorable state of the Achaemenid palaces shocked him. Two years later during his campaign against Sheikh Khazal's southern tribes, he visited Susa for the first time. He was unimpressed with the French work and regretted how much Muzaffar ed-Din Shah had given away in the 1900 concession.[10]

Government ministers regularly complained about the loss of antiquities to France, with virtually no benefit for Iran. In response to these complaints, in January 1924 the foreign minister formally asked France to enter into conversation with a view to modifying the existing agreement.[11]

The visit in 1925 of an extraordinary American scholar and publicist, Arthur Upham Pope, helped to crystallize thinking among influential Iranians and seal the fate of the French monopoly. Pope was first attracted to Iran through encounters with Iranian art and especially carpets, which he believed showed "real superiority of mind and spirit." His love affair lasted on and off for over forty years and led him to found the American Institute for Persian Art and Archaeology. Pope received mixed reviews from all who knew him. Although many agreed that he did much to increase interest in Iranian art, architecture, and handicrafts at home and abroad, they also considered him a charlatan, who always had some questionable scheme to recommend to any who would listen. More troublesome for some was the fact that he bought Iranian antiquities on commission for individuals and museums in Europe and the United States. Although proceeds of these transactions supported his philanthropic interests, they opened him to continual charges of illegal dealing from which suspicion he would never clear his name.[12]

All this lay in the future, however, when the enthusiastic Pope arrived in Tehran for his first, and arguably most important, visit. Pope's host, Samuel Jordan, president of the American College, introduced him to Muhammad Ali Foroughi and other prominent individuals to whom he expounded his views on the glory of Iranian art and its contributions to the world. Foroughi pressed him to deliver a speech to government leaders on this topic, and Pope, never one to pass up such an opportunity, readily agreed. The audience on April 22, 1925, was a who's who of prominent Iranians—members of parliament and the cabinet, including Riza Khan, then prime minister and soon to be Riza Shah Pahlavi, Abdul Hussain Taymurtash, Hassan Pirnia, Seyed Hassan Taghizadeh, Murteza Quli Buyat, and Muhammad Musaddiq. Representing the American community were U.S. Chargé d'Affaires Wallace Murray, a lifelong supporter of friendly relations with Iran, and Arthur Millspaugh, administrator general of Iranian finance.[13]

Iran, according to Pope, had made a great impression on the whole history of civilization. Even in the Islamic age the empire "was largely in its greatest period sustained by Persian brains." Iranian architecture was superior to that of ancient Egypt; Turkish arts were all of Iranian origin. "Cloisonné is a Persian invention, the most magnificent example," he explained, "being the so-called Cup of Chosroes now in the Bibliothèque Nationale. . . . Too much of the history of Persian art unfortunately still lies locked under the soil awaiting the releasing spades of the archaeologist." From earliest times, he continued, Iranians had displayed "a high order of energy, intelligence, lively-mindedness and intellectual superiority." The revival of arts was essential. Yet Iran lagged behind other Middle Eastern lands, which had already set up museums. Iran, the mother of Islamic art, was still without any important collection of its own best work. It was the historical task of monarchs to support the arts, not, as Fath Ali Shah (1797–1834) had done, to destroy them. Here he referred to an incident when the shah had defaced a Sasanian (226–641 C.E.) rock carving to substitute a "stupid carving of himself and his family." Castigating this notorious example surely appealed to Pope's audience.[14]

Although there was little in his speech that was new to his audience, Pope's call to action came at the right psychological moment. Riza Khan seemed "keen, alert and responsive," at least for half an hour, after which he became restless, causing Pope to cut short his speech. A few days later in Isfahan the prime minister ordered his own funds used to repair the beautiful Sheikh Lutfullah Mosque, which had fallen into disrepair like so many other buildings in the former capital (1597–1736) of the Safavid dynasty. Isa Sadiq, the young Iranian scholar who had served as translator, concluded with boyish enthusiasm that Pope's "statements about the significance of our culture and its influence upon other cultures kindled fires within us like magic. We became proud of ourselves." Pope's speech was published in the newspapers, and the minister of public instruction had it printed as a text and delivered to schools throughout Iran. At Riza Shah's coronation several months later, Foroughi, now prime minister, spoke words filled with references to Iran's glorious past. He compared the shah to many of Iran's ancient rulers "who had emerged and led the nation to glory after periods of decay." Building on the Aryan theme of the Orientalists, Foroughi announced to the assembled deputies that "the Iranian nation realizes that today a Shah who is of the pure Iranian race has ascended to the throne."[15]

The American minister came away in a jubilant mood, for the question of the French monopoly concerned others as well as the Iranians; it had become an international issue. When archaeological concessions were involved, Western diplomats frequently used every stratagem to benefit their countrymen. For weeks Murray had attacked the French "closed door" in his dispatches to Washington, claiming that they had achieved little in the immense field of Iranian archaeology and that Iran should adopt an open door policy, admitting the archaeologists of other nations, who would undoubtedly make marvelous discoveries. The French, he knew, felt guilty about their concession. This seemed a good opportunity for American archaeologists. He had offered to speak with Riza Khan if the State Department instructed him to do so. Now, he exulted, the department could well imagine "the dull stupefaction which this universal acclaim of an American authority on Persian art has caused among the French here." [16]

And Pope was not one to leave a task half done. At Philadelphia in 1926 he organized an international exhibition of Iranian art, to inaugurate which Seyed Hassan Taghizadeh, minister of finance, traveled to the City of Brotherly Love. Pope wrote to Murray, newly returned to the State Department, to explain all the arrangements he had made. He urged the diplomat to see that the department was represented, if only informally, at the welcome for scholars attending the international congress on Middle Eastern art. In the course of his letter he devoted considerable space to disparaging the efforts of both the German archaeologist Ernst Herzfeld (1879–1948) and the French, who were busily vying for control over Iranian antiquities, when neither knew much about setting up museums, Iran's greatest need. This was vintage Pope. [17]

Even after leaving Tehran the previous year, he had continued to recommend establishment of a government department of art and antiquities and a national museum and the ending of the French monopoly. "The policy of those advising the French government in archaeology matters is to release nothing except under pressure," he wrote to influential friends. Their policy was an intolerable infringement on the sovereignty of Iran and "an affront to the spirit of science itself." He advised the Iranians to raise the issue in the press and at the League of Nations and, if necessary, to launch their own archaeological expeditions. [18]

The monopoly issue came up for discussion in parliament, where Hussain Ala, former minister to the United States, and Foroughi argued that the Majlis had every right to withdraw concessionary privileges if they had not been fully exploited. This argument made some European nations nervous, especially Britain, France, and Belgium, which feared for their own concessions, but the United States, Germany, and Italy, having little to lose, did not support them.[19]

The whole issue of the French monopoly was working out in the best interests of Iran, and this had surely been one of Foroughi's calculations in sponsoring Pope's address to the assembled Iranian and American dignitaries. It had become clear that the Americans were taking a lead on the issue, running interference for the Iranians in the ongoing discussions. The U.S. and German chargés had already pressed the French to learn more about their archaeological activities. This, Paris thought, was not a good sign. The French suspected that the British, too, might be ready to move against their interests but not so openly as the brash Americans. The French diplomats were troubled by the fact that the Germans and especially the Americans were expanding their cultural interests and giving scholarships to Iranian students. This despite the fact that France had a natural constituency among the elite, most of whom spoke French, and should have exploited its advantage.[20]

The French minister had summoned de Mecquenem to Tehran to control the damage. Incredibly, he had not visited the Iranian capital in years, despite his position as head of the French archaeological mission. Even then he refused to give in to Iranian pressure. When officials suggested that the French should work elsewhere in addition to Susa and that de Mecquenem should provide antiquities for a national museum, he spoke only of giving duplicates of pieces collected from Susa or of providing Tehran with casts of unique pieces bound for the Louvre. The minister of public instruction protested the existing convention as a virtual gift to France of Iranian antiquities. In twenty-five years, he claimed, the Iranian government had gained nothing from this. Years would pass before de Mecquenem set foot again in the capital, having concluded that his presence there only incited Iranian officials to complain.[21]

De Mecquenem seemed at first unprepared to respond positively to the changes in Iranian archaeology. He had begun working at Susa under the old regime, when no one interfered with the work of the expedition. Perhaps he had stayed too long, for now he had to cope with the increasing demands of officials in an age of rising nationalism. Throughout the late 1920s he encountered growing problems, leading him to criticize not only the Iranians but French diplomats as well, whom he believed did not support him as strongly as they should.

In 1926, while officials in Tehran were still discussing the monopoly, customs officers stopped de Mecquenem at the border and would not let him leave the country with his antiquities. He protested in vain until permission came from Tehran to let him pass. The French minister reported that de Mecquenem complained more than was necessary, for he had been a lord at Susa and now had difficulty conforming to changing conditions, which put new restrictions on his work. De Mecquenem feared he would soon be ousted from the château to make room for the governor of Susa, despite the fact that the expedition, he claimed, had made "this corner of desert . . . a center of culture" and the home of disciplined workers. All this, he predicted, the Iranians would soon forget.[22]

What they would not forget were the petty insults such as the director's insistence on flying the tricolor from the top of the citadel, which he claimed was French territory. His government made no such claim. When Iranian officials complained, politely suggesting that in future he fly the Iranian flag on formal occasions, he took it down. Privately they were furious.[23]

Grudgingly, de Mecquenem agreed that changes would have to be made, but they should give up as little as possible. He suggested dividing the country into two zones, of which the south and west would remain under French monopoly—everything from Kermanshah to the Gulf, including Isfahan and Shiraz. What remained could be opened to the archaeologists of all nations.[24]

French diplomats had to be more realistic, to save what they could from a difficult situation. They met with the ever-ambitious Pope, who brought his suggestions directly to the Quai d'Orsay in Paris. He met with Professor Paul Pelliot, dean of French archaeologists, and members of the Ministry of Foreign Affairs to discuss the deteriorating French position at Tehran. Rather full of his own importance, Pope wrote to a friend at Harvard University that he had had many talks with Pelliot, "he representing the French Foreign Office and I speaking for our State Department." Pope counseled Murray that the State Department should impress upon the French the great pressure being exerted by university archaeologists and archaeological societies in the United States against monopoly, which only the French practiced.[25]

Early in 1927 the Iranians appeared on the verge of appointing the well-known German archaeologist Ernst Herzfeld of the University of Berlin as director of antiquities. Herzfeld had spent years in the Middle East and was perhaps the leading foreign scholar of ancient Iran. He had carried out a survey of important archaeological sites for the Iranian government, showing how much he had done and by comparison how little the French had accomplished. This list set the agenda for future archaeological work in Iran, indicating what was valuable and what could be ignored. He had remarkable technical ability and a sincere interest in Iran's past. With his many influential friends, he seemed a natural choice for this newly created position.[26]

The French minister, Gaston Maugras, intervened at the last moment to thwart Herzfeld's appointment, for French pride could not tolerate such a German victory so soon after the Great War. He told Court Minister Taymurtash that the appointment of a German to the post could well end all hope of revising the French concession. While denying the right of the ignorant Qajars to traffic in the national heritage, Taymurtash offered Maugras a way out of the impasse. Iran would be prepared to accept a French national as director of antiquities in return for ending their monopoly. Maugras strongly advised his government to accept the proposal. The French position could only become worse, he reported. International opinion was entirely against them, and Iranian anger would grow with the increase of education and nationalism. This seemed to him the best solution available.[27]

The new agreement was signed on October 15, 1927. Under its terms the French monopoly would end as soon as the contract with a French expert had been signed. This expert would serve for an initial term of five years as director general of antiquities under the orders of the responsible minister. The Iranian government promised to engage a French expert for twenty years to show its sincere desire to have a learned Frenchman in charge of archaeological work. Following the ending of the monopoly, the French government could no longer interfere in matters connected with the excavation of antiquities in Iran. According to Chargé Paul Ballereau, this accord, although by no means perfect, was the best the French could expect. He pointed out to Paris the contradiction in article 4, which granted France the continued right to excavate at Susa "under present conditions," but went on to say that the archaeologists should observe the new regulations concerning excavations and division of antiquities. In future this contradictory article would cause problems. In 1928, for example, General Farajollah Agholi, military governor of Khuzistan province, visited Susa at the end of the excavating season and was astonished at the number of fine antiquities being prepared for shipment abroad. He telegraphed Riza Shah, asking if this export had his approval. The shah replied that this had to be allowed under the existing treaty, but shortly thereafter the terms of the French concession were modified to provide for a fifty-fifty division.[28]

The legation did what it could to fix conditions of employment for the French expert, but Taymurtash had been distracted by efforts to end various capitulations with other foreign powers, and thus even the expert's salary remained undetermined. Ballereau explained to the Foreign Ministry that whoever accepted the position in Tehran would need an extraordinary amount of patience to keep smiling through all the frustrations—refusal of funds, incompetent assistants, the intrigues of his competitors—that he would certainly encounter. All this while he tried to expand the French presence in Iran.[29]

What fortunate French archaeologist would fill this position? The Advisory Commission on Archaeological Excavations in Persia, a semigovernmental body, including officials and archaeologists, began a search for a suitable candidate even before the diplomats had reached agreement, for they hoped to counter Herzfeld's influence at Tehran. After the signing they pressed their search with vigor and by November 1927 had recommended André Godard, a young French archaeologist who had carried out fieldwork in Afghanistan and Iraq. The members admitted that he was not a great scientist, but he knew Islamic art, was diplomatic, and apparently was acceptable to the shah. Furthermore his wife, Yedda, had interests in the field of archaeology, and according to the commission she knew "well how to carry out the responsibilities of such a position."[30]

As Godard prepared to depart for his new post at the end of 1928, the shah was touring the south of Iran accompanied by Herzfeld. This made the French minister very uncomfortable, for he knew that they were visiting ancient sites along the route. The shah, he wrote, "although very modern in his thinking, is very respectful of the traditions and the history of his country." It was Godard, not "the German scientist," who should be accompanying the sovereign. Much to the minister's relief Godard finally arrived in Tehran on January 31, 1929. Remarkably, he would remain at his post for twenty-four years.[31]

Godard's longevity was a considerable achievement, proving perhaps that the commission had chosen wisely. No one, however, could have predicted this at the outset, for the Frenchman was sniped at from all sides. Pope considered him a third-rate man and believed that the Iranians had no great respect for him. The minister of public instruction under whom he worked blocked much of what he proposed regarding a national museum. Taymurtash himself put Godard's position clearly in focus during an interview with Herzfeld. "The appointment," he explained, "was the price paid to get rid of the French monopoly and having done that the

Persian government would be glad to pay the whole of five years salary in one lump, if they could, in order to get rid of Godard." Ironically, it was Taymurtash who soon disappeared and Godard who remained.[32]

Yet Taymurtash's influence was lasting. He had taken the initiative in forming the Society for the Preservation of the National Heritage, and its constitution, drawn up in 1922, made clear its agenda to instill in the public knowledge of Iran's historic heritage. Throughout the years of the Pahlavi dynasty, the group took action to achieve its goals. Its members also supported modernization in Iran, which they believed could only be achieved with a strong monarchy, hence their focus on the powerful kings of the pre-Islamic dynasties, who had ruled Iran at the height of its glory.[33]

The passing of the French monopoly had been engineered in such a way that all parties could take some satisfaction. Iran had gained the most; its government could now look forward to complete control over ancient sites, although there were as yet no trained Iranian archaeologists. The French had made a rather successful transition under difficult circumstances. They could boast that French archaeologists now served as directors of antiquities in both Egypt and Iran, two of the most significant centers of archaeology during the interwar years. This certainly pleased officials in Paris, who espoused an expanded cultural mission for France in the Middle East. The other Europeans and the Americans also benefited. They could seek concessions from the Iranian government in territory hitherto closed to them. A new phase of Iranian archaeology was about to begin.[34]

# 7. WINNING PERSEPOLIS

American archaeological interests came to dominate in Iran in the decade following the end of the French monopoly. This was arguably the most important U.S. commitment in the country up to the arrival of the Yankee Brigade in the middle of World War II. This fact helps to explain the extraordinary level of diplomatic activity there on behalf of the archaeologists and their sponsoring institutions. The diplomats took a more active role than they did in Egypt, where the British and French still dominated, or in Turkey, where they had to move cautiously for fear of provoking a nationalist backlash. In Iran the nationalist movement was somewhat weaker than in neighboring Turkey.

Americans had more money to lavish on expeditions, at least until the mid-1930s, and they hired European archaeologists, often Germans, to run their excavations. American institutions, the Metropolitan Museum of Art, the University Museum of the University of Pennsylvania, and especially the Oriental Institute of the University of Chicago, negotiated with Tehran for new concessions. In their efforts they were fortunate to have a strong advocate at the State Department. Wallace Murray, chief of the Division of Near Eastern Affairs from 1929 until 1944, had begun his diplomatic career as chargé d'affaires in Iran, a post he occupied from 1922 to 1925, and he would end his distinguished service as ambassador there in 1945–1946. He had been present on April 22, 1925, when Pope made his now-famous address to the assembled leaders of Iran. He cared deeply about U.S.-Iranian relations and took an active part whenever problems arose between the expeditions and the government of Riza Shah Pahlavi.

The directors of the University Museum (Horace Jayne, 1928–1939) and the Oriental Institute (James Breasted, 1919–1935) competed for the choicest sites, while that other American, Arthur Upham Pope, now director of the American Institute for Persian Art and Architecture, tried constantly to gain advantage with one or the other by offering (sometimes threatening) to use his extensive contacts in the Iranian government. Long before passage of a new antiquities law, which encountered significant opposition from landowners in parliament, Pennsylvania and Chicago were marshaling their forces.

The prize was Persepolis, what Iranians knew as Takht-i Jamshid, the most important archaeological site in Iran, some would argue in the entire Middle East. Persepolis had been the ceremonial center of the Achaemenid rulers (547–330 B.C.E.), founded by Darius I (521–486 B.C.E.), whose successors had embellished it with palaces, grand entrances, and royal stairways, much of which in 1929 still lay buried under 2,300 years of deposits left by wind and water. The complex had fallen to Alexander the Great in 331 B.C.E., and tradition held that he had ordered his troops to set it ablaze before he set out for further conquests to the east.

Persepolis captured the imagination of the growing number of Iranian nationalists in ways that Susa could not; for decades the French had excavated that winter capital of the same dynasty, but most of its treasures had gone to the Louvre. By contrast, Persepolis was relatively untouched since ancient times and held the prospect of yielding a great store of antiquities as well as a store of historical knowledge about one of Iran's most illustrious dynasties. The site lay at the heart of the Iranian homeland in Fars province, not far from the fabled city of Shiraz.

Iranians had never quite forgotten Takht-i Jamshid, and over the long centuries one could find repeated references to these ruins, which provided settings "for affirmation of a notion of continuity with more ancient traditions as well as for symbolic practices of rulership and religious observation." Two inscriptions attributed to Shapur II (309–379 C.E.) provided testimony of the visit by the great Sasanian ruler and later by two of his nobles, who prayed there and performed divine rituals in the monarch's name. In the Islamic era, a Buyid prince (955) had an inscription in Arabic carved, telling of his visit. In his *Rubaiyat*, the poet Omar Khayyam referred with melancholy to the site: "They say the Lion and the Lizard keep the Courts where Jamshid gloried and drank deep." Other medieval writers visited and marveled at the remains, considering them too incredible to have been built by mere mortals.[1]

In March 1924 Ernst Herzfeld had carried out an extensive survey of the site at the request of the Iranian government, which expressed the hope that his work at these ruins from "the most wonderful epoque" of Iran's history would lead to measures to stop its decay or even its total disappearance. Herzfeld readily agreed to take up the task and at his own expense, referring to the site as the most magnificent memorial of the ancient world, surpassing even Nineveh and Babylon in its complexity and state of preservation.[2]

**Figure 7.1.** Persepolis, Colossi of the porch of Xerxes, c. 1900. Glass Negative. Myron Bement Smith Papers, Freer Gallery of Art and Arthur M. Sackler Gallery Archives, Smithsonian Institution, Washington, DC, Gift of Katarine Dennis Smith, 1973–1985. Photographer: Antoin Sevruguin, negative number 31.10b.

In his report he complained of the desecrations by so-called scientists, who had removed pieces of sculpture "with their profane hands, to enshrine them in the museums of Europe." He offered to raise the necessary funds to clear the site if the government would give its support to this project. For Herzfeld this would be the culmination of a long and distinguished career.[3]

When discussions began concerning a new antiquities law, Herzfeld succeeded in lobbying the government to decree that Persepolis would remain outside any law and that no excavation could take place there without the cabinet's direct approval. This special status, which revealed Herzfeld's great interest in the site, seemed a good idea in 1929, but it would cause repeated problems for American excavators throughout the 1930s.[4]

Herzfeld discussed with Pope his prospects for gaining the concession,

**Figure 7.2.** Persepolis, Apadana [probably 1923]. Ernst Herzfeld Papers, Freer Gallery of Art and Arthur M. Sackler Gallery Archives, Smithsonian Institution, Washington, DC, Gift of Ernst Herzfeld, 1946. Photographer: Ernst Herzfeld, negative numbers 2255 and 2256.

knowing that the latter was working as an agent for Jayne, who wanted to expand Pennsylvania's activities in the region. Pope whetted the director's appetite, reporting that Persepolis was to Iran what the Valley of the Kings was to Egypt or the Manchu tombs (where Jayne had once excavated) to China. And, he boasted, "I can get it if anyone can."[5]

Jayne had another agent at Tehran as well, David Williamson, U.S. chargé d'affaires and son-in-law of the president of the Pennsylvania museum, who served on Jayne's board of directors. Williamson sent detailed reports to Philadelphia regarding the prospects for concessions and acquired antiquities for the museum as occasion offered. Apparently untroubled by any notion of conflict of interest, he continued collecting information—and artifacts—for Jayne until he was transferred to Istanbul at the end of 1929.[6]

Pope, too, kept up his efforts on behalf of the University of Pennsylvania. He tried to recruit Herzfeld, writing to Jayne in August 1929, "[Herzfeld] had made a definite and positive agreement with me that he would direct any American expedition that I could arrange for." Pope made clear, however, that he was indispensable to the whole operation for he had support from both the shah and Minister of Court Taymurtash, who was then at the height of his power. Herzfeld, by contrast, had numerous deficiencies, which made him unsuitable as a negotiator, confided Pope. Iranians considered him selfish and unethical.[7]

This cautionary note did not prevent Jayne from contacting Herzfeld himself and seeking his advice regarding suitable excavation sites. The director reiterated the importance of maintaining a fifty-fifty division of any finds, for "contributors . . . insist upon visible, and, if possible, spectacular results from the excavations." It was this concern that kept Jayne closely allied with Pope, despite the flurry of rumors about his unsavory methods in obtaining antiquities for Pennsylvania and numerous other museums and private collectors in the United States and Europe.[8]

Pope, Jayne knew, was not a trained archaeologist, but he offered good prices for rare pieces, and this was a priority. Jayne raced to beat out the Boston Museum of Fine Arts to purchase forty Luristan bronzes and then told Pope that he might find the money to purchase even more. Later Pope told him of a possible joint expedition to the ancient Iranian capital of Ctesiphon, where, he exulted, "good loot is absolutely assured . . . and a killing might possibly be made." Such racy language was common within the archaeological world of the 1920s and 1930s. Museum directors felt they had a primary obligation to acquire fine pieces however they might, and agents such as Pope seemed a godsend. Jayne himself had worked on two expeditions in China in 1924–1925 with the infamous Langdon Warner, and not only had they acquired many fine antiquities from the interior, but they had departed the country under a cloud of suspicion concerning their methods.[9]

Pope could not clear his name of wrongdoing, but the charges appear not to have troubled him excessively. Some observers claimed that his Iranian associates scoured the countryside, encouraging locals to dig secretly or to remove fine examples of artwork from existing monuments. Pope would live long enough to see an almost complete rejection of such methods. The final repudiation came, ironically, at the Fifteenth Congress of Iranian Art and Archaeology in Tehran and Shiraz in April 1968. There, three hundred delegates from twenty-eight countries formally decried the traffic in antiquities "except through official and authorized channels." Pope, who had consistently argued that antiquities were the best ambassadors from one culture to another, cast one of only two dissenting votes.[10]

As scientific knowledge had grown, archaeologists came to realize that an object had importance principally in relation to the location where it was found. A pot in isolation revealed little about the culture from which it came. Ripped from the earth, most of its historical record was irretrievably lost. Even in the 1930s these progressive ideas were becoming more commonly accepted.[11]

All too soon Pope's plans began to unravel. He learned that Breasted had been communicating with Herzfeld regarding the concession for Persepolis and neighboring Istakhr. Pope rushed to head off Breasted, writing to his good friend, Hussain Ala, now Iranian minister to France, to lay out all the reasons why the Oriental Institute would be an inappropriate choice for such an important concession. He wondered how carefully Breasted would follow the spirit of the law, and he shared with his friend a rumor that the American archaeologist had taken a precious golden relic out of Palestine without the government's permission. He claimed that Breasted was an imperialist, hoping to dominate all archaeology in the region, that he was a Johnny-come-lately to Iran, having shown little interest previously and done nothing to help amend the archaeology treaty with France. Following this list of complaints, Pope avowed that he had no intention of putting obstacles in Breasted's way, but, of course, he did. Ultimately he hoped for a broader program for archaeological work in Iran, a consortium perhaps, in which there would be ample opportunities for Pope and his associates.[12]

Despite Pope's intervention, Herzfeld won the concession at Persepolis, and he immediately contacted Breasted to ensure that the Oriental Institute would provide the money needed. Herzfeld had always worried about the high costs of living in Tehran, four times what it would have cost him in Berlin, he claimed, and even in the field his expenses were significant. He had borrowed money from the German minister to cover costs for a recent expedition to Sistan in eastern Iran. He spent a good deal of time, as did many in his field, looking for support. He could count on his salary as a professor at the University of Berlin, but that was hardly sufficient. He kept with him in Iran four expert Arab excavators, and he had to provide for them as well as keep a house in Tehran, make occasional purchases from antiquities dealers who came knocking on his door, all this plus the costs of outfitting expeditions.[13]

This hand-to-mouth existence had led him to ally with Breasted, who, it was widely known, was still receiving generous funding from John D. Rockefeller Jr. Furthermore, Herzfeld had come to dislike Pope intensely. Perhaps he was jealous of the American's excellent contacts at court, his audiences with Riza Shah and Taymurtash, despite having no scientific training whatsoever. One diplomat aptly observed that Herzfeld "wants the Persian field to himself." With Breasted's support Herzfeld could get to work without further worry.[14]

Breasted did not immediately welcome the news that Herzfeld had requested and received the Persepolis concession. His resources were stretched with expeditions in Egypt, Iraq, Palestine, and Turkey, and he doubted that he would be able to begin work there immediately. He told State Department officials that he had thought Herzfeld was going to ask only for an option on Persepolis, not for the actual concession.

The diplomats were deeply disturbed at this revelation, for they considered archaeological work in Iran the one bright hope for American interests there. Chargé Hugh Millard wrote that there had been one "flub after another in American efforts in Persia." "I am tired of it," he added. He was referring to a series of setbacks throughout the 1920s, beginning with the murder of Vice Consul Robert W. Imbrie on July 18, 1924, by a Tehran mob, the disastrous financial mission of Arthur Millspaugh (1922–1927), and the withdrawal of the Ulen group from the railroad syndicate at the end of the decade. He believed that "archaeology is about the only thing [the United States] are likely to be interested in which stands much chance of bringing results." Wallace Murray urged the diplomats to support these efforts because if successful they would greatly enhance American prestige.[15]

Frederick Wulsin, curator of anthropology at the University Museum and Jayne's new representative in Iran, explained the seriousness of the situation to the director. "To have the greatest scholar [Herzfeld] ask for the most famous Persian site, in the name of the richest archaeological institution in the world [the Oriental Institute] and then to give up right away would discredit all Americans and all archaeologists and make them a laughing stock."[16]

Assistant Secretary of State William Castle passed directly to Breasted a warning from American diplomats in the Iranian capital that "American prestige in Persia would greatly suffer if the Persian offer were rejected." Under such pressure Breasted could hardly refuse. He explained to Castle that America had gained a very influential position in the region in science as a result of the efforts of his institute. The position, he said, constantly involved him in political relations with local governments, and he appreciated the deep interest and support of the State Department in his work.[17]

Having reluctantly taken up the concession, Breasted looked forward to the early arrival in Chicago of Persian antiquities, for these were what spurred donors to contribute, and he had to fill a large new museum on the Chicago campus. He urged Herzfeld to do all he could to get some of the finds to the United States to stimulate, he said, American interest in Iranian history. He wrote to his friend George Hale, referring to Persepolis as "the Versailles of the Persian royal family," and reported important finds there that would mean new additions to their exhibition halls. Later, after Herzfeld found the two monumental staircases, Breasted excitedly revealed to his friend that this would mean "the leading collection of Persian sculpture in the world here at the Oriental Institute."[18]

At the same time that Herzfeld was negotiating for this most important concession, the Iranian parliament and cabinet were considering various drafts of a new antiquities law. The path to approval was tortuous. Landowners, resenting the fact that early drafts made it almost impossible for them to dig on their own lands, offered stiff opposition. Herzfeld and Godard supported the original version, as did the minister of court, but the minister of public instruction, who would administer the law and was himself a landholder, wanted changes. And so the bill languished. Pope worked tirelessly to get it passed. Not surprisingly, he saw no harm in allowing landholders to dig on their own lands as long as there was some government supervision. This was the compromise that brought passage in early November 1930. The minister of court had given his support, which hastened passage but only by a narrow margin.[19]

Over the next several years, concessions were granted in all parts of Iran, many of them to Americans. Wulsin excavated at Turang Tepe in the northeast. Erich Schmidt, having abandoned Turkey, headed another University of Pennsylvania dig at Tepe Hissar and later at Rayy near Tehran. Joseph Upton carried out a smaller excavation for the Metropolitan at Takht-i Abu Nasr near Shiraz, followed by work at Nishapur in Khurasan province.

Pope continued to come and go in Iran, all the while photographing ancient monuments for what would eventually be his six-volume *Survey of Persian Art* (1938-1939). To meet expenses, he bought antiquities for his clients in the United States and Europe, taking 10 to 15 percent of the price as his commission. He bought at bargain prices, giving as an example an Achaemenid burial urn worth $1,000.00 for which he paid $22.50. He urged friends of the museum in his native San Francisco to make important acquisitions through him now or suffer eternal inferiority in Iranian art, fine pieces of which were becoming scarce.[20]

None of this endeared Pope to André Godard, who told Wulsin that there were almost no rare art objects that could be legally sold in Iran, and Pope knew this. The two men were constantly at loggerheads. Godard kept his distance, never passing up an opportunity to criticize the American; Pope wrote the director long letters, expressing his dismay and urging reconciliation. And so they carried on throughout the 1930s.[21]

Iranian officials became increasingly concerned about the illegal flow of antiquities to Europe and the United States. When reports reached Tehran that ancient statues from the vicinity of Persepolis were being sold in America and that the Boston Museum of Fine Arts had purchased one of them, the Foreign Ministry ordered the legation to investigate. It also asked the legation to inform relevant U.S. authorities that these statues represented Iran's ancient glory and their export was forbidden. It also wanted answers to three questions: How exactly did the antiquities get to the United States? Could museums be sued under U.S. law for buying stolen goods? What other protests from countries such as Italy, Greece, and Egypt had been made and with what results? The Iranian minister could obtain little precise information on questions one and three, and the answer to number two was disheartening. Apparently, museums could not be sued unless the purchaser knew the article had been stolen. Officials would have to be content with trying to tighten control on Iran's porous borders.[22]

In spite of all the unsavory tales circulating in Iran, Europe, and the United States about the infamous Professor Pope, he seemed to remain surprisingly influential. In 1931 he organized the Second International Exhibition of Persian Art in London, which was a great success. For months he had used this project as leverage with the Iranian government, claiming that he needed to bring the finest art objects to England. The shah granted his wish, saying that anything Pope selected from the royal collection, the imperial library, the national museum, or the great mosques at Qum, Ardabil, or Mashhad would be shipped along with objects from recent excavations. Pope obtained special permission to photograph previously forbidden mosques. He believed firmly that one good turn deserved another, and he expected to be able to advance his own interests in Iran as a result of his efforts at London.[23]

Pope informed Hassan Taghizadeh, now Iranian minister in London, that the exhibition and his own *Survey* would together "advance the prestige of Persia more than anything that has happened in centuries." Developing this theme, he emphasized the importance of making progress on archaeology during the exhibition, especially with passage of the then-stalled antiquities law.[24]

Not everything turned out so well for him; he had far more ideas than he could ever carry to fruition. But underneath everything lay a genuine interest in Iranian art, which he did more perhaps than anyone at the time to advertise abroad. Unfortunately, his methods and his braggadocio offended a host of former friends and associates, who willingly related their particular Pope stories, few of which reflected well on him.

Herzfeld must have been near the top of the list of complainers. After the London exhibition he reported to Jayne that Pope had shipped boxes belonging to various antiquities dealers along with those destined for display in Britain; none of them had been inspected. Some of these boxes, he claimed, contained sculptures stolen from Persepolis, which eventually turned up for sale in Paris. Herzfeld had come to the south of Iran

**Figure 7.3.** Persepolis, at the time of Reza Shah's visit. Fourth from left: Lotte Brodführer (Mrs. Bradford), her son, Herzfeld wearing doctor's hat from the University of Berlin, F. Krefter, H. Kuhler, Muhammad Taghi Mostfavi (commissioner), and M. André Godard, October 28, 1932. Gelatin silver print. Ernst Herzfeld Papers, Freer Gallery of Art and Arthur M. Sackler Gallery Archives, Smithsonian Institution, Washington, DC, Gift of Ernst Herzfeld, 1946. Photographer: Unidentified. Photo file 5, volume 3 #66b.

**Figure 7.4.** Excavation crew at work at Persepolis. Courtesy of the Oriental Institute of the University of Chicago.

**Figure 7.5.** Persepolis, Apadana, Eastern stairway. Professor Ernst Herzfeld, field director of the Persepolis expedition of the Oriental Institute of the University of Chicago, standing in front of an inscription of Xerxes. Photographer: James Henry Breasted Jr., February 23, 1933. Courtesy of the Oriental Institute of the University of Chicago.

to escape Pope's constant meddling in his affairs. Imagine his annoyance, then, when he discovered Pope one day photographing the site without his permission.[25]

Despite such occasional interruptions, Herzfeld made good progress in uncovering the terrace and its surroundings and in reassembling the columns. At the end of 1932 Breasted was able to announce the discovery of magnificent sculptured stairways leading up to the terrace. The shah visited Persepolis with his entourage in late October 1932. He told Herzfeld that he was "doing here a great work of civilization," for which he thanked him.[26]

The following year the discovery of four inscribed silver and gold foundation tablets brought a personal letter from the court, expressing the shah's satisfaction with the discovery and the work generally being undertaken at the site. Because of their importance in throwing new light "on the grandeur and extent of territory of the Persian Empire" and because the shah was especially interested in the Achaemenids, he decided to keep two of the tablets at his palace. He invited government officials, members of parliament, and other dignitaries to visit the Marble Palace to see them, and when he gave an important speech to officers several months later, he recited in detail the story of their discovery.[27]

Riza Shah had a longtime interest in his country's ancient monuments, and he made a point of visiting them whenever he traveled. He took Herzfeld with him on one memorable, rain-soaked journey through southwestern Iran in November 1928, and they toured a number of sites along the way.[28]

News of important discoveries by archaeological expeditions combined with the court's campaign to revive interest in Iran's ancient glories contributed to an outpouring of articles and letters in the local press throughout the 1930s. At first these showed concern for the fate of the nation's treasures, as in an editorial in *Shafaq-i Sorkh* that asked, "Are Antiquities Beets or Carrots?" The editor questioned the fifty-fifty division of antiquities and wondered who was looking out for Iran's interests. Could it be the French director of antiquities? Better to leave these objects buried, he concluded, than that they should be dug up only to decorate foreign museums.[29]

Such advice was the exception, however, and as the decade proceeded, with confidence growing that the new dynasty had the situation under control, articles focused on the glories of Iran's past, relating them to the great possibilities of the present reign. Mention of the foreign contribution to archaeological discoveries in Iran remained very limited, and frequently there was no mention at all. *Ittila'at*, Iran's principal daily newspaper, and its French edition, *Journal de Tehran*, commented frequently on developments in archaeology. *Iran-i Bastan* (1933–1937) focused almost exclusively on the history of ancient Iran, its masthead a visual feast containing a sketch of the Zoroastrian supreme deity, Ahura Mazda, the swastika, an ancient symbol, at his feet, paired with another of the Achaemenid rulers, and over all the Zoroastrian creed "Good thoughts, good words, good actions." When not featuring stories of Iran's remarkable past, the paper devoted its columns to friendly articles on the Third Reich; Berlin subsidized this obviously pro-German publication. Another interesting paper was *Iran-i Imruz* (1938-1942), sponsored by the Department of Information and Propaganda under Riza Shah. All these papers focused on the pre-Islamic period, especially the Achaemenid (547-331 B.C.E.) and Sasanian (226-641 C.E.) dynasties, which they viewed as being particularly Iranian in origin. As in Egypt and Turkey, where for many nationalists the coming of Islam seemed to herald a decline from former greatness, so, too, in Iran secular nationalists harked back to the "golden" years before the Arab conquest.[30]

Attention centered on Takht-i Jamshid, where, according to one editor, one found "the source of [Iranian] honor and pride today." He encouraged the holding of annual celebrations there to remember Darius and his successors. Foreigners came to view these grand monuments, and Iranians should, too, for the study of the ancients provided the inspiration necessary to make a nation. Such visits instilled a faith in the destiny of the eternal fatherland. On his return from his second visit to the site in 1928, Riza Shah had told officials that the magnificent ruins filled him with national pride. Editors took pains to emphasize the importance of these monuments for Iranian youth, and the minister of public instruction agreed, sending collections of photographs of the most important monuments to the nation's schools to be used in the study of Iran's ancient history. The objective was to create in the minds of students "a living consciousness of the past by showing the great achievements of the race." Pilgrimages there not only taught the lessons of the past but also instilled an ardor for the future.[31]

From the early 1920s, textbooks were tailored "to forge a uniform and obedient national culture." Most of Iran's exemplary models were monarchs, some of them mythical, drawn from the pre-Islamic centuries, rulers such as Fereydun, Cyrus, and Anushirvan. The texts often stressed the fact that Iranians belonged to the white race, for whites, it was widely believed, were "smarter and more civilized than the other races." A leading member of the intelligentsia, Hassan Pirnia, wrote a number of histories of ancient Iran. He corresponded with foreign archaeologists, including Ernst Herzfeld, and despite his intense patriotism, the resulting work was free from "biased interpretations." In 1928 he became a member of the Commission of Education for which he wrote a textbook, *Ancient Iran* (1929), which was used in high schools for two decades.[32]

Recent archaeological discoveries proved that Iran was the cradle of civilization, whose glories were being restored under Riza Shah. One poet lavished praise on him, citing his restoration of the ancient splendor of Takht-i Jamshid and concluding, "The shade of the great Darius returns to his cold stone and on his couch of granite, happy, satisfied, says to himself, sleep in peace, oh my soul, you live again."[33]

Nothing could be more important than bolstering the confidence of Iranians after two centuries of bad government under the Qajars, when they had lost the sense of their glorious traditions. This was the new dynasty's message. Now the people had become more aware of their past, symbolized by the remains at Persepolis, which made concrete the genius of an era and a race. Iranians were making up for lost time. They had received the torch of civilization from their ancestors, but they had much yet to do to live up to the record of their forebears.[34]

Pride in the past and in one's race at times spilled over into a narrow chauvinism, especially in the late 1930s, encouraged no doubt by the spread of Nazi pseudoscientific theories of Aryan superiority. Some editors claimed that by the sixth century B.C.E., the Aryans had subdued the Semites and were dominant everywhere in western Asia. Darius had established his great empire in the East; the Greeks had made similar progress in the West. The two peoples were comparable for they were both of the Aryan race. As in Turkey and, to a lesser extent, Egypt, Iran's nationalist elite used such conclusions to argue that their nation also deserved the recognition and respect of Europe.[35]

What one scholar has labeled "dynastic nationalism" was in full bloom by the end of the 1920s. The movement had built on works going back to the nineteenth century. The move to impress upon the Iranian public, especially the growing numbers of students and soldiers, respect for the nation's ancient history and monuments had the full support of the state. This program would strengthen Iranians' resolve to lead their country by means of progressive reform into the circle of great nations once again.[36]

As attention to ancient monuments grew, so, too, did official scrutiny of the work of foreign archaeologists, especially those at Takht-i Jamshid, which had become a nationalist shrine. Iran did not yet have its own trained archaeologists, so the government depended on foreigners, whom it did not always trust. Even Godard, who directed Iranian antiquities for twenty-five years, never fully escaped suspicion that his real objective was furthering the interests of his own nation and seeking treasures for himself.

Herzfeld was no less the object of suspicion. He had built up a sizable personal collection of antiquities over decades of traveling around the region; even when accompanying the shah in 1928 he had added to his collection. Rumors circulated that he shipped antiquities illegally out of the country and that he was pilfering at Persepolis.[37]

In spite of the shah's apparent approval of Herzfeld's work at Takht-i Jamshid, such an important symbol of Iranian grandeur was bound to receive special attention from Tehran. As time went on, a number of unresolved issues developed between the Persepolis expedition and the Iranian government, and these led in summer 1934 to full-blown crisis, drawing in American diplomats and threatening to disturb friendly relations between the two nations.

It began with a long letter from Herzfeld to Breasted on April 7, 1934, in which he detailed his complaints against the government in Tehran. It had delayed unnecessarily a division of the finds made thus far by the expedition. These included the library of Darius, thirty thousand unbaked clay tablets with Elamite inscriptions that were in danger of crumbling to dust. Better to have left them undiscovered, opined Herzfeld. The minister of public instruction regularly gave professional photographers access to the site, which violated accepted practice. Finally, many of the books and other supplies shipped to Iran for Herzfeld had been held up indefinitely in customs. Tehran never gave a clear response to his complaints, so the annoyances mounted. He was also piqued by the fact that the role of the Oriental Institute had been slighted in a recent publication of the Ministry of Culture that seemed to indicate that the Iranians had done everything at Persepolis themselves.[38]

Breasted determined immediately that Herzfeld would not be firm enough to deal with the situation and that he would have to take action himself. Writing to his son, Charles, he noted, "The Oriental has to be told very decidedly where he gets off." He turned to Wallace Murray for advice. Apparently, the Iranian government had now reaffirmed that the palace of Persepolis was a unique treasure and therefore not subject to the ordinary provisions of the antiquities law regarding division of finds. Breasted and Murray found this unacceptable, especially for pieces of sculpture that could not be restored to their original positions on the palace and for the glazed bricks and clay tablets. The Persepolis concession had come after passage of the antiquities law and thus must be subject to the regulations of that law, they reasoned. Neither of them seemed to be aware of Herzfeld's earlier lobbying to gain a special status for the Achaemenid site.[39]

After years of experience dealing with Iranian officials, Murray advised Breasted to come to a clear agreement with Tehran "as to whether it proposed to live up to its contract." If it did not, the director might inform the government of his intention to withdraw entirely from Persepolis. The diplomat pledged the State Department's support in impressing upon the Iranian authorities the importance of living up to their obligations.[40]

Murray's incautious, perhaps even undiplomatic, response fed Breasted's determination to settle matters once and for all. This straight-forward approach was often the one he favored when dealing with "Ori-entals." Thus he strongly supported Herzfeld's decision to suspend work at Persepolis until the government had clarified its position.[41]

Meanwhile, Breasted prepared a strong letter, laying out his complaints and demanding that the Iranian government act. He sent a draft to Mur-ray, who made suggestions, which he incorporated. On July 10 he sent a copy of the final draft to Murray, saying that he would send the original whenever the State Department felt prepared "to proceed further in the matter."[42]

The key passage of the revised letter stated that the Oriental Institute "desires to emphasize herewith its purpose to suspend all work at Persepo-lis and to discontinue operation until the Persian government accedes to its claims" regarding delays of equipment, issuance of photography per-mits, and a just division of finds at Persepolis. The director also took credit for restoring to the Iranians for the first time "the vanished glories of their ancestors."[43]

In the cover letter to Murray, Breasted compared what the Iranians were trying to do to Lacau's actions in Egypt, where he had placed each concession outside the antiquities law, which made each expedition sub-ject to the vagaries of the ministry rather than to the certainty of the law. He also pointed to the Iranians' current challenge to the contract with the Anglo-Persian Oil Company to show their readiness to disregard con-tracts and obligations. Writing to his son at the end of July, Breasted con-cluded, "It is a big contract to undertake the education of the Persian gov-ernment, but I have no doubt we can improve matters if we stick to the job, and at least show them that they can't bluff us. I am enormously thankful for Wallace Murray."[44]

In the time between the suspension of work on the plain of Persepo-lis and the delivery of Breasted's demands, the Iranian government issued an ultimatum of its own, informing the institute that unless work began again by August 10, the concession would be canceled. There were rumors that the minister of public instruction, Ali Asghar Hikmat (1933–1938), a member of the Society for the Preservation of the National Heritage, and his subordinate, Godard, would be only too happy for Iran to assume direct control over the prestigious site. More pointedly, it could not have been easy for the shah, always prickly about such matters, to accept calmly the increasingly obvious intervention of the American diplomats—and, to a lesser extent, of the German minister, representing Herzfeld—in what could plainly appear a matter between Iran and a private institution. Only recently had Riza Shah succeeded in ending foreign capitulations in Iran and unequal relations with Western nations; this brewing crisis must have seemed all too familiar.

Furthermore, successes in neighboring Turkey, where Riza Shah made a state visit in June 1934, and in more distant Egypt in bringing foreign archaeological expeditions firmly under state control must have emboldened the Iranian authorities. The Foreign Office files were full of materials documenting how relations with European and American archaeologists in those two countries had been developing since the end of World War I. There was, for example, an article from a Swiss newspaper comparing the stringent controls over the export of antiquities from Egypt, Italy, and Greece with the much looser restrictions of Iran. As early as January 1926 officials at the Department of Foreign Affairs informed their minister that the Egyptians had set the norm for excavations in the region. Like their colleagues in Cairo, who had recently defended their control over the tomb of Tutankhamun, Iranian officials had already determined that Persepolis would not be treated as just another site. Herzfeld himself had acknowledged this when he wrote to Jayne in October 1929, "Persepolis . . . is and always will be outside any possible law of antiquities."[45]

The Iranian démarche arrived while Breasted senior vacationed on a leisurely cruise from New York to San Francisco, and Charles had to deal with the issue. He turned once again to Murray, who cautioned that one could not temporize with the Iranians. "If the Persian government refused to come to a reasonable settlement . . . the obvious step to take was to close up shop and withdraw." Charles agreed and endorsed Murray's recommendation that the American minister in Tehran ask the government to take no action until it had received his father's letter to the prime minister.[46]

Charles Breasted drafted a letter to Dr. Frederich Krefter of the Persepolis expedition, reminding him that his responsibility was only to deliver the institute's ultimatum, not to negotiate. He was ordered to leave Prime Minister Muhammad Ali Foroughi in no doubt that Chicago would withdraw if its conditions were not met. Murray sent this letter out to the Tehran legation over the signature of Undersecretary of State William Phillips, who fully concurred with the stand the Breasteds were taking.[47]

On September 3 the Council of Ministers refused to accept Breasted's letter of July 25, saying that it was insulting to the Iranian government and suggesting that it be resubmitted with the objectionable threats removed. The prime minister, a man of letters and an ardent nationalist, advised U.S. Minister William H. Hornibrook that if that were done a division of finds could take place "without recognizing application of the antiquities law," and discussions regarding shipment of the clay tablets to Chicago could begin.[48]

Charles Breasted, rarely the diplomat, drafted a sharp response, which, fortunately, he did not send. Murray had come to his senses, and on being advised about this latest missive, invited the younger Breasted to Washington for discussions. There, the diplomat recommended—and Breasted accepted—a little bargaining that would allow the Iranians to save face but would result in the institute achieving its objectives.[49]

Subsequently, Hornibrook undertook a series of meetings with Foroughi seeking compromise. He cautioned his superiors at the State Department that he doubted the Oriental Institute would get everything it wanted in a division. Breasted, freshly returned to Chicago, suggested that the minister might get the small ornamental staircase for the institute if he played on Iranian pride, saying that Iraq had given an enormous, five-meter-high sculpture and Egypt a royal statue over five meters. "Shall Persia be represented in America by nothing equally as impressive?" The ploy, if used, did not succeed, for the movable staircase stayed at Persepolis.[50]

The minister of public instruction would have preferred dealing with a representative of the institute rather than with an American diplomat, but Hornibrook refused to take the hint. He had visited Persepolis for a week in October to familiarize himself with every detail, and by mid-November they had reached agreement.[51]

The institute would receive five hundred of the clay tablets, a collection of sculptures, a part of the enameled brick frieze of the Apadana, or audience hall, of Darius I at Persepolis, and numerous small objects, including some gold. For future reference, none of the excavation within a one-mile radius of the Apadana would be governed by the antiquities law; rather the finds would be divided according to amicable agreement as in the present case. (This was hardly the firm decision Breasted had been seeking.) The law, however, would operate for any finds beyond that distance. Other clay tablets could be transported to Chicago for preservation and translation and later returned to Iran at the institute's expense. The minister of public instruction retained the right to issue special permits for photography.[52]

Murray was highly pleased with Hornibrook's accomplishment. He explained to the minister that the department had taken such extraordinary interest in this affair because the institute brought credit upon American scientific endeavors, occupying an outstanding position in the field of archaeology. No other organization, he declared, was so well equipped to carry on this important work.[53]

Privately, Breasted could hardly contain his anger at the behavior of the Iranian government and the shah. Riza Shah, he reported, had displayed the gold foundation tablets at the palace, and the Ministry of Public Instruction had publicized them, yet neither had even mentioned the work of the Oriental Institute expedition. "To put it very mildly," he told his friend Hale, "if there are any loathsome vermin anywhere on the surface of the earth worse than the Persians I do not know where it might be!" Regaining his composure, he paradoxically ended his letter by pointing to the prospect of a favorable division after all.[54]

Everything seemed settled at last, and yet the Iranians had not had their final say. In Tehran the government had determined to be rid of Herzfeld for offenses both real and imagined. Opposition to the German director had been building slowly, but once officials came to a decision, they proved inflexible.

With the crisis apparently resolved, Herzfeld prepared to leave Iran for the winter. Much of the time before the start of a new excavation season he would spend in Chicago, preparing his reports for publication, discussing expedition affairs with the director and his son, meeting with important contributors, and perhaps giving a few lectures on his work at Persepolis.

Herzfeld did not like the United States, for he felt slighted there; people did not show him the respect he deserved—or so he believed. This despite the fact that the institute organized a three-day lecture series for him as well as a dinner honoring his accomplishments, which Wallace Murray, making his first visit to the Oriental Institute, attended with great enthusiasm.[55]

In normal times Herzfeld would have spent the months in Berlin with friends and colleagues, but with the Nazis in power his homeland was becoming increasingly inhospitable to Jews. Breasted made reference to this changing climate when he visited briefly in May 1933 to see old friends from his university days and to undertake "the unpleasant task of persuading the Jew-baiting Hitler ministers that Herzfeld was a valuable asset to Germany in Persia and that his leave ought to be extended." He was surprised to find all his old friends who normally abhorred politics "deeply interested in Hitler's newly acquired leadership and *all of them in favor of him!*" Breasted had excellent connections in the scholarly community. This and his fluent German earned him a "courteous and kindly reception" at both the Foreign Office and the Ministry of Culture, where his proposals regarding Herzfeld were immediately accepted.[56]

Nevertheless, Herzfeld was about to become a double exile, not only from his homeland but from Iran as well, which, for the leading scholar of Iran's ancient history, would become the more bitter of the two. He would never be allowed to return to the land of his greatest discoveries.

Why had Herzfeld become so unwelcome in Iran? He was a master at offending people. Even Breasted had become frustrated with his total lack of administrative ability and "his jealously and disregard of his subordinates." Relations between Herzfeld and his chief assistant, Frederich Krefter, a fellow countryman, had become so difficult that Krefter had offered his resignation. Of far more serious concern, however, was the realization that Herzfeld had lost the support of Iranian authorities in Tehran. As a result Breasted began secretly searching for an American to head the expedition. Charles Breasted, who served as the enforcer in his father's frequent absences, dispatched a long memo to Herzfeld in August, setting out all the unpleasant incidents in the institute's relationship with him and accusing him of presenting "an attitude of increasing discouragement and hopeless resignation." If Herzfeld wanted to resign he should just send a letter to that effect to Dr. Breasted and stop threatening to resign. Otherwise, he should get on with the important scientific work there.[57]

The decision rested with the Iranian government, however, not with the Oriental Institute, and Tehran's determination to be rid of Herzfeld became increasingly apparent. Authorities made clear their desire to keep the Persepolis expedition and to replace the director. Herzfeld had not helped his cause by appealing to the diplomatic representatives of Britain and Germany to take up his case. According to Hornibrook, this was "a masterful indiscretion," and the intervention of the German minister only created more problems for the archaeologist. Further, when Herzfeld had been invited to participate in the celebrations marking the millennium of the birth of the great Iranian poet, Ferdowsi, he had not responded to the official invitation, prompting the cancellation of a proposed government-sponsored tour for visiting scholars to Persepolis.[58]

This last discourtesy on Herzfeld's part was no trifling matter. Beginning in the late 1920s, the Society for National Heritage had launched a campaign to locate the site of Ferdowsi's grave in Tus and then to build a suitable memorial. Members raised the sums necessary through public subscriptions and with generous support from the government. The image of Ahura Mazda was located on the central front facade of the completed structure, copying the Throne Hall at Persepolis. Following a congress of Orientalists in Tehran, at which Minister of Public Instruction Hikmat addressed the delegates, they made the long bus journey to eastern Iran to Ferdowsi's birthplace outside Mashhad for the official inauguration. Riza Shah gave a brief address. Although Herzfeld had been involved in earlier stages of the project, his decision to absent himself from this celebratory event was the height of folly.[59]

Hornibrook spent more than two hours with Hikmat on December 23, trying to understand the Iranian point of view. The minister accused Herzfeld of smuggling, and not for the first time. At the end of 1933 customs agents at the Russian border had confiscated a number of antiquities, mainly seals and coins, because Herzfeld did not have a permit to take them out of the country. These were later returned to him by decree of the cabinet after the minister of public instruction had certified that the items were not of great value. More serious was a subsequent charge that several of Herzfeld's trunks had exited the country amid the baggage of the visiting Swedish crown prince, whose luggage, of course, left Iran without a customs inspection. Although the Swedish minister strongly disputed the Iranian claim, he admitted that Herzfeld had recommended that the crown prince purchase some antiquities and send them out as part of his official baggage. The crown prince refused to buy anything for which he could not obtain an exit permit.[60]

The minister made other, similar charges, and he traced all the recent difficulties between the government and the institute to the German director, who had offended Tehran with his long list of complaints. He went on to say that the Council of Ministers was firmly opposed to Herzfeld's continuing at Persepolis and that the shah agreed. In the course of the discussion the Iranian official made several anti-Semitic remarks, referring to "that German Jew" and to Herzfeld's "Jewish blood," which indicated how complex the crisis had become.[61]

Although being a Jew would not alone have accounted for his dismissal, it likely provided one more mark against him, for official records showed a heightened concern with the possible role of Iranian Jews in the smuggling of antiquities. In January 1930 the Ministry of Public Instruction sent a Berlin newspaper article to the Foreign Ministry. The article explained that the Berlin Museum had just purchased a stone carving from Persepolis, which an Iranian Jewish antiquities dealer had smuggled out of the country. In March 1933 the embassy in Paris reported that an Iranian Jewish dealer, residing in the French capital, had offered to give information about smuggling from Persepolis in return for a fee. Later the minister of court announced that two young Jews from Isfahan had used the proceeds from the sale of stolen carvings from Persepolis to flee to Palestine. Ayoub Rabenou, a Jewish dealer with close ties to Pope, was often accused by the authorities of removing pieces of Islamic art from unguarded sites. Whether or not these charges were true, Hikmat certainly knew of them, and they may have contributed to his outburst to the American minister.[62]

Hornibrook tried to impress upon him the importance of keeping Herzfeld, saying that his indiscretions "might properly be overlooked in the interest of science . . . and of restoring the ancient treasures of Persia." This practical advice was in keeping with the department view that Herzfeld was most qualified to carry out the archaeological work at Persepolis unless the Iranians "were merely looking for a jovial and tactful person," who could keep them in good humor. He also hinted at the string of recent diplomatic misunderstandings between the United States and Iran. Failure of the Persepolis negotiations at this late date would naturally leave an unfavorable impression in Washington.[63]

In spite of these arguments, the Iranians held firmly to their demand that Herzfeld must go. Hornibrook, in a long dispatch to the State Department, observed that although the German had become something of a scapegoat, he would have no choice but to leave.[64]

Breasted then sought permission for Herzfeld to stay on at Persepolis as an advisor to the new director, but again the government refused. Hikmat told Hornibrook that "it would better promote the success of the expedition if he [Herzfeld] refrains absolutely and under no pretext whatsoever from visiting Persepolis during the life of the concession." Shortly thereafter the government explained that it did not want Herzfeld to return at all.[65]

Breasted broke the news to Herzfeld at the end of January, telling him that his poor relations with the Iranian government would have made it impossible for him to continue to lead an expedition anywhere in that country. Herzfeld was angry, charging that the institute had done a poor job of supporting him against unfounded charges, which would now be used to block his return to Iran.[66]

Herzfeld passed much of the next decade in a country that never fully appreciated him. He returned briefly to Berlin in 1935, but conditions were unbearable. The government canceled his passport, and he was fortunate to be able to leave for a teaching position at Princeton University. Donald Wilber, then a junior archaeologist, worked for him during those first months and later recalled that Herzfeld had the "haughty manners of a Prussian . . . and would bristle at the suggestion of any slighting remarks or fancied insult." His old acquaintance Gaston Maugras, the former French minister in Tehran, told him he was a man who had fulfilled his destiny. Still, he added, "it makes me a little wistful to know that you are exiled in America in surroundings so different from those which were the object of your studies."[67]

In his final years, Herzfeld remained as difficult as ever in his relations with the Oriental Institute. The new director, John Wilson, referred to his letters as "mystically psychopathic." Nor did his anger lessen during the war. In response to Wilson's invitation to attend a preview of the new Iranian hall at the institute in Chicago, Herzfeld replied, "In view of the fact that I have not been consulted in the preparation of the Hall, I do not feel called upon now to accept your invitation." He ended by reminding the director that the Iranian expedition would have been impossible without him. Wilson sent him a pleasant reply. When the war ended he left the United States for his beloved Middle East. There, he received the kind of fawning attention he relished, telling a friend of a party in Ankara given in his honor by Afet Inan where all his publications were spread out on tables for guests to peruse and admire. He settled in Cairo, where he died of cancer in 1948.[68]

The American minister in Tehran traced the origin of the case against Herzfeld to André Godard, who, he argued, exercised increasing influence over the minister of public instruction. According to the American, Godard was "the master mind directing the French cultural offensive" in Iran. He described him as "shrewd, calculating, agreeable, intelligent and a veritable master of intrigue." His success could be gauged, wrote the minister, by the fact that the Iranian government had just conferred a decoration on him at the request of Hikmat. Godard brought the charges against Herzfeld late in the negotiations in the hope that they would be rejected by the Oriental Institute, forcing the concession to revert to the Iranian government. In that eventuality Godard would either head the excavation himself or bring in another French archaeologist. All of this, naturally, would increase French prestige in the country.[69]

But Hornibrook saw more in Godard's scheme. He discerned a controversy between French and German cultural ambitions in which the institute had become an innocent victim, having backed—in the interests of science—the wrong party, that is, the German, Herzfeld.[70]

Although the idea of an ongoing Franco-German rivalry in the Middle East in the 1930s is not without substance, and there is certainly evidence to support this in Egypt and even more in Syria, the American diplomat might have looked more closely at the nationalist movement in Iran to explain Herzfeld's difficulties. Murray had already written that "the spirit of rampant nationalism is abroad and such an impulse must naturally come in conflict with archaeological endeavor."[71]

Yet neither Murray nor Hornibrook nor Breasted looked at the rejection of Herzfeld as anything more than a power struggle among the Europeans, with a measure of anti-Semitism, which seemed predictable. Godard, they concluded, had manipulated Hikmat, and yet they had before them ample evidence to account for Iranian actions. Hikmat had told the U.S. minister that he opposed Herzfeld's bullying tactics in unilaterally stopping work at Persepolis. He knew, of course, how the Egyptians had responded at Luxor a decade earlier with considerable success when Howard Carter had ceased work at Tutankhamun's tomb. By seeking diplomatic assistance, Herzfeld also reminded officials of the capitulations only recently—and reluctantly—relinquished by foreign powers. Finally, his apparent attempts to send antiquities abroad, without going through customs, angered those nationalists who had seen European and American museums grow fat on a steady diet of illegal antiquities. When Herzfeld's belongings were being packed at the end of 1935 under Godard's watchful eye, a number of items from his collection of antiquities were retained for the museum. Whatever Godard's other motives, he made clear his commitment to stopping the illegal antiquities trade and to preventing Iran's monuments from being stripped any further of their artistic treasures.[72]

Perhaps foreign observers missed the significance of these incidents because they could not or would not see that what archaeologists did was political. Murray actually wrote to Breasted toward the depths of the crisis that archaeology by its very nature was "nonpolitical." How mistaken he was. The nation's past as embodied in its ancient monuments had become almost sacrosanct, as the nationalist elite constructed a mythic tale of past glories that would come again once they had instilled new vigor and commitment in their fellow citizens. Naturally, any foreigner working at Persepolis was bound to come under suspicion, and Herzfeld, who had been working for decades in the region, seemed insensitive to these more recent developments.[73]

Murray believed that Iranians and other peoples of the region had been spoiled by American largesse, and he cautioned that "scientific, philanthropic and educational benefits should not be lavished gratuitously." As they had never been asked to make any contribution to the efforts, they had no appreciation for what the Americans had been doing all these years.

Besides, to give them something for nothing could be mistaken as weakness. In fact, he briefly wondered whether Americans should be spending such large amounts in foreign countries at all, at a time when their own countrymen were on relief. After the breakthrough in negotiations in Tehran, however, he apparently put such moralizing aside.[74]

The American diplomats had become deeply enmeshed in the affair of the Oriental Institute. Murray admitted that he had urged Breasted to demand five hundred of the clay tablets from Persepolis and that without State Department support the institute would have received much less compensation for its efforts. This reward became part of the national treasure of the United States, boasted Murray, "contributing to the cultural advantage and advancement of the American people."[75]

# 8. TROUBLES OVER IRAN

Ernst Herzfeld's departure marked another stage in the gradual transformation of archaeological relations between Iran and the West. In 1929 Iran had successfully ended the long period of French monopoly over its ancient sites. Now, five years later, the government had succeeded in enforcing its rules governing the excavation of its most important site.

With Herzfeld gone, the expedition's work could resume, and Breasted wasted no time selecting a new director. Godard had hoped that his friend, Friedrich Krefter, would be chosen, but Breasted turned instead to Erich Schmidt, another German but one who had recently become an American citizen. Schmidt was in Chicago at the time and was able to meet with Herzfeld before leaving for Iran. Schmidt had worked several years earlier for the Oriental Institute at Alişar in central Anatolia and currently headed the University of Pennsylvania expedition at Rayy, not far from Tehran, where he was quite successful. He had encountered few problems with Iranian authorities, and he now recommended taking the Persepolis question out of diplomatic channels for that was a line of support to call on only in emergencies. All the same, before he left the United States, Schmidt traveled to Washington for a private meeting with Wallace Murray.[1]

When Schmidt arrived in Tehran Hornibrook advised him to use the utmost tact with the minister of public instruction and especially with Godard "in view of his own desire to maintain French cultural ascendancy in Persia." Flattery would work better than reason in dealing with the director of antiquities and would smooth Schmidt's tenure as field director.[2]

Godard apparently believed that Schmidt was not experienced enough, nor did he have the stature to be appointed director at Persepolis. Then, too, he was a German. It was one thing for Herzfeld, the Einstein of his field, to occupy that position, quite another for Schmidt. The U.S. chargé d'affaires, James Rives Childs, agreed, telling the State Department that it reflected badly on the United States and did not add to American pres-

**Figure 8.1.** Erich Schmidt (left), director of the University of Pennsylvania expedition at Rayy, with Iranian officials, 1932. Courtesy of the University of Pennsylvania Museum, Philadelphia.

tige. On the one hand, Breasted could sympathize with such arguments; on the other, he complained that American universities had failed to produce a new generation of Orientalists. He had no choice, therefore, but to turn to Germany.[3]

Despite these early doubts, Schmidt's arrival seemed to go well. Prime Minister Foroughi, a firm friend of the United States, and Hikmat suggested that he treat visitors to the site generously and cooperate with government authorities, to both of which he agreed. Godard himself agreed to come to Persepolis to verify Chicago's share of the previous season's antiquities, which would then be sealed and sent on their way to the United States. He arranged to give Schmidt the same government commissioner he had had at Rayy the previous year. In early July Schmidt notified Chicago that his relations with officials were excellent.[4]

Two issues, however, were raising concerns in Tehran. The lesser of these was Schmidt's decision to continue as director at Rayy while pursuing his work at Persepolis. Godard and his superiors wanted Schmidt to give his full attention to the latter, in order to clear the site and where possible to reerect scattered materials such as fallen columns as quickly as he could. This, the premier site in Iran, was surely worthy of Schmidt's undivided attention. When Schmidt asked permission for yet a third concession, this one in Luristan in western Iran, in cooperation with Arthur Upham Pope, Godard initially refused. He relented only after Schmidt agreed to withdraw as soon as possible from the expedition at Rayy, which then would become the site of the first scientific excavation by an all-Iranian staff. Godard was able to call upon the assistance of three inspectors from the archaeological service who had worked on foreign excavations in recent years, Muhammad Taghi Mostafavi, Muhammad Minui, and Hussain Ravanbodh. Although it would be six years before a fully trained Iranian archaeologist, Fereydun Tavalloli, became available, the press touted Rayy as "a brilliant beginning."[5]

The other issue turned out to be far more problematic for Schmidt. The new director proposed to bring an airplane into Iran to facilitate his work and to carry out aerial surveys of archaeological sites throughout the country. This was, of course, an extremely sensitive subject, but Schmidt seemed not to realize this at first. No one in Tehran welcomed foreign aircraft in Iranian skies, even with the best scientific motives. That Schmidt did not prepare Iranian officials adequately only made the problem worse. From the Iranian perspective, this was a military-security issue, which could only be resolved by the highest authority.

The U.S. legation first learned of this proposal from Godard, who had been notified of Schmidt's intentions in a personal letter. Childs, who had already criticized Schmidt's appointment, went right to the point, telling Washington that the new director had prejudiced authorities against him by his ready assumption that approval for the plane would be accorded as a matter of course.[6]

Schmidt explained to the prime minister that use of the plane would herald the application of modern techniques to the science of archaeology. Iran would become a leader in the region in the use of "the most advanced means for tracing and studying the remains of its glorious past." Westerners were always asking local authorities to put themselves into the forefront of scientific advance whatever the issue at hand.[7]

Schmidt could be very determined. He went behind the backs of Hikmat and Foroughi to ask the chief of the air force if the Iranian military had opposed his bringing in the plane, and then in the face of continued official opposition, asked that the question be submitted directly to the shah. Despite his earlier decision to keep the diplomats out of expedition affairs, he also asked the institute if it thought Washington could help him. To make his proposal more attractive, Schmidt decided to offer the plane, which had been purchased by his wife's family, as a gift to the government of Iran once his work was finished. While the shah pondered Schmidt's request, the director continued to meet with Iranian military leaders to discuss uses of the plane, areas to be surveyed, and other such details.[8]

On July 15 the royal assent to bring the *Friend of Iran* into the country was communicated to institute headquarters in Chicago. Schmidt had to agree to turn over all negatives to the Iranian government and to fly only when a representative of the government was on board and only to previously agreed upon locations.[9]

Schmidt received the news with enthusiasm, viewing the shah's decision as the opening of the door to a long sought after enterprise full of grand prospects for expanding archaeological efforts. The U.S. minister was less sanguine, declaring to Murray that the plane would provide a constant source of irritation and any advantages would hardly compensate for the friction with the authorities that would surely result.[10]

Schmidt continued his association with Pope, and they would eventually obtain from Godard the concession in Luristan. Pope found raising money during the Depression difficult, and he was gratified when the Iranian government, that is, the shah, agreed to contribute 500 pounds toward the long-term project of publishing Pope's magisterial *Survey of Iranian Art*. He gave a lecture in Tehran in early May, which many top officials attended. To enhance his position at court, Pope had undertaken yet another international project, this time in the Soviet Union. He served as international secretary for the Congress of Iranian Art and Archaeology held in Leningrad in September 1935.

Pope had suggested to Hikmat that the Oriental Institute be invited to send a photographic display of its work at Persepolis and that Breasted be urged to attend. The U.S. minister thought this an excellent idea, and he cautioned Schmidt that there would be "hell to pay" if the institute did not cooperate even if Breasted and Pope did not get on. The photos arrived late, and Breasted did not appear at all.[11]

Pope's wife, Dr. Phyllis Ackerman, received a decoration from the shah for her work on Iranian textiles; the shah had had her husband decorated at London in 1931. The U.S. minister assured Washington that this must have come as a rebuff to Godard.

The Leningrad exposition provided another occasion for an outpouring of nationalist rhetoric. Hikmat spoke there of the mission to protect the ancient monuments, which had value for the entire civilized world, and to reestablish the ancient culture and values of their ancestors. Isa Sadiq, president of Tehran Teachers' College, explained that Tehran University, founded only the previous year, had established a chair in archaeology so that in future Iranians could undertake scientific excavations themselves. The exposition, wrote one editor, had "the value of a grand symbol—the symbol of a formidable heritage such as one discovers when rising from a long and debilitating illness [Qajar rule]."[12]

The French were continuing to have singular success in Iran. The new French minister, Jean Pozzi, had a great deal of experience in archaeological matters, and this may have accounted for his appointment to Tehran. He never tired of praising French accomplishments at Susa. To existing excavations at Nihavand, Kashan, and Susa, the French added two more organized by the Louvre at the Sasanian sites of Kazerun and Shapur, showing that their cultural offensive under Pozzi had made a considerable advance.[13]

The Americans, meanwhile, received a serious and unexpected setback in December with the death of James Breasted, who had been the driving force behind much of the archaeological activity taking place throughout the Middle East since the end of World War I. Frances, his wife of forty years, had died in July 1934, and the following year he had married her younger sister, Imogen. Their wedding trip took them to Europe and the Middle East, and at the age of seventy Breasted seemed to have found new energy, writing to Charles, "I am as keen as a boy to get back to my desk." On the return voyage, however, he became gravely ill from an infection, which, before the availability of sulfa drugs, almost always proved fatal. He died soon after reaching New York.[14]

Although Breasted had interests throughout the region, he had been especially excited at the prospect of excavating the ancient Achaemenid center. He once touted Herzfeld's discoveries there as the greatest in western Asia since the Germans found the great altar at Pergamon in the 1870s. Through years of controversy he had been able to ensure that work there went forward. With his passing, the future looked decidedly less promising.[15]

Already in early 1935, faced with declining contributions, which he attributed in part to Franklin Delano Roosevelt's new tax on wealthy Americans, Breasted had made a personal appeal to Rockefeller for increased support. He claimed that the loss of Persepolis would mean "the loss of magnificent monuments which America has almost in her grasp." That appeal had succeeded because, as a trusted advisor noted, "Mr. Rockefeller has great confidence in Breasted and great admiration for his work. [He] has a feeling that his function as interpreter of ancient cultures is unique. Such men do not appear often."[16]

In spite of the close, almost spiritual bond between these two men,

Breasted had to make the case again in August, arguing to David Stevens, director of humanities for the Rockefeller Foundation, that Persepolis was "the most valuable concession in the world." The State Department, he explained, had fought for many months on the institute's behalf to keep Persepolis. Should it now be sacrificed? Again, there was a reprieve. The "Donor" felt compelled to write again in late November, just two days before Breasted's ship would arrive in New York City. He reiterated in the strongest terms that Breasted would somehow have to pare his operating expenses. In these difficult financial times, Rockefeller had no intention of making further contributions. Breasted never read this letter.[17]

With Breasted gone, the link to Rockefeller had weakened. John Wilson, James Breasted's longtime associate, who would soon succeed him as director of the institute, wrote to Stevens only two weeks after Breasted's death. He realized that the time had come to cut back many programs, a development Breasted had been able to delay. Wilson referred to Persepolis as the late director's favorite site but suggested that the wisest step might be to withdraw completely and at once. Wilson pointed to continuing problems with the Iranian government, citing an example from Leningrad where the Iranians had displayed the gold foundation tablets from Persepolis, presenting them as having been discovered by its own archaeological service.[18]

Yet six weeks later Charles Breasted, whose authority at the institute had declined considerably with the death of his father and the appointment of Wilson as acting director, asked Murray to send Wilson a letter emphasizing the importance of Persepolis to maintaining American prestige in Iran. This could, he hoped, be used to convince the Rockefeller Foundation to continue its support. Murray had no problem drafting a letter that revealed his true feelings and getting Undersecretary Phillips to send it out over his own name. In it Murray praised the work of the institute, pointing out that precipitous withdrawal would not only affect other American archaeological projects but also impair "the efforts of the Department to obtain favorable consideration for other legitimate American interests in Iran," including educational institutions, missionary activities, and even commercial enterprises.[19]

The Oriental Institute struggled through the 1936 season, but finances became desperate. When Wilson informed Schmidt that the institute would have to pull out of Persepolis, the site director convinced George Edgell, director of the Boston Museum of Fine Arts, and Jayne, of the University Museum, to share costs with Chicago beginning in 1937. This arrangement worked reasonably well and lasted until Schmidt departed in October 1939.

Solving the financial shortfall was in some respects the easiest of Schmidt's problems. Relations with the Iranian government went up and down like a roller coaster, and he could not always account for the dramatic shifts. When he visited with the chargé d'affaires, Gordon Merriam, in Tehran in April 1936 he was, according to the official, "in a perturbed state of mind." The authorities had grounded his plane once again, had returned to him a beautiful volume of aerial photographs he had prepared as a gift for the shah, and had asked him when the expedition would finish its work. Murray was surprised that Schmidt seemed so little prepared for such difficulties, which seemed to go with the position. The diplomats thought that he needed to be more realistic.[20]

And they were right. Schmidt had angered the minister of public instruction by complaining directly to the military of a lack of cooperation, warning them that other expeditions would be affected if he were continually denied permission to fly. Hikmat reminded the Foreign Office that he was responsible for all foreign archaeological missions and that Schmidt should have come to him first before complaining elsewhere. Yet the director seemed unaware of his offense.[21]

Instead, Schmidt attributed all his troubles to the deteriorating relations between the United States and Iran. After the Djalal incident, in which Maryland police officers had unknowingly arrested the Iranian minister for speeding, thereby violating his diplomatic immunity, the government recalled its representative from Washington. Then a critical article in the *New York Daily Mirror* had antagonized the shah. Iranians, who were unfamiliar with American institutions, believed it was the duty of the U.S. government to prevent publication of articles offensive to the shah.[22]

Pope weighed in on this crisis as he did on most issues in these years affecting U.S.-Iranian ties. He wrote letters to prominent Iranian friends explaining how unimportant and disreputable the *Daily Mirror* was. He told Hikmat that only servant girls, chauffeurs, errand boys, hangers-on in the theatrical world, "and other riffraff and low brows" read the paper. Respectable and intelligent people never looked at it, and, he assured the minister, it had no status or influence in the United States.[23]

Schmidt was at least partly correct in his assessment. By the mid-1930s the Persepolis expedition had become an important symbol of American activity and enterprise in Iran, and the Tehran government could signal its pleasure or displeasure toward the United States by its treatment of the archaeologists there. Thus the State Department and the legation watched developments carefully for any hint of a changing attitude toward Washington.

The Americans were not alone in this predicament; Iran's relations with France had suddenly worsened and for similar reasons. The shah's visit to Susa, also in 1937, provided the opportunity for a royal outburst against the rapaciousness of the French "thieves," who had taken all the treasures to the Louvre and left Iran only the cement. He had long known about this "thievery," of course, but his words seemed carefully chosen at this time to signal his overall displeasure to Paris.[24]

In June Schmidt faced another mini-crisis when the crew at Persepolis accidentally damaged a bull-shaped capital that was being moved to storage. The Iranian commissioner at the site immediately reported the incident, and Hikmat used it to criticize the work of the expedition generally. He referred to the recklessness and carelessness of those responsible and demanded that the expedition compensate Iran for the damage. This, he claimed, was an example, and not the first, of the indifference and inattentiveness of the expedition. He concluded with a warning that should conditions not improve, the ministry would have to reconsider its concession to the Oriental Institute. Schmidt responded with a detailed explanation, carefully avoiding any hint of confrontation.[25]

He discovered that part of the ministry's disapproval arose from the fact that he was still serving as director at Rayy, the implication being that had he given all his attention to one site such an accident would have been less likely. There was also the possibility that Hikmat, who was said to be politically ambitious, might have found this an excellent opportunity to climb on "the anti-American bandwagon." Whatever the reason, this would definitely be Schmidt's last season at Rayy.[26]

Schmidt, too, had his ambitions, and he and Pope were pressing hard for the concession in northern Luristan. Pope wrote to Hikmat to explain the importance of what they proposed. In one short paragraph he set out many of the reasons—repeated again and again by other Western archaeologists—why Iran should approve their request. A sound scientific exploration would be regarded as world news in every civilized country. Attention would focus on Iran and bring prestige for its enlightened archaeological policy. The expedition would enrich the new museum, soon to open, and provide an intellectual and artistic service to the whole world. Despite Pope's blandishments, the authorities still refused, and it became clear to Schmidt that work could not begin in Luristan before spring 1937.

He decided, therefore, to concentrate on Persepolis, which was exactly what Iranian officials wanted.[27]

By year's end Schmidt was complaining again about a lack of support from the Iranian authorities. Not only had they denied him permission for photographing flights, but they were also insisting that Americans would have to pay Iranian income tax. Schmidt claimed that the Iranians considered them antiquities dealers, therefore merchants, and hence they should pay the tax. Coming at the end of a line of petty harassments, Schmidt believed that they represented the anger of the shah at the United States rather than any shortcomings on the part of the expedition.[28]

Nevertheless, Schmidt counseled an early withdrawal from Iran if the government's attitude did not change. When he met with Murray in Washington, he asked if there was nothing the department could do to press the Iranians as it had done in the case of Persepolis in 1934. The division chief admitted that conditions had deteriorated; bilateral relations were seriously strained and partially severed. Direct channels of communication with the shah had been cut, and Murray could not think of a single Iranian who would dare to approach the shah to ask for more cooperation with the institute in its work at Persepolis.[29]

Although Murray blamed Iran, he did not want the institute suddenly to withdraw, for precipitate action could negatively affect other American interests there. He asked Wilson to synchronize any such steps with the State Department, but the new director said he could not assure Murray that this would always be possible, for the institute might not be able to delay its response if a suddenly unfavorable situation arose.[30]

In the middle of this most recent crisis, Murray and the chargé in Tehran exchanged letters that revealed very different assessments of the root of the problems at Persepolis. Merriam believed that everything could be traced to Schmidt's methods in Iran, which he considered "too complicated, spectacular, and expensive." It aroused the suspicion of the Iranians and the envy of the French. The plane had proved an endless source of controversy, forcing Schmidt to "abandon archaeology for diplomacy." Schmidt, he concluded, should work on a more modest scale. "The watchword should be: decentralize and simplify." This had been a problem for Schmidt in Egypt earlier, where he and Merriam had served at the same time. As Merriam concluded, "Sometimes I wonder if Schmidt is not too ambitious for a scientist."[31]

The chargé's well-intentioned analysis received a surprising rebuke from Murray, who claimed that Schmidt was in a completely different category from all the other American archaeologists in Iran, for he was always in the spotlight. It was not the job of the diplomats to complain about his joint directorships or his plane. These were issues between him and the Oriental Institute. The diplomat's job was to do his best to help when they needed assistance, said Murray, concluding testily, "We would not pass on the policies of Standard Oil or General Motors, neither should we on the Oriental Institute and Schmidt." After the series of crises that had developed since 1934, Murray had clearly had enough of Iranian officialdom. He wanted no more sympathetic understanding for them from junior diplomats in Tehran.[32]

Then, as suddenly as the clouds had gathered, they parted, and the Iranian sun shone brightly again for Schmidt. The shah had decided to make one of his infrequent visits to the site; the most recent one had been in 1932 when Herzfeld was director. Riza Shah chose his dates carefully. He and the crown prince, Muhammad Riza, only recently returned from his studies in Switzerland, would travel to Persepolis just after the Iranian new year (March 21) and during the thirteen-day period when since ancient times Iranians had celebrated the vernal equinox and the coming of spring. Many Iranians traveled during the period to visit family and friends, and the significance of the shah's "pilgrimage" to the ancient capital could not be missed.

Schmidt and members of the expedition worked overtime for two weeks to prepare the site, disregarding all other duties. With flowers planted, floors swept clean, and bad patches plastered, the expedition had, according to Schmidt, "an almost unnaturally sleek appearance." The small museum was spruced up with dark maroon cloth and photographs and maps laid out on tables. At nearby Istakhr, a separate room housed the so-called aeronautical department, including cameras, maps, and enlarged photographs from earlier flights. At the last moment it was decided that the royal party would spend the night at Persepolis, and thus Schmidt abandoned his quarters for a tent next to the hangar where the *Friend of Iran* was parked.[33]

When the royal party arrived, the provincial chief of education spoke briefly, as arranged with the monarch, concerning Schmidt's hopes for his aerial work, especially along the Gurgan River on the Turcoman Steppe in northeastern Iran. The shah immediately granted permission, emphasizing that this was solely for Schmidt and that no one else would get such approval.[34]

As they toured the site looking at reliefs recently cleared, the shah and the crown prince stopped to gaze upon a scene showing the great Darius and his son, Xerxes. Everyone was impressed by the parallel nature of these

**Figure 8.2.** Persepolis 1937. Shah and crown prince in front of the Darius treasury relief. Courtesy of the Oriental Institute of the University of Chicago.

two scenes, one ancient, the other modern. Just before his departure the next morning, the shah expressed his general satisfaction with the expedition. Schmidt concluded his report by observing that "the man whose word in this country is law has expressed his satisfaction with the expedition although he knows well enough that it is an American enterprise." Wilson found it ironic that earlier the authorities had objected to Herzfeld because of his nationality and asked for an American director, yet now the shah was appeased in his anti-Americanism upon hearing that it was headed by the German, Schmidt.[35]

While at the site, the shah indicated that he wanted the platform cleared as quickly as possible, and the director agreed to do all he could. In the days that followed, this request was not forgotten. Hikmat urged Schmidt to reset fallen columns on the terrace at Persepolis as the shah had requested, to which Schmidt replied that his whole workforce of two hundred fifty men was engaged in that very task. Clearly, Schmidt was facing new demands, and with all this coming just after the tragic death of his wife, Mary-Helen, he felt intense strain. He implored Hikmat and the other authorities in Tehran to support his work "with kindness and consideration and to protect it against attacks."[36]

Murray thought that unlikely. He attached a less positive interpretation to Schmidt's report, one that fit well his own earlier pronouncements. The shah, he concluded, had given only grudging appreciation for the important work already done at Persepolis. This visit, he thought, threw further light "on the curious mentality of the Iranian sovereign," who had given "peremptory orders that operations should be expedited."[37]

Better relations were short lived, and by the end of 1937 Schmidt was complaining again about the authorities' growing indifference to the expedition. In January his plane was grounded, and he concluded that it was becoming so difficult to work in Iran that he would try to finish everything up by 1939.[38]

Although all these developments clouded U.S.-Iranian relations generally and the work of American archaeologists in particular, the Iranian government continued to affirm its interest in and attachment to the nation's ancient past. The government required foreign nations to refer to the country as its citizens had always known it, "Iran," not "Persia," as it was called in the West, a name derived from the Greeks. A course in the ancient Pahlavi language—also the name of the new dynasty—was instituted at the university. In 1937 a department of archaeology was established there as well. These steps, it was hoped, would encourage Iranians and others to become more conscious of their nation's past.[39]

A movement grew also to build a national museum to house Iran's growing collection of antiquities. The former minister of court, Taymurtash, had been instrumental in laying plans for a permanent home, and on April 22, 1933, the Majlis made the necessary initial appropriation. Skeptics referred to the project as "Godard's Dream" because the director had helped to sketch the plans and was such a strong advocate. These were difficult times economically, however, so the project took longer than expected; it was not completed until 1938. The Museum of Ancient Iran, its facade inspired by the Sasanian palace at Ctesiphon, sat in the center of the capital. Hikmat had acquired extra land for its Ferdowsi library by asking the shah to donate property originally set aside for stabling police horses. The shah could hardly refuse as the nation was then celebrating the millennium of the poet's birth. Nevertheless, the land set aside for the museum was small and would restrict its future growth.[40]

To build a museum and library had long been objectives of the Society for the Preservation of the National Heritage, and its members took pride in their role of bringing the project to completion. To them it seemed only proper that the museum should house treasures from the pre-Islamic

**Figure 8.3.** Arch at Ctesiphon, former Sasanian capital, near Baghdad. Vehicle of the University of Pennsylvania expedition in the foreground. Courtesy of the University of Pennsylvania Museum, Philadelphia.

centuries. It would privilege that era over the Islamic period and thereby reinforce a particular historical memory.[41]

When the museum finally opened, the crown prince and his young bride, Fusieh of Egypt, made a much-publicized tour. Both her father, the late King Fuad (d. 1936) and her brother, King Faruq (1936–1952), had shown great interest in Egypt's antiquities. Although in comparison to Cairo's Egyptian Museum, Iran's new structure must have seemed small to Fusieh, to Iranian nationalists, who had waited so long, the museum showed "Iran as the most glittering civilization of the world." People who visited it, wrote one editor, would "get to learn of their past and speak with their ancestors." Despite its size, the museum came to be considered one of the finest in the Middle East.[42]

Arthur Upham Pope applauded these developments. He continued to collaborate with Schmidt up to the outbreak of World War II. He wrote countless letters to friends in Iran and Europe, always seeking to raise

**Figure 8.4.** King Faruq (left), Fusieh, his sister, and her future husband, Crown Prince Muhammad Riza Pahlavi of Iran. Cairo, March 15, 1939. Courtesy National Archives.

funds and to suggest new schemes for Iran. They were unlikely partners, frequently at odds. Pope admonished Schmidt not to be so quick and dogmatic with his opinions regarding the age and authenticity of ceramics, especially when it was Pope who had sold some of them to key contributors. He cautioned Schmidt "to study [his] ceramics more carefully." As funds dwindled Pope reminded Schmidt to remember the sacrifices he and his wife had made to keep the Persian Institute going. Dr. Ackerman had been forced to sell what remained of her textile collection, and he had long ago parted with his own antiquities. Even in hard times, the resourceful

Pope kept coming up with new ideas. He wanted Schmidt to announce an archaeological survey of Azarbaijan as part of the society's program. In fall 1937 he took several Iranian art and architecture students, including Foroughi's son, Mohsen, on tour with him around Iran. The Iranians were immensely pleased at the attention given to their up-and-coming young artists.[43]

Despite Pope's reputation for shady methods and questionable tactics, he never lost sight of the issues he considered fundamental. It was a matter of pride that he had never gone through the U.S. legation for help because of Iranian sensitivity to foreign influence. In August 1937 he sharply criticized a piece his friend Robert Byron had written in the *London Times* regarding the "new" Iran. Pope had introduced Byron to government officials there, and he knew they would assume that he shared Byron's critical assessment, hence his quick response to the *Times*, dissociating himself from the piece. In long letters to Byron and to a third friend, the eminent British archaeologist Sir Aurel Stein, he explained that there were many in Iran, including some of the shah's military associates, who regarded "archaeology as nonsense and diverting interest from modern accomplishments to indolent attention to the past." Iran had a good antiquities law and helpful personnel, who had little formal training. It was not, he said, his intention to spare the Iranians any rebuke that they deserved, but such criticism had to be fair in the present context. "If you had made your trip in 1910 or 1925 — those halcyon days for which you sigh," wrote Pope, "you would have got almost nothing done and might have lost your life." Pieces such as Byron's could easily undo much good resulting from the efforts of Iranians and Westerners alike.[44]

Pope was fiercely anti-Fascist, supported the republicans in Spain, and despised Mussolini and Hitler. He did all he could to bring German Jewish scholars to safety in the United States. He also gave a boost to many young scholarly careers, including those of Donald Wilber, Joseph Upton, and Gustav Von Grunebaum, some of whom broke with him in later years.

Pope continued his interest in things Iranian into the early postwar years, when he welcomed Muhammad Riza Shah (1941-1979), who was making his first visit to the United States, to New York City in 1949. The speech was typical of Pope, full of references to Iran's ancient greatness, its service to world civilization, and favorable comparison of the present reign to those of the great kings of Iran. The shah was clearly impressed, and years later he would repay Pope's kind words, rescuing him and his wife from a penurious existence in rural New England. He set them up in a fine old house in Shiraz for the last few years of their lives and at the end arranged for their burials in a simple tomb on the banks of the Ziandeh Rud in Isfahan.[45]

For Schmidt, work in Iran was drawing to a close, and he prepared to move on. The outbreak of war made it unlikely that the expedition could work effectively, and permission in wartime for aerial photography was out of the question. On September 7, 1939, Schmidt informed the Department of Antiquities that the expedition would be departing by mid-October due to conditions beyond its control.[46]

Schmidt had received approval from the Iraqi government to do aerial photography there, but after war began the Iranians refused to release the plane. Schmidt thereupon donated it (a second time) to Iran. His *Flights over Ancient Cities of Iran*, a collection of the best aerial photographs from these years, was published in 1940. During the war, Schmidt made available to the U.S. Office of Strategic Services (OSS) and to the army air force his photographs from those flights, thus contributing, as did many archaeologists, to the Allied war effort.[47]

It had been clear all along to those who knew Schmidt that his greater interest lay in aerial photography. He told one acquaintance that digging had no more attraction for him, that he wanted only to do the flying work. He told Wilson that he would put every ounce of his strength into the fight to obtain permission for his flights. Wilson sometimes became infuriated that Schmidt always put the aerial surveys before the Persepolis expedition. Could Iranians, then, be faulted for their concern about the neglect of their most important historical monument?[48]

When the expedition hastily departed, the Oriental Institute's share of the final division, ten cases of antiquities, remained, becoming the subject of continued negotiation during the war. U.S. Minister Louis G. Dreyfus (served 1939–1943) discussed with Godard the likelihood of their release, but the director of antiquities said they would never leave Iran, that the shah had made that decision and no one would dare to suggest he reconsider. He accused Schmidt of having constant contact with known German spies and of having used his plane for illegal activities. Hornibrook had certainly been correct when he wrote in 1935 that the *Friend of Iran* would become an unending source of irritation.[49]

The cabinet resolved the standoff prior to the abdication of Riza Shah in September 1941, just before the entry of British and Soviet forces into Iran. This was a time when matters had become critical politically, and the government no doubt hoped this friendly action would encourage American support for Iran in the current crisis. Of the 519 articles in the ten

cases, the Tehran Museum retained only 33 items for which it had no duplicates in its collection. Officials packed the remainder in six cases and one
crate, sending these to the southern port of Bandar Shahpur on November 4, 1941. In late March they were loaded onto the SS *City of Alma* for
transfer to the United States. During the night of June 2, 1942, the vessel
was torpedoed and sunk by a German submarine in the Caribbean only a
few days short of its destination. All the antiquities were lost.[50]

Once the American expedition had departed, the Department of Antiquities took control at Persepolis, and Godard put two hundred men to
work under an Iranian director to continue the excavation. Article 3 of
the 1922 constitution of the Society for the Preservation of the National
Heritage had hinted that only Iranians could fully appreciate and protect
their cultural heritage. Now that the nation's premier archaeological site
was at last in trusted hands, they could breathe more easily.[51]

# 9. ARCHAEOLOGY AS USUAL

To the west of the Iranian plateau lay Mesopotamia, the land between the two rivers, the Tigris and the Euphrates; it had witnessed the rise and fall of numerous city-states and empires, among them, Ur, Nippur, Babylonia, and Assyria. The region was rich in the history of the development of human society, competing in importance with Egypt itself.

Buried under fertile riverine soils or desert sands lay largely untouched the relics of these ancient societies. As in Egypt, Turkey, and Iran, the revival of interest in these peoples and their long-buried cities was nurtured by European adventurers and Orientalists, who appeared in increasing numbers in the second half of the nineteenth century. The names of many of these ancient sites were known from the Old Testament, where they figured prominently, and much of the early fieldwork was motivated by the desire to prove the historical accuracy of the Bible.

Of the adventurers, the first was Paul Emile Botta, French consul at Mosul, who combined the roles of amateur diplomat and amateur archaeologist. The Englishman Austen Henry Layard came soon after him. In the 1840s they each dug separately into Assyrian mounds at Nimrud, Nineveh, and Khorsabad in northern Iraq. From there they shipped to their respective capitals astounding treasures, stone slabs with intricate reliefs of ancient kings, winged animals and other mythical figures, and whole libraries of clay tablets with indecipherable cuneiform writing. Layard "used an army of peasants wielding picks and shovels to cart away as many of the huge reliefs . . . as he could. . . . In the process, [he] lost quite a few, which sank to the bottom of the Tigris."[1]

This was a time of plundering, and Ottoman authorities had little success in controlling the export of antiquities, which soon appeared on display in the private collections of the wealthy and, of course, in the Louvre and the British Museum. Layard became famous for his exploits, and the displays of artifacts he uncovered stimulated general interest in and admiration for the skills of ancient craftsmen. New histories traced the

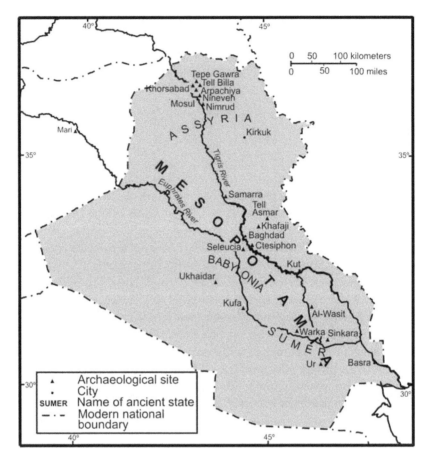

Iraq

roots of Western civilization to these ancient peoples. Out of this interest came more European and American adventurers to discover for themselves what they could. Toward the end of the century, as in Egypt and
elsewhere in the region, excavation methods became more refined for recovering the ancient record, and antiquities were less likely to be ripped
thoughtlessly from the soil, without first giving some attention to the context in which they were discovered. The Americans and especially the University of Chicago and the University of Pennsylvania sent out a number
of expeditions, but Chicago's efforts ended in scandal in 1904 when the
field director, Edgar James Banks, was accused of smuggling antiquities.
This affair ruined his career and the expedition as well for as one scholar
observed, "receiving stolen property was fine, but the direct and public

accusation of robbery was damning." Countless antiquities continued to flow into the United States up to World War I, many of them purchased from dealers, who obtained them for a pittance from illicit diggers, usually local peasants.[2]

The outbreak of World War I brought a halt to all expeditions except that of the Germans, who continued working until driven off by British forces moving up the Tigris in April 1917. Robert Koldeway, supported by the German Orient Society, had worked continuously at Babylon for eighteen years, 1899–1917. He abandoned 536 crates of antiquities from that site to the victors. At war's end Britain and France imposed their control formally over much of the region in the guise of mandates under the League of Nations. France obtained Syria; Britain, Palestine and Iraq. Britain added the northern *vilayet* (province) of Mosul, largely inhabited by Kurds and Turks, to those of Basra and Baghdad to form the new state of Iraq with its capital at Baghdad. In neighboring Turkey, Mustafa Kemal, facing many challenges farther west, reluctantly chose not to protest the British move by force of arms.

The provinces of this modern nation of Iraq had for centuries been part of the Ottoman Empire, forming the often-troubled eastern border of the empire with Iran. Following its days of glory during the Abbasid Empire (750–1258), Baghdad, the former imperial capital, and indeed all the territory that would make up this modern successor state, had become a backwater of the Islamic world.

It took some time for conditions to settle down there, where there was tribal opposition to British rule and a full-scale uprising during summer 1920, which Britain put down at great expense. In a famous conference at Cairo in February–March 1921, Britain's Middle East experts, among them T. E. Lawrence, Gertrude Bell, Sir Percy Cox, and, of course, Winston Churchill, colonial secretary, decided to make Faisal, son of the Sharif of Makkah, king of Iraq. Faisal had cooperated with the British during the war with the expectation that an independent Arab state would be established in the Arabian peninsula, Syria, and Palestine at war's end. Instead, the French had driven him out of Damascus, and the British did not protest. Their decision a year later to make Faisal king evolved in part out of strategic considerations and in part out of a guilty conscience. Then, too, there was the influence of the intrepid Gertrude Bell, Oriental secretary in Baghdad, who admired Faisal's military and administrative experience, "his diplomatic skills, his depth of character and his charisma." She believed he would be best able to win the loyalty of his Iraqi subjects and to establish a stable regime.[3]

After putting down some local opposition, Faisal was crowned king on August 23, 1921. His Hashemite dynasty would rule Iraq for thirty-seven years. High-strung and calculating, he kept his intentions hidden. He took his new position seriously, doing all he could to attach leading Iraqis to the new dynasty. Yet until the end of the mandate in 1932, Britain held the upper hand in the country, and even after that, until the 1958 revolution, it maintained a strong influence.[4]

In the early postwar years, with so many urgent problems to resolve, archaeology was not a priority of the India Office, which exercised control in Iraq until February 1921. This troubled archaeologists, who were planning to return there even before the guns of war fell silent. In October 1918 officials at the British Museum suggested that the government give attention to its needs. Director Sir Frederick Kenyon hoped that there would be no tightening of controls over the export of antiquities. Among other suggestions, he urged that all antiquities be brought home for scientific treatment and publication and that roughly one-half could be returned "if and when required to do so." It was one thing to extend such controls in India and Cyprus, where there were highly intelligent and educated classes, he argued, but this was hardly the case in Mesopotamia. It would be ironic if as a result of control there by Britain the museum should be prohibited from adding to its collection.[5]

Kenyon corresponded with George Gordon, director of the University Museum in Philadelphia, encouraging him to make a formal application for an expedition to Mesopotamia so that the India Office would understand the international scope of the desire to renew excavation. In June 1920 Gordon applied for a concession, stressing the need to remove finds to the West, where alone scholars could carry out the essential scientific work. His request was temporarily denied.[6]

After the signing of the Treaty of Sevres with Turkey in August 1920, the need for a new antiquities law for the successor states, including Iraq, became urgent. Once again, Kenyon wrote the Foreign Office with suggestions for the new law. He urged that it not be too restrictive and, most important, that it allow for a fair division, that is, fifty-fifty, to encourage high-quality expeditions.[7]

With the fate of archaeology unsettled, James Breasted arrived in Baghdad on his combination survey tour and purchasing expedition, which had begun six months earlier in Egypt. He reported to his wife that the acting civil commissioner, Captain Arnold T. Wilson, was a man of "decided views," who spoke of protecting the rights of the Arabs. "Imagine," he wrote, "Arab rights based on their appreciation of cuneiform documents!" Breasted feared he would not be allowed to take out a single thing. This would be especially unfortunate now, for there were many antiquities available for purchase. Without doubt the finest of these was a six-sided terra-cotta prism, eighteen inches high, inscribed with the royal annals of Sennacherib (705–668 B.C.E.), king of Assyria. The dealer offered it at $9,500, which, given the generally deflated prices of the day, provides some indication of its immense value.[8]

After several weeks in Iraq inspecting an assortment of sites and visiting with various dignitaries, Breasted decided to return overland, crossing the desert and the Euphrates into Syria. He arrived in early May 1920 at Aleppo. This was an arduous and dangerous journey; the tribal uprising began within days of his departure. Pictures of the expedition, showing their vehicle prominently displaying a large American flag, remind one of frontier scouting parties in the Wild West. Breasted was able to bring to Allenby in Cairo much information on political conditions in the region, and the high commissioner requested that he meet also with officials in London on his way back to the United States.

On this journey Breasted carried with him the six-sided prism and some other antiquities, all of which likely left Iraq without approval from the British authorities. He wrote in his diary, "We must say simply that they were acquired in Western Asia." Today, the Sennacherib prism has pride of place in the Oriental Institute museum at Chicago.[9]

When control of Iraq passed from the India Office to the Colonial Office, Kenyon exulted, for, he pointed out to Gordon, now they would be dealing with men who were sympathetic to archaeology. He was right. In fact, T. E. Lawrence, who had begun his own career before World War I at the Hittite site of Carchemesh, now had principal responsibility for such affairs in the mandate. Early in 1922 Lawrence invited Gordon to apply for a permit to excavate, informing him that a committee had been established in London to advise the Colonial Office on each application. This would keep excavations at a high quality, he reported, "as Mesopotamia has suffered so much in the past from unscientific work." Gordon need not be too concerned, he assured him, for it was to be a practical and quite representative body, with Sir Frederick Kenyon as its chair. The irony of this situation would have been immediately apparent to Gordon, who had been discussing combining forces with Kenyon to carry out a joint expedition in Iraq. According to Kenyon, Pennsylvania would bring the money and the British Museum the goodwill with the authorities and some expertise. This would prove a highly successful combination, continuing for twelve years, 1922–1934.[10]

**Figure 9.1.** Iraq: Madan. Caravan of the University of Chicago expedition, flying the U.S. flag, 1920. Courtesy of the Oriental Institute of the University of Chicago.

**Figure 9.2.** James Breasted and Governor of Aleppo at citadel entrance, 1920. Courtesy of the Oriental Institute of the University of Chicago.

Negotiations for the joint venture continued throughout the remainder of the year, with Kenyon dangling before Gordon the prospect of obtaining a good selection of antiquities. Eventually they reached agreement and selected Leonard Woolley, the former director at Carchemesh, to head the expedition at Ur in southern Iraq, the birthplace of Abraham. Woolley had been trained as a theologian, and "he thought that by going to Ur he would bring to life the Old Testament."[11]

The new director received a wonderful reception in Baghdad when he arrived in October 1922, visiting all the leading dignitaries, including King Faisal, who, he remarked, was "very affable and keen on the work." Perhaps his most important meeting was with his countrywoman Gertrude Bell, whom Faisal had appointed honorary director of antiquities the previous year, for she would oversee the work of the expedition. The antiquities regulations she had proposed had not yet become law, so the minister of works gave Woolley a provisional permit to begin excavating.[12]

Conditions were difficult in southern Iraq. Aside from the isolation of the site and the difficulty of living in a tent, Woolley had trouble finding trained workmen and dealing with the local sheikhs and the general insecurity in the area. These matters notwithstanding, he concluded that the first season had been a remarkable success. Bell visited the site in January and seemed pleased with the work. At first Woolley did not know who would conduct the division of his finds, for there was no one in the country with enough expertise, he thought, but Bell and the minister of public works carried out the task, in which the expedition did very well. He noted, especially, the award to the museums of the best examples of goldsmith work found that season.[13]

**Figure 9.3.** Gertrude Bell, director of antiquities, and archaeologist Ernest Mackay during division at Kish, near Babylon, early 1920s. Courtesy of the University of Pennsylvania Museum, Philadelphia.

Woolley realized that present conditions in Iraq worked greatly to his benefit. The government had no way properly to treat the more delicate items, so by default most of them went to the expedition "on the plea of the interest of science." Also, they received more than their share as a reward for agreeing to repair some of Baghdad's antiquities in London. At the end of each season, Woolley lectured in Baghdad on the year's excavation at Ur and in his talk would inevitably emphasize how much the Iraqi government was getting for nothing. These lectures in English were not well attended, but Bell would drag along the king, who was not hugely interested in archaeology, and any other officials she could persuade.[14]

As Bell's political influence declined, she devoted more time to Iraq's antiquities. Her dream of having a museum building came true in June 1926, and again she persuaded Faisal to attend the opening ceremony. Until then a room in the palace had held Iraq's share of antiquities from the various expeditions, which were rapidly increasing in number. She frequently visited excavation sites and became convinced that the discovery of the "achievements of the early Mesopotamians helped to substantiate her claims that Iraq would return to its former greatness."[15]

For all her enthusiasm and long hours, she was not an expert, and the antiquities did not always receive proper treatment. Breasted spoke with King Faisal when the latter visited Cairo at the end of 1925 to urge upon him "some organization of the antiquities which are now receiving no attention at all." Although Breasted may have exaggerated, his concern was not misplaced. In March 1926 Woolley donated his time to assist Bell with some repairs of valuable objects from Ur. He found the copper bulls from another site in a "lamentable state."[16]

Even in these early years of the mandate, there were indications that informed Iraqis wanted to exercise more control over the country's antiquities and that, justified or not, they had strong suspicions about the commitment of the honorary director to the interests of Iraq. As a result, the law she proposed in July 1922 with the king's support faced stiff opposition in the government, where, Woolley reported, debate had been acrimonious. Some officials objected to a fifty-fifty division as Bell proposed. There was, of course, much talk in Iraq of developments in Egypt and the Tutankhamun affair, and Woolley thought Iraq might follow in Cairo's footsteps by tightening restrictions on foreign expeditions. Sati' al-Husri, who would become director of antiquities (1934–1941) and was at that time director general of education in the Ministry of Education, urged Bell to tighten restrictions on antiquities, allowing only duplicates to be assigned to foreign expeditions. Everything else should stay in the country. He claimed she bypassed his opposition by transferring her office from the Ministry of Education to the Ministry of Public Works, where, in his words, there was "no native influence." [17]

The law did not pass until 1924, and even then it contained several important modifications from the original. All antiquities privately held were to be recorded with the government, which had the right to purchase any of them. The director of antiquities would have the right to appoint a representative to reside at each site during the season at expedition expense. As to divisions, the director could take any objects thought necessary for the scientific completeness of the Iraq Museum collection. Of the remainder, the expedition should be given a representative share of the whole. As later events proved, these terms were open to various interpretations. They showed clearly, however, the influence of Egyptian nationalist thinking.

Under Gertrude Bell and her immediate successors after her death in July 1926, foreign expeditions received generous treatment, and as a result they flocked to the country from Germany, Italy, Britain, France, and, of course, the United States. In 1929 seven of the thirteen expeditions were American sponsored. On learning of Bell's death, expedition leaders and their sponsors had shown some concern that interpretation of the law might suddenly change for the worse, but a series of European directors, Britishers Richard Cooke (1927–1928) and Sydney Smith (1928–1931) and the German Julius Jordan (1931–1934), maintained the practices first introduced in 1923.

This seemed surprisingly generous given Woolley's remarkable discoveries, which began at Ur at the very end of the 1926–1927 season. In excavating an ancient cemetery, he discovered sixteen royal burial sites over the course of the next four seasons. These contained a vast array of Sumerian treasures, statues, jewelry, weapons of great artistry, many made of precious metals, "the like of which," according to Max Mallowan, "had never been seen before and is never likely to be seen again." The University of Pennsylvania's share would become the centerpiece of its already well-endowed collection. These discoveries became front-page news in England and the United States. If they did not attract quite as much attention as had the discovery of Tutankhamun in Egypt because of their greater distance, their staggered discovery, and the lesser familiarity of the American public with Iraq, they returned to their sponsors magnificent additions to their collections, which Howard Carter's had not. [18]

During the years 1927–1934, the Iraq Museum still lacked proper facilities to treat and restore Woolley's rare finds, and thus the museum was

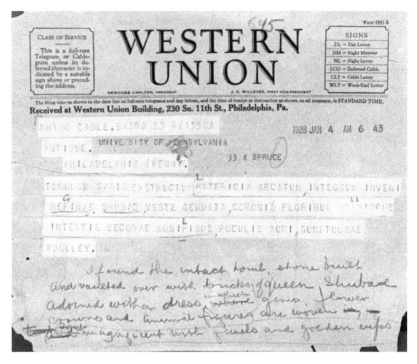

**Figure 9.4.** Telegram from Woolley announcing a marvelous find (in Latin) at Ur, January 4, 1928. Courtesy of the University of Pennsylvania Museum, Philadelphia.

chary of choosing items requiring a lot of care. Much of the finest work had to be sent to London as in the days of Gertrude Bell, Iraq's share to be returned later. The government received an equal share of the divisions during these years, but the correspondence of field directors at Ur and Kirkuk, two of the most important sites, confirmed the high quality of what they were able to send home. Woolley reported in 1930 that "on the whole the result of the division was greatly in the expedition's favour." Edward Chiera of Harvard University's dig at Kirkuk reported to David Lyon of the Semitic Museum, "You will have a splendid display in your museum, even after the Iraq Museum has taken its share"; and the next year his successor admitted, "The division was very fair. Most of the things of importance to which I attached a value came to us," and again in 1930, "Harvard retained by far the better half of the spoils."[19]

Then, too, some archaeologists were still purchasing antiquities from dealers as budgets allowed. Richard Starr reported that he had purchased a small Sumerian head of excellent craftsmanship. He had a struggle to keep it from Sydney Smith, director of antiquities, who wanted it for Iraq's museum, but Starr prevailed. He also had the opportunity—but not the money—to purchase a fine statue from a dealer, who would deliver it to him in Syria, for the Iraqi government might not allow it to be exported by normal channels. Starr saw no moral problem, arguing that antiquities bought in Europe, which everyone knew had been smuggled, caused no one a crisis of conscience. Why should this arrangement?[20]

Following John D. Rockefeller Jr.'s $10 million offer to Egypt and the subsequent agreement to build a museum in Jerusalem, successive Iraqi governments tried to interest Americans in providing the country with proper facilities for the care and research of its collection. At the end of 1926 Prime Minister Jafar al-Askari asked the directors of the American Schools of Oriental Research (ASOR), a consortium with offices in Baghdad, for help raising money for this purpose. This initial request came to nothing.[21]

A more specific proposal followed in 1928, one that Edward Chiera, now working for the Oriental Institute, appears to have solicited on his own. According to Breasted, in exchange for $1 million from the institute to build a museum, the government would turn over the site of ancient Nimrud with all of its antiquities; $2 million would bring an additional site with the same conditions. Breasted wrote enthusiastically to Raymond Fosdick, obviously hoping to interest Rockefeller in the offer. "This means such an *extraordinary* opportunity so *entirely* unprecedented, that I think I should be culpable if I did not let you know about it." It was, he concluded, "a perfectly good business proposition."[22]

The response from Thomas Appleget, another Rockefeller advisor, was not what Breasted had expected. In a meeting Appleget told Breasted that he thought such an exclusive arrangement was a bad idea. How could Rockefeller build a museum in Iraq to preserve that country's antiquities at the same time that the Oriental Institute was relieving it of the very best Nimrud had to offer? Appleget thought that many of the problems archaeologists faced in the 1920s were the result of simple looting. More consideration in the past, he believed, would have made those countries more generous in the present. If the Oriental Institute wanted to excavate at Nimrud, it should do so but under existing rules.[23]

This scheme seems to have lapsed with the change in directors at Baghdad from Cooke to Smith and the cool reception from Rockefeller's advisor. Breasted wrote to the new director of antiquities in late 1929, explaining that it had been solely Chiera's idea and that he had rejected it once Chiera had informed him! Having repeatedly come up empty-handed, the Iraqi government would eventually build its own museum.[24]

Given Breasted's penchant for grand schemes, it is little wonder that

Chicago faced periodic criticism from fellow archaeologists. Rumor of the discussions about Nimrud might have contributed to this. The news that Chiera had bypassed the director of antiquities and gone directly to the responsible government minister for a concession at Khorsabad in northern Iraq would not have enhanced the institute's reputation. Many of those working in the region were suspicious, perhaps jealous as well, of Breasted and his grandiose plans, for he had access to resources about which they could only dream. One critic writing about Tell Asmar noted that "Chicago has built a *palace* at their new dig here—a scandal among expedition houses [that] . . . cost here £6,000."[25]

These suspicions sometimes translated into problems with British and French officials, who were responsible for affairs in the mandates. Breasted had already had assorted feuds with the French in Turkey, Syria, Egypt, and Iran. In Iraq it was the British, or so Breasted thought, who caused him difficulties. He wrote his friend, Hale, in October 1929 to complain of the anti-American attitude of Europe generally. He may have been referring as well to other political and economic issues that troubled U.S.-European relations but which indirectly affected the institute's work. Whatever the reasons, European scientists were attempting to present the institute as a predatory organization. They begrudged the Americans their small representative collections even when they boasted "museums crowded from cellar to garret with magnificent monuments 'acquired' by their grandfathers." From London, where he was trying to elicit more support from the Colonial Office, Charles seconded his father's view, recalling that Teddy Roosevelt had been right when he said, "if you are going to hit at all, hit *hard*." Charles urged his father to be firm with British officials, who had to learn that they could not push Americans around as they used to when they dominated the Middle East.[26]

Soon, however, they both had something more serious to worry about. Britain announced in September 1929 that it had agreed to recommend that Iraq become a member of the League of Nations in 1932. This was followed by the Anglo-Iraqi Treaty of 1930, which would come into effect when Iraq entered the league. These developments contributed to growing concern among Western archaeologists, who wondered what an independent Iraq would mean for the future of their expeditions. Breasted, always sensitive to such threatened changes, wrote to Rockefeller's advisors, attributing all the problems in the region to Lacau's misguided efforts in Egypt. Although the Frenchman's policies would have some impact in Iraq, where they were already well known, Breasted thought Iraqi nationalists were more moderate than those in Egypt.[27]

In January 1930 Sydney Smith called a conference of all archaeologists in Iraq to discuss the future of their work. In a confidential statement he told them he was not optimistic, detailing "the xenophobic character" of a new antiquities law being discussed, which would restrict concessions to Iraqis and forbid the export of antiquities. Those attending concluded that they would have to present a united front. Also, they would need to advertise both in-country and abroad the advantages of their expeditions for Iraq.[28]

Despite the uncertainty and the remarks by some that they should get all they could before a new law became operational, the divisions changed remarkably little, even when Julius Jordan, German director at Warka, replaced Smith as director of antiquities in fall 1931. Woolley informed Horace Jayne that the recent division had been quite satisfactory, including in the expedition's share "the finest object of the season." The following year Ephraim A. Speiser at Tell Billa described his division as the best one he had ever seen, in which he had obtained everything that he had wanted badly.[29]

Such good times could not last indefinitely. News of discoveries such as Woolley's at Ur contributed to growing nationalist opposition to the continued export of antiquities. An important turning point came with the so-called Cooke-Starr incident, which helped to sully the reputation of foreign archaeologists, putting it almost beyond repair. The former director of antiquities, Sydney Cooke, was accused of trying to smuggle antiquities out of the country with the help of Starr of the Harvard expedition, who was to receive them in Syria. The crate was opened at the border, the antiquities were discovered, and Cooke very quickly left the country. Friends doubted that the pair had acted with criminal intent, suggesting that the former director was merely shipping home antiquities he had acquired legally over the years. Whatever the truth, the Iraqi press and informed opinion would not let the issue rest. For years they used this as a favorite example whenever explaining why Iraqis must always be suspicious of foreigners in positions of authority in their country, especially in the Department of Antiquities. Western archaeologists lamented the impact the incident had on their standing in the country.[30]

Even without this unfortunate incident, opinion in the country was strongly anti-British, for Britain held the power. After the end of the mandate in 1932, its representatives in Baghdad still exercised considerable influence, as they did in Cairo. Speiser reported at this time that the surest way to block a measure was to have it supported by a Britisher.[31]

All these antagonisms toward foreigners grew with the nationalist

movement in Iraq. To understand this development, we should go back
to the early postwar years. When Faisal became king in 1921, he had in
his entourage numbers of Arabs who had served in the Ottoman army
or bureaucracy and later in his short-lived government in Damascus. In
Baghdad they held senior positions in the government and the military,
among them habitual officeholders such as Nuri al-Said, Jafar al-Askari,
and Yasin al-Hashimi. Some of these, al-Said and al-Askari in particular,
became so accommodating to British policies in Iraq that they lost their
earlier nationalist credentials.[32]

Others ended up espousing Pan-Arabism and opposing British and
French control anywhere in the Arab world. One of the most important
members of this group was Sati' al-Husri (1880–1968). Born to Syrian par-
ents in Yemen, where his father served as an Ottoman official, he studied
in Istanbul and became a distinguished educator, with a successful career
in the empire. He published an influential journal in Istanbul and gained
a well-deserved reputation for commitment to duty. He once debated
the Turkish nationalist Ziya Gökalp, Mustafa Kemal's mentor, arguing in
favor of multiculturalism within the empire. By 1919, however, he had become a convert to Pan-Arabism.[33]

In Baghdad, al-Husri and others like him emphasized the brotherhood
of all Arabs instead of focusing exclusively on a narrower Iraqi nationalism. The Pharaonists in Egypt and those who extolled the ancient glories
of the Hittites in Turkey and the Achaemenids in Iran preached their
messages to populations that were more homogeneous than that of Iraq,
with its slight majority of Shiite Arabs, who clustered mainly in the south,
and the large minority of Kurds in the north. The minority Sunni Arabs,
therefore, looked to strengthen ties with their brethren in the larger Arab
world. Then, too, al-Husri and some other leading nationalists were not
Iraqi by birth. This fact made it awkward for them to build their nationalist ideology around the glories of ancient Iraq. Instead they glorified the
Arab past.

Al-Husri rarely missed an opportunity to praise the glories of Arab history. He lectured Iraqi youth as well as visiting foreign Arab groups on
the importance of the past, knowledge of which provided a catalyst for
the revival and reawakening of nations. He likened the feelings of nations
to those of individuals and warned that to forget a nation's history was
"to surrender to the oblivion of sleep." Imperialists tried to encourage
such forgetfulness in order to make their domination more successful.
Arabs must look to modern Turkey for a model of how a nation could
use history "to consolidate the national spirit" and bring about modern-

ization and radical reform. He urged Arabs to visit the sites associated with the great Abbasid Empire as a way of stimulating "a belief in the vitality of the Arab nation and the ability of gaining new glory like that of the past."[34]

Al-Husri eschewed politics, preferring to work through the schools to spread his secular nationalist message. He saw compulsory education and military conscription as "the two most important mechanisms for cohesion of the nation." Faisal made him director general of education, a key post, where he served until 1927. He was in a perfect position to influence the curriculum in the new system being established under the mandate. Although British advisors were meant to wield the real power in Iraqi ministries, one leading scholar has argued that they lost control over education by 1923.[35]

Thus the director general had years to ensure that a Pan-Arab, nationalist ideology was inculcated in Iraq's classrooms. The teaching of history had an especially important part in the entire process, for through this medium young minds could be influenced to appreciate the glories of the Arab past. History, he believed, contained the memory and consciousness of the nation. In a manner similar to Turkey, with its emphasis on ties to the ancient Hittites, in Iraq the idea became widespread that the peoples of ancient Mesopotamia had been the descendants of Arabs who had migrated out of the "cradle of the Semites," Arabia. What became clear through successive textbook revisions, however, was that heroes came overwhelmingly from the Islamic period.[36]

Al-Husri focused on elementary education because school attendance was not yet compulsory, and many students would abandon their studies as they grew older. He encouraged young Iraqis to become teachers, which, he argued, was the greatest profession and one that could be very influential. He inspired intense loyalty among his protégés, one of whom, Talib Mushtaq, left a flattering account, relating how the director general had convinced him to stay in education when he planned to resign and had obtained for him a two-year fellowship to study in Britain. Al-Husri also brought in non-Iraqi teachers from Syria and Palestine to contribute their skills and Pan-Arab zeal. He urged the writing of textbooks with the nationalist message.[37]

He earned the grudging admiration of the British colonial authorities for his efforts to secure efficiency and high standards for both teachers and students. "No other Iraqi," they claimed, "combines his enthusiasm, his experience and knowledge of education systems, and his fearlessness." Lionel Smith, who served as al-Husri's British advisor, resigned several

**Figure 9.5.** Iraqi boy scouts visiting the excavation at Fara, 1931. Courtesy of the University of Pennsylvania Museum, Philadelphia.

times because of disagreements but repeatedly returned to work with him.[38]

Although al-Husri left his post in 1927 in a dispute with Iraqi colleagues, by then he had established a system that, like those of France and Germany earlier, would nourish the nationalist spirit. Long before he became director of antiquities (1934–1941), his efforts had begun to affect the thinking of young Iraqis, many of whom would come to occupy important posts in the late 1930s. This educational process took place without much notice from Western archaeologists, intent on their narrow concerns, but it would affect their activities in almost predictable ways.[39]

What did get their attention were the heated discussions that took place periodically in parliament over the control of antiquities and foreign expeditions. As early as 1929 two deputies from Mosul, in whose environs several important excavations were located, asked Prime Minister Tawfik al-Suwaydi if proper measures were being taken to monitor the expeditions. Al-Suwaydi, a friend incidentally of James Breasted, expressed his confidence in the honesty of the missions. He was immediately challenged by a deputy from Baghdad, who wondered how they could trust the antiquities department when its former director [Cooke] had himself sold antiquities. He also reminded him of the troubles the Egyptians had experienced in 1924, quoting admiringly Ahmad Shawqi's verse, "Does the person who would steal from the reigning monarch, make a virtue of not stealing from kings in coffins?"[40]

Over the next three years the parliamentary education committee suggested a number of changes in the antiquities law to tighten the government's control. Members expressed their belief that Iraq had not been receiving its fair share, as they put it, of "treasures left by ancestors to grandsons as symbols of their great civilization." With complaints such as these, archaeologists had good reason to feel uneasy.[41]

The stage was set by the early 1930s for a confrontation. Throughout the region, especially in Egypt, Iran, Turkey, and now, of course, in Iraq, the nationalists were taking steps to ensure tighter control over archaeological sites and the antiquities associated with them. Wherever possible they wanted their own nationals to take command. Some foreign archaeologists understood this and from time to time referred to coming changes, but all of them wanted to put off that day as long as possible.

# 10. THE REIGN OF SATI' AL-HUSRI

Nineteen thirty-three proved pivotal for Iraq. It brought the first full year of independence and the death of King Faisal, whose steady hand was removed suddenly and unexpectedly. His heir, Ghazi (r. 1933–1939), was decidedly less friendly to the British than his father had been. "Ghazi represented the new Iraqi, the younger generation which grew up during the 1920s, now actively expressing its animosity toward the British . . . and its support for Arab nationalism." [1]

The first crisis for archaeologists began in July 1933, even before Faisal's death. Since 1929 control over the Department of Antiquities had returned to the Ministry of Education, and now the minister refused the British Museum an export permit for its share of antiquities from Arpachiyah, a site in northern Iraq. With rising antagonism against Britain and growing suspicion of foreign archaeologists, a British expedition seemed a natural target. The director at Arpachiyah was Max Mallowan, a former assistant to Woolley at Ur and the husband of Agatha Christie. Christie accompanied him almost every season, whether in Iraq or, later, in Syria, and her experiences there formed the background for a number of her best novels. [2]

Mallowan's current predicament unfolded like one of his wife's mysteries. His share had been approved by Julius Jordan, so the minister's refusal came as a great surprise. There had recently been a campaign in the nationalist press against Jordan, who, it was charged, had let priceless treasures leave the country. The hope was that after this attack Jordan would feel obligated to resign. The editors wanted to bring about a total stoppage of excavation until the time when Iraqis themselves could undertake the work. The ministry hoped to present a new, stricter antiquities law and in the meantime wanted to keep additional antiquities from being sent abroad. Officials also complained that there were not enough inspectors to monitor all the expeditions and that the Iraq Museum had no space left to house additional antiquities. This last may, of course, have been a stratagem for attracting foreign funding for museum facilities, the absence of which had angered Iraqi officials.[3]

The archaeologists responded immediately to this challenge. George Hill, Kenyon's successor as director of the British Museum, urged the Foreign Office to protest the action through its representative in Baghdad, Ambassador Sir Francis Humphreys. He was duly instructed to caution the Iraqi government that how it acted in the matter of foreign archaeologists would be regarded by many "as a test of whether Iraq is really a modern and progressive state."[4]

Hill realized, however, that joint action would be more effective than a single diplomatic protest from London. He sent duplicate letters to the institutions and archaeologists of the five Western nations working in Iraq, urging them to ask their respective governments to coordinate a joint protest. He also encouraged them to consider their own protest against changes in the antiquities law, perhaps by refusing to continue excavating in Iraq if that government completely prohibited the export of antiquities.[5]

Most of the institutions he contacted agreed that they would not return if the government were to impose more stringent controls. The response was not unanimous, however, for Breasted refused to commit the Oriental Institute in advance to such drastic action. His reluctance surprised Wallace Murray, who had already acceded to Breasted's urgent request that the State Department support the Foreign Office protest at Baghdad. Naturally, he had assumed that the institute would take every step possible to press Iraq to maintain the 1924 law.[6]

Breasted found himself in a dilemma. He believed in the efficacy of presenting a united front to the nationalists, yet he did not want to commit himself not to excavate in the 1933–1934 season until Iraq made clear its policy. He was not certain that the action against Mallowan was more than an isolated incident, for other export permits had subsequently been issued. He needed some assurance that the minister of education's action represented a change in policy in Baghdad. Struggling to come up with an alternative approach, Breasted even suggested taking the issue to the League of Nations, "for feeble powers like Iraq set great store by its actions." Hill agreed that might be a good tactic but reminded Breasted that the nationalists were testing the situation to see how far they could go, just as the Egyptians had done earlier, when Chicago had taken the lead in organizing a united front.[7]

Henri Frankfort, the Dutch archaeologist and director of the institute's excavations in Iraq, suggested that without a commitment not to dig, the present law could not be retained. His interference angered Breasted, who fired off a sharp rebuke, warning Frankfort that if he did not approve of what headquarters was doing, he was free to find himself another position. "No more letters of petty criticism," he warned, "will be tolerated."[8]

In another letter circulated to museum directors, Breasted argued that they had an important educational role to perform in Iraq. They must explain that popular interest in archaeological discovery and in the ancient monuments of Iraq provided the chief bond between that nation and the West. This interest, he believed, far surpassed any Western interest in petroleum. The government in Baghdad must be made to understand this truth. Furthermore, it would be to their advantage if Western archaeologists indicated a willingness to help the Iraq Museum become one of the greatest in the world, a rival to the Egyptian Museum in Cairo. They should know, also, that a withdrawal of the Western expeditions would lead to plundering of the sites and heavy losses for Iraq. At the end of his proposal, Breasted apologized to his correspondents for omitting any reference to science in his long letter. He had learned, he said, in long years of dealing with "Oriental cabinets made up as they inevitably are of fanatical Nationalistic Orientals" that one had to emphasize purely material interests.[9]

After all this correspondence among the interested parties on both sides of the Atlantic, Breasted still refused to threaten to withdraw his expeditions from the four sites where they were currently working in Iraq. The institute had arrived relatively late on the scene, long after the University of Pennsylvania, for example, and the thought of abandoning such a fertile field was anathema to him. He hoped that a united protest to Baghdad would be sufficient.

Breasted had earlier made some interesting comments that shed light on his response to the Arpachiyah incident. In January 1930, at the time of Sydney Smith's special conference in Baghdad, Breasted had warned that the day would surely come, as it had in Egypt, when the government would place more rigorous restrictions on the export of antiquities. This, though inconvenient, would not stop Western institutions from uncovering the vast written record on clay tablets, for these, he could not imagine, would ever be subject to the restrictions. Thus the great scientific work of the West in Iraq could continue. Three years later these same thoughts must have influenced him still. He even remarked to Frankfort that they had learned to tolerate inspectors on sites in Iran and Turkey, and they could adjust to them in Iraq also if necessary. Showing interest in these "budding native" archaeologists was a way to foster good relations.[10]

Murray was clearly disappointed to learn that the Oriental Institute had returned for the new season to excavate at Khorsabad and Tell Asmar. Most other foreign expeditions had decided not to take up their work again, and he did not know how the U.S. consul general in Baghdad should respond if asked about the position of American institutions. Breasted replied, pointing out the differences between the institute and other institutions. Unlike the others, he remarked, Chicago's fieldwork "is not conditioned on a division of antiquities." Scientific work must go on even if there were no division. Murray must have thought this strange indeed, given the director's strong protests earlier against restrictive policies in Turkey and Egypt.[11]

Fortunately for Breasted, the crisis was resolved without his having to make a further commitment. The government released Mallowan's impounded cases and promised to show the British ambassador a draft of any new antiquities law before introducing it to parliament. According to Paul Knabenshue, the U.S. consul general, a bill had been drawn up by Abdul Razzaq Lutfi, curator of the Iraq Museum and a strong nationalist, that seemed to borrow freely from the Egyptians. Lutfi, it was rumored, had his eye on the post of director of antiquities. In late November 1933 a new cabinet, minus the former minister of education, who had caused the brouhaha, withdrew the draft antiquities legislation, which, remarked Frankfort, was more than anyone had expected.[12]

Everyone assumed that the threat of a four-power protest contributed to this decision. Yet the crisis had an impact. The French archaeologist, André Parrot, had not returned to Sinkara, deciding to dig instead at Abu Kemal (Mari) on the banks of the Euphrates in French-controlled Syria.[13]

At the end of the 1933–1934 season, Jordan was as generous as he could be in the divisions, given heightened nationalist concern. He took all precious metal and almost all unique items and divided what remained. The expeditions at Ur, Khorsabad, and Warka faced the same kind of foot-dragging from the Ministry of Education that Mallowan had encountered the previous year. The British, German, and American diplomats had to intervene to get the export permits signed. This was the last straw for Woolley, who after twelve seasons chose not to return to Iraq. Mallowan joined him in relocating to Syria and did not return until after World War II.[14]

British archaeologists complained bitterly to the Foreign Office regarding the Iraqi excesses, concluding that the new antiquities proposals in Baghdad were conceived "in so narrow a spirit of unintelligent nationalism that the government is inevitably laying up for itself a legacy of universal condemnation from the learned world." To which an official minuted that nothing would be gained by adopting such a condescending attitude toward Oriental countries. Bellicose memoranda such as theirs, he added, do more harm than good.[15]

At Khorsabad Frankfort struggled on, trying to cope with criticisms from Chicago and challenges from his hosts. Jordan refused to separate a monumental Assyrian gateway and attendant reliefs, one of which Chicago dearly wanted. Then on his way to visit Parrot in Syria, Frankfort and his wife were stopped by police and their luggage searched meticulously for stolen antiquities. Frankfort remarked stoically, "Cooke's conduct makes it difficult for us to protest as vigorously as we should." Nevertheless, he notified the American minister, who filed a formal complaint with Dr. Naji Beg al-Asli, director general of the Ministry of Foreign Affairs.[16]

Breasted decided that the institute must continue its scientific work in Iraq, knowing, he admitted, that, like other Orientals, the Iraqis had only financial and political interest in their monuments. Strangely, he held the British responsible for much of what was ailing Middle Eastern archaeology. The collapse of their influence had spelled disaster for the Cairo Museum project, and now he was worried about associating too closely with them in Iraq. This might lead to increased "native" prejudice against Chicago.[17]

Breasted did have some interesting news to send Frankfort. Two young Iraqi students, Fuad Safar and Taha Baqir, had just enrolled at the University of Chicago to study archaeology. Breasted had met with them briefly. They had received five-year scholarships from the Iraqi government, and, remarked Breasted, after that time they could well be prepared to take an influential part in the antiquities situation in their country. It seems remarkable that Breasted had known nothing of their coming. For all the discussion about the lack of trained Iraqi archaeologists, none of the Western institutions working there had seen fit to support students on their own initiative.[18]

Amid all these minor irritations, a major change was about to take place in the administration of antiquities in Iraq, and Westerners were largely unaware of its significance. They knew that Jordan's contract was ending in 1934 and that thereafter he would serve only as technical advisor to the Ministry of Education. They worried that Abdul Razzaq Lutfi, who had reportedly been at the center of so much agitation against them, would replace the German. When they learned that the new director would be Sati' al-Husri, formerly director general of education, they were relieved.

The British conveyed their concern to Foreign Minister Nuri al-Said that al-Husri was not an archaeologist, but al-Said assured them that he would have the expert, Jordan, at his side.[19]

Had they paid close attention to al-Husri's response to the foreign minister, they would have found reason for concern. He immediately rejected the idea that he would be taking advice solely from the former director. He would be seeking advice also from Iraqis at the museum, headed, of course, by Lutfi. Al-Husri would serve in this position until 1941 and prove a formidable adversary.[20]

By his own account, al-Husri immediately took stock of the situation in his new department. What he found disturbed him greatly. Thousands of antiquities had been loaned abroad for a variety of purposes, but records on them were incomplete; many had been absent for years. Records of what the museum held were also incomplete. Facilities to repair and photograph materials were inadequate. The library had fewer than five hundred books, much smaller than his own personal library. The museum's role as a vehicle of culture had been sadly neglected. Lectures were mainly in English and attracted little interest even among intellectuals.[21]

Most of the museum's possessions came from the pre-Islamic period, illustrating the usual bias of Western archaeology, which focused primarily on cultures related somehow to the Bible or to what was believed to be the roots of Western civilization. For centuries the West had neglected, denied, or remained ignorant of the contributions of Islamic civilization to its own development, and this offended many scholars in the Islamic world. The result was that there were almost no antiquities from the Islamic period, that is, after the early seventh century c.e., in the museum, and what few there were lay neglected in a corner of the building. After touring the museum, one visiting foreign archaeologist remarked to al-Husri, "I was so astonished at not finding Arab or Islamic antiquities in the museum of a city that was once the Abbasid capital." The new director determined to correct all these problems, especially the last one.[22]

Al-Husri drafted a new antiquities law, which various officials had struggled to do for years. At the request of Nuri al-Said, he circulated it to heads of expeditions, who found much to criticize. At that point he decided to put plans for a new law on hold while studying the laws of other countries. Meanwhile he would strictly enforce the 1924 law, several articles of which had only been loosely observed.[23]

Al-Husri began with article 19, the regulation that each excavation should be subject to inspection during the work season. This had rarely happened. When he asked Jordan why he had neglected to do this, Jordan responded that expeditions were technical, scientific, and specialized and that it would not be proper "to doubt their intentions or to observe their work." Al-Husri sent a letter to all the expeditions, reminding them of the article and asking them to receive representatives from his department whose salaries they would have to pay. He indicated that these high school graduates might in future be employed by the museum and that such practical experience as they would gain in the field would be useful to them. Before sending them out, the new director briefed the young men as to their observational work and asked them to send him weekly reports.[24]

The various expeditions had little choice but to accept this change for it was the law, but they complained vigorously in private. Millar Burrows, president of the ASOR, described the requirement as extremely bothersome; the presence of such an individual inevitably led to trouble with the workers and friction all around. The government should just trust them. The Germans told Frankfort that the Iraqis did not make their work easy, and he responded that the students being sent had no background in either history or archaeology and seemed poor material from which to develop specialists. Breasted was not pleased either, but he noted to his field director that students were preferable to mature men, who might be more troublesome. At Khorsabad al-Husri's representative apparently started off badly, accusing the archaeologists, especially the director, Gordon Loud, of infinite dishonesty.[25]

In February 1935, as the end of the excavating season neared, al-Husri prepared to take a second step, this also under the 1924 law. Article 22 stated that the director of antiquities should select and remove from the antiquities recovered those items that in his opinion were necessary to complete the collection of the museum. Then a part of the remainder would be assigned to the expedition to reward it adequately for its efforts. This should be as far as possible a representative share. Thus a strict reading of the existing law indicated that unique items belonged to Iraq and that there was no legal requirement for a fifty-fifty division of antiquities. Since the early 1920s successive directors had interpreted this article loosely to the great benefit of Western expeditions. Al-Husri would soon change this practice.

To prepare himself, al-Husri had increased his visits to excavations during the 1934–1935 season, examining their finds and comparing them to items in the collection of the Iraq Museum. He chose the hapless Frankfort's site at Khafaje as his first target because it was close to the capital, which meant he could visit it more often, and because the season would finish there earlier than elsewhere.

On the day set for the division, the director, Jordan, and Salim Lowi, assistant curator of the museum—al-Husri left Lutfi behind because of feuds he had had with Jordan and other foreign archaeologists—arrived to find all the antiquities laid out in two equal rows on a long table. Traditionally, a toss of the coin or a drawing of lots would determine which row the museum received. Al-Husri asked Frankfort to leave the room so the three officials could examine the antiquities. When they were alone, he asked Jordan to point out items that were significant and different from those already in the museum. After this discussion, he had Lowi put seventeen items on a side table, announcing to a stunned Jordan that these would not be part of the division. When Frankfort learned what was happening, he complained loudly, thinking the director was acting under new guidelines, but the director assured him that this procedure was in accordance with the provisions of the existing law. Jordan carried out the division of the remainder, with Frankfort all the while protesting and warning that his director, Professor Breasted, would be informed and that all his colleagues on other expeditions would be watching.[26]

Frankfort immediately contacted the Oriental Institute with the results of the division, referring to al-Husri as a fanatic, unusually strong language for the Dutchman. He reported that the new policy on clay tablets was impossible, for al-Husri insisted that the museum's share must be studied in Iraq; he would no longer allow them to be loaned abroad. Frankfort knew better, however, than to recommend a course of action.[27]

Breasted was angry, for this was one of his own expeditions. Furthermore, the Iraqi had targeted clay tablets along with everything else. He contacted his friend Murray for assistance, telling him that it was extremely important not to accept this unjust division at the hands of Iraq's first "native" director of antiquities. To do so would set an unfortunate precedent. Apparently untroubled by any inconsistencies in his earlier letters to Murray, Breasted now warned that if necessary he would withdraw to Syria where divisions were fair. He wanted the U.S. diplomatic representative in Baghdad to tell the Iraqi government that the institute would leave if this injustice were not rectified. The State Department dutifully sent instructions to Knabenshue to take action at once.[28]

The next two weeks saw an intense round of meetings in an attempt to resolve the crisis at Khafaje. In these Paul Knabenshue took a prominent part. It was fortunate for the Americans that they had such a strong

advocate. His predecessor, Alexander Sloan, had shown almost no interest in archaeology, being concerned largely with petroleum issues, but the
present consul general had a genuine interest in the scientific work of the
expeditions. And he was tenacious. He had served earlier in Beirut and
Jerusalem, in the latter of which he had managed to antagonize the Zionists, who did not soon forget him. In his new post he would have many
opportunities to serve the interests of American archaeology.[29]

Knabenshue met with Nuri al-Said, now foreign minister, to discuss
the affair and to lodge a formal protest. He knew al-Said well. They often
played tennis together at the legation, and the American had taught him to
swim. The American minister told al-Said that he felt especially responsible because he had encouraged the archaeologists not to withdraw from
Iraq and to trust the Department of Antiquities to be fair.[30]

The foreign minister summoned al-Husri to his office for an explanation, arguing that this was no time for stirring up trouble, for the government faced a host of political problems. The director refused to back
down, saying his actions were completely legal. At that point Knabenshue
left so that they could discuss the matter in private.[31]

In their discussions over the next several days, the two Iraqi officials
agreed only that there could not be a redivision, for that would set a bad
precedent of giving in to foreign demands. Then the Iraqi cabinet fell, and
Knabenshue had to wait for a new one to be set up. Fortunately for him,
when the process was over, his friend was still foreign minister.[32]

Meanwhile, Frankfort met again with al-Husri to discuss the recent
division. This time he stressed the interest of science, saying that by losing
its best pieces, the expedition would be unlikely to continue, and archaeology would be the loser. Al-Husri replied that the Oriental Institute had
received a valuable collection of antiquities and had earned the honor of
discovering the items that would be placed in the museum. He would duly
note their contribution. Rather than spread important items in far-flung
museums, to the extent possible they should be kept together where they
were found. These items were not lost to science; they would become part
of the greatest collection of Mesopotamian antiquities in the world, available for all to see and to study. The Iraq Museum would become the collective work of all archaeologists. When Frankfort then raised the issue of
security for antiquities, alluding to possibly unstable conditions, the Iraqi
official reminded him of all the antiquities and art that had been lost in
Europe during World War I.[33]

In his final line of defense, Frankfort asked, "What will Professor
Breasted say?" He indicated that this action might lead Breasted to aban-

don Iraq for Syria, as the French and British expeditions had done earlier. Al-Husri assured Frankfort that he would write a letter to Chicago, setting out all the arguments he had given him. He also offered the archaeologist a little sweetener for the institute in the form of a copper bull's head, which had originally come from Woolley's excavation at Ur, and he promised a more generous division the following year. He put these proposals in writing and gave Frankfort a copy.[34]

Frankfort did not want to press the issue further, confiding to Knabenshue that he thought the exchange of the bull's head for the seventeen items set aside before the division was probably fair. The diplomat agreed and recommended that Breasted accept this arrangement as the best possible under the circumstances. If he refused, al-Said would seek to bring a motion in the Council of Ministers to have al-Husri dismissed. This would likely destabilize the present moderate government and make the director a martyr for the nationalist cause. All this would likely strengthen Yasin al-Hashimi, leader of the opposition. That result, he concluded, would be damaging for foreign archaeologists.[35]

Breasted reluctantly acquiesced but with grave concern for what was to come. Once again he traced all the problems in Iraq to Egypt and Pierre Lacau. He would take upon himself, he said, the responsibility of educating a small group of "these ignorant and fanatical Iraqis."[36]

Frankfort had generous words for the American diplomat, who had used a combination of tact and forcefulness to obtain at least a little satisfaction. He also saw the influence of Egypt in what was taking place in Iraq. He even had some slight praise for the director of antiquities, seeing him as an exceptionally able exponent of the prevailing nationalist view of antiquities as part of the national heritage. Any government would have to take up the issue, and, to be fair, he reminded Breasted, agitation had begun long before al-Husri took office at the end of 1934. If the institute wanted to stay in Iraq, "it would simply have to accept the situation."[37]

In his correspondence with the director of antiquities, Breasted did take a more reasonable position, offering him the institute's full support. He reminded him, however, that antiquities assigned to foreign institutions were not lost to Iraq, for they contributed to growing interest in the country and to increasing numbers of tourists. Egypt's great collection was the result largely of foreign expeditions, and, he hinted, since it had abandoned liberal divisions, it was receiving almost nothing, for most expeditions had withdrawn.[38]

After this affair, al-Husri decided to distinguish more carefully between university expeditions and those representing museums, whose principal aim was to expand their collections. He would try to conciliate the former to gain favor with the scientific community. Such a distinction did not always make sense, however, for the universities, Chicago, Michigan, and Pennsylvania, had museums on their campuses. Filling them, of course, was perhaps not their primary purpose in Iraq.[39]

Just as debate with the Americans was winding down, Leonard Woolley published an article in the *London Times* that rekindled nationalist fervor. Woolley had already withdrawn from Iraq, so he could speak out with impunity, not that he had ever worried about being blunt. His comments did little to help the cause of foreign archaeologists. He criticized the proposed antiquities law, saying that it would ruin archaeological work in Iraq and far beyond its borders and pointing to the great work done by foreign missions to bring the country's treasures to light.

In response, one Iraqi editor pointed out that those expeditions had been so handsomely rewarded that the great museums of the West had better Mesopotamian collections than did the Iraq Museum. Oh, for the day, he concluded, when Iraqis could bring the treasures to light on their own. In a follow-up interview, al-Husri explained that the time had come for a revised law, and he was consulting the laws of other countries before presenting a draft to the Council of Ministers. He ended by observing that the former Ur expedition had on loan from Iraq more than five thousand objects.[40]

Al-Husri continued the debate privately with Woolley, sending him a letter requesting information on a number of antiquities for which he could not account. The former director at Ur responded that his responsibility had ended once the then director of antiquities and his staff took charge of the museum's share. There were no pleasantries in this exchange, and the tone was reminiscent of that which Woolley had been using for decades with officious natives. It was unwelcome and unwise in late 1930s Iraq. Even British Ambassador Humphreys deplored the former site director's confrontation with the Iraqis over the proposed law. He reminded the Foreign Office that the Iraqi government had been very good to Woolley over the years.[41]

The crisis over Khafaje was no sooner settled than Knabenshue faced another, concerning the writings of the well-known Arab American, Amin Rihani. He was a member of a prominent group of Christian Arab poets and writers, among them Kahlil Gibran and Nadeem Naimy, who had emigrated to the United States at the end of the nineteenth century. Rihani traveled frequently in the Arab world, where he became an important voice in Arab affairs. After the French banished him temporarily

from Lebanon, he lived in Iraq during 1933–1934 at the invitation of King
Ghazi. During his residence, he gathered material for his travel book, *The
Heart of Iraq* (1935), several inflammatory passages of which brought him
suddenly to the American diplomat's attention.[42]

In his book Rihani accused the German archaeologists and their diplomats in Iraq of stealing antiquities. As a result the Germans began a lawsuit against the author and his publisher. The German minister sent a copy
of the offending passages to Knabenshue, hoping perhaps that he would
be able to get Rihani to retract them. After some correspondence with
Knabenshue and discussions with Nuri al-Said, Rihani agreed to remove
the most critical statements and replace them with newly edited pages to
be inserted in those volumes that had not yet been sold. This seemed to satisfy the Germans, though the unedited accusations had already appeared
in March in the nationalist paper, *Al-Bilad*.[43]

Even without the offensive paragraphs, what remained contained plenty
of strong criticism of foreign archaeologists. Rihani claimed that his information came from a letter that Abdul Razzaq Lutfi had written to the
minister of education. In it he had criticized the former director of antiquities, Jordan, for not looking out for Iraq's interests because he favored
the foreigners and especially his fellow Germans. Iraq would be wise to
leave its treasures buried in the earth until it could have its own trained experts rather than see them flying away over the sea. Lutfi's words, gaining
credence from their insertion in the *Heart of Iraq*, fed popular suspicions
of conspiracy.[44]

Rihani wrote to Knabenshue, explaining that part of his self-appointed
task was to defend the interests of the Arabs. He wanted Europeans and
Americans to realize that only fair play and mutual respect could lead to
the establishment of friendly relations between Westerners and Easterners. The evidence he had collected in regard to archaeology, however, was
not very encouraging.[45]

Perhaps the new, more restrictive antiquities law would silence nationalist critics. After much discussion al-Husri's draft antiquities law was
promulgated on April 20, 1936. A much longer statement than that of
1924 — seventy-three articles versus thirty-three — the new regulations at-
tempted to eliminate earlier ambiguities and put more control into the
hands of the Iraqi government. Article 49, one of the most important,
detailed how divisions would be carried out. As had occurred in Egypt,
Iraq declared that all antiquities discovered belonged to the state. As a reward for their work, however, excavators would be given half of duplicate
items and any of the remaining antiquities that the government decided to

dispense with, owing to the existence of "similar objects" in the Iraq Museum. Excavators also had the right to make casts of any of the surrendered antiquities.

When shown an earlier draft, Knabenshue had suggested the words "similar objects" in place of the original "exact duplicates," leaving room for the director of antiquities to be more or less generous as he chose. The difference now was that archaeologists had less justification for demanding their rights because legally all antiquities belonged to the state.[46]

The remaining American expeditions received reasonably fair treatment during the last season under the old law and the first under the new. Charles Bache, director at Tepe Gawra, reported to Jayne that his division was "quite alright," but, he added, "no thanks to the bastard Abdul Razzaq Efendi, who Allah deplore." Bache had had enough and recommended withdrawing to Syria, "where you are regarded as something human." A note from al-Husri in April, confirming that the government would be keeping a whole vase and returning a small potsherd of the same ware and motif to the expedition, must have triggered some choice words from the American and confirmed for him that Syria was the new Promised Land.[47]

During the 1936–1937 season, Clark Hopkins of the University of Michigan reported that al-Husri and Jordan had done everything possible to facilitate his work at Seleucia, and in the division Michigan had received a splendid series of objects. His colleague, Enoch Peterson, who formerly excavated in Egypt, reported likewise on the favorable treatment at the division, indicating that in some cases, because of their greater knowledge of the material, the archaeologists had a definite advantage over the representatives of the director of antiquities.[48]

The Oriental Institute also received a favorable division as al-Husri had promised. Finances, however, forced Breasted's successor, John Wilson, to end all the Iraqi digs after the 1936–1937 season. In response to a request from Ambrose Lansing of the Metropolitan regarding the climate for archaeology in Iraq, Wilson replied optimistically that prospects under the new law looked very promising, and he regretted deeply the necessity of withdrawing.[49]

Replying to the same query, Horace Jayne passed along Bache's pessimistic advice. Unlike Wilson, he viewed the 1936 law as a barrier to successful work in Iraq on a par with the Egyptian law, and he encouraged Lansing to look to Syria if he wanted to enter the region. Yet Pennsylvania remained in Iraq for another four seasons.[50]

Ephraim Speiser, Bache's successor as director, reported that the divisions at Khafaje and Tepe Gawra had been fair. This information may have convinced Jayne to remain. Pinhas Delougaz (1901–1975) continued working for Pennsylvania at Khafaje through the 1939–1940 season, and he received friendly letters from al-Husri and his new British technical advisor, Seton Lloyd, urging him to return the following year. Jayne, however, decided that international conditions by then were too unsettled to continue the expeditions any longer, thus ending the last American expedition in Iraq. By then only the Germans remained.[51]

In these years al-Husri did not spend all his time on foreign archaeologists. There were many other issues to keep him busy. In the period 1935–1940 he oversaw the writing and publication of several guidebooks, all of them concerned with Arab monuments and antiquities. He traveled widely, visiting many countries, including Morocco, Spain, and Egypt. In 1937 he attended an international conference of excavators in Cairo, where it was rumored the new Iraqi law would come in for criticism. Al-Husri stoutly defended the legislation and ended by winning the admiration of many of those attending for its precise language. As a result of contacts made there, al-Husri was appointed a member of the International Consultative Committee on Museums, which was affiliated with the League of Nations.[52]

In 1939 he engaged in a heated literary exchange with the great Egyptian intellectual and Pharaonist, Taha Hussain. According to al-Husri, Hussain had denied any contribution of the Arabs to Egypt's history and claimed that the Pan-Arabists wanted Egyptians to renounce their pre-Islamic past and destroy their Pharaonic monuments. Nothing could be further from the truth, declared the director of antiquities. Hussain must recognize that he could not excise the past thirteen centuries from his country's history. Egypt's long history had relevance for the whole Arab world, but Egypt, too, had drawn its historical memory from several sources, just like a large river.[53]

The director of antiquities planned for his department to sponsor its own excavations. Soon after he was appointed, articles began to appear in the press, indicating that such a program would soon begin. Al-Husri was determined to focus on Islamic monuments, which had been neglected by Westerners. This work would serve to strengthen Pan-Arab nationalism among the general population by focusing on the glorious history of Arab/Muslim dynasties, especially the Abbasids. There was also a very practical reason for this approach. The remains at these sites were close to the surface and therefore within the range of ability of Iraqis, who did not yet have much field experience. Finally, monuments from the Islamic period, with their Arabic inscriptions, would be easier to study than those from ancient Mesopotamia, which required mastery of long-dead languages.⁵⁴

They began with Samarra, the short-lived Abbasid capital one hundred kilometers north of Baghdad, where Herzfeld had excavated before 1914. Jordan supervised the work, which provided an essential training ground for department employees. They went on to work at the great mosque at Kufa and the Umayyad site of al-Wasit. The department undertook restoration work as well at Ukhaidar and on various Abbasid monuments in Baghdad.⁵⁵

To house the finds from these various projects, al-Husri set up a museum of Arab antiquities in a medieval khan, or warehouse. To gain control of the building, he had to outmaneuver another government agency by persuading the prime minister, Yasin al-Hashimi, of the need for such a cultural institution. The prime minister not only gave him the building but also ordered the Ministry of Public Works to pay the costs of repairing it. The museum opened in 1937 with a visit from the king and the Council of Ministers.⁵⁶

With the work about to begin at Samarra, al-Husri renewed his acquaintance with Herzfeld, who was now living in the United States. The director had been one of a group of Iraqis who had come to see the famous German off in May 1923 when he left Baghdad for Tehran. Herzfeld's name had been prominently mentioned in 1928 as a replacement for Cooke at the Department of Antiquities. Al-Husri now asked him specific questions concerning what he had found at the Abbasid site, explaining that the department was about to recommence digging there.⁵⁷

Al-Husri may have had more on his mind, however, and one is reminded of his ruse at Khafaje, where he got Jordan to reveal the value of antiquities without telling him what he planned to do with the information. When the Germans abandoned Samarra in 1917, they left behind sixty-five cases of antiquities, which the British inherited. After the war it was decided to ship these to London for safekeeping, and Herzfeld was invited to the British Museum to oversee the unpacking and to add scientific information. Finally, the British authorities decided that Iraq would never use everything in the crates, so after putting aside something for Iraq, they shared out the antiquities among British and foreign museums, including Chicago, Michigan, and the Metropolitan. Herzfeld got a share as well.⁵⁸

Years later, at the time of al-Husri's letter to Herzfeld, al-Husri asked for the return of all the captured antiquities. The British Museum delayed, saying that the Samarra materials were in bad condition when they arrived in 1922 and that Baghdad probably had better examples in its collection. Among themselves, officials agreed that Iraq had no legal claim to the antiquities. The Iraqi Ministry of Foreign Affairs asked the British embassy to intervene to return the materials, but by 1936 that request was almost impossible to satisfy.[59]

Al-Husri encountered problems with officials of his own government as well, men who wanted to modernize Iraq and would destroy whatever monuments stood in the way of achieving their goals. The most persistent of these was the mayor of Baghdad, Arshad al-ʿUmari, who planned to tear down part of a medieval mosque to construct a new boulevard. The director was able to frustrate his plans. In another case, to forestall city encroachment on a triangular piece of land reserved for the future museum, al-Husri reconstructed an Assyrian gate at one point of the triangle, placed a Babylonian lion at another, and built a temporary storehouse on the third. The land was saved. In a third battle, this time to protect an ancient tower on the old city wall, he had to admit defeat when the mayor obtained the support of Bakr Sidki, military strongman of the day. Even then the director warned that future historians of the city would point accusing fingers at those who had supported such wanton destruction. Al-Husri did not give up easily.[60]

The reconstruction of the Assyrian gate from Khorsabad brought congratulations from John Wilson. To move such large monuments successfully from northern Iraq was difficult and showed the increasing sophistication of the Iraqis. Wilson wondered if al-Husri intended to use all of the gate and its associated reliefs inside the new museum. The Oriental Institute's expedition had discovered these in 1934, and Wilson wanted to express his interest in obtaining one of the winged figures if it were not to be used.[61]

Al-Husri replied that he could not consider separating the components of the gateway. They must stay together. He would be happy to have a cast of a bull or some other figure made for the institute, if Wilson in turn would provide a cast of the winged bull given to Chicago in 1930. As for its use, he intended to restore the monument to its original function; it would serve as the gateway to the museum grounds, for, he remarked tellingly, "I don't want to transform these into museum objects."[62]

When the two Iraqi graduates, Fuad Safar and Taha Baqir, returned at last from the University of Chicago after five years of study, the department could begin work at pre-Islamic sites as well. It was they who, working with Seton Lloyd, had removed the Assyrian sculptures to Baghdad. Then they proceeded to carry out soundings and excavations at pre-

**Figure 10.1.** Iraq, 1929, Khorsabad. Transporting the crated Assyrian Bull on a three-ton truck and trailer at the start of its voyage to the United States. Courtesy of the Oriental Institute of the University of Chicago.

historic sites. They were the first generation of Iraqi experts and would provide continuity into the post–World War II period.

Seton Lloyd had taken the place of Jordan, who left Iraq under a cloud in May 1939. Jordan was a confirmed Nazi, and he did nothing to hide his convictions. He became a recognized German political organizer while still an official of the Iraqi government. He conducted anti-British propaganda and frequently exhibited his anti-Semitic prejudices. According to Agatha Christie, when she and her husband, Max Mallowan, were visiting Jordan, someone casually mentioned the Jews. Suddenly he became a changed man, blurting out, "You do not understand. Our Jews are perhaps different from yours. They are a danger. They should be exterminated. Nothing else will do but that." Christie stared at him unbelievingly. He quickly became an embarrassment, and the government used the crisis associated with the accidental death of King Ghazi to send him home to Berlin.[63]

By 1940 there was only one foreign expedition remaining in Iraq, the Germans at Warka, which some suspected of serving largely political purposes. What happened to the others became a much-debated question. Westerners and some of their supporters in Iraq claimed that the unfriendly attitude of the Department of Antiquities had chased them away, largely to Syria where the mandate government went out of its way to encourage foreign expeditions, thirteen of them by 1936. The nationalists countered that these charges were nonsense, that the expeditions had departed for a variety of reasons: some had completed their work; others had run out of money due to the Depression; and then, in the late 1930s, the unsettled international situation had caused them to pack up and go home. To argue otherwise, they believed, was simply propaganda.[64]

The work of the department, with its emphasis on Arab-Islamic monuments, continued through the early stages of the war, but the pro-German coup under Rashid Ali al-Kaylani in spring 1941 brought a temporary halt to all such activities. The Iraqi archaeologists went off to join their military units, and British subjects, including Seton Lloyd and the famous travel writer Freya Stark, were interned at their embassy, where they waited out the coming confrontation between British and Iraqi forces. For several weeks in May, Iraq became the focus of the war in the Middle East.

With defeat of the nationalist forces and the impending return of the pro-British Nuri al-Said and the regent 'Abd al-Ilah—the late king's son, Faisal, was too young to rule—Sati' al-Husri's position became precarious. The new government removed him as director of antiquities and then, using a law passed years earlier to deal with a domestic disturbance, stripped him of his citizenship. It ordered him to leave the country immediately and assigned him a guard to make certain he did. Abdul Razzaq Lutfi, the nemesis of the foreign archaeologists, went into exile as well. The new regime executed the top leadership, but al-Kaylani escaped abroad. The former director of antiquities settled in Lebanon, where he continued to write in support of his beloved Pan-Arabism until his death in 1968.[65]

Sadly, Paul Knabenshue had little time to enjoy the return to power of his longtime friend. He died quite unexpectedly from an infection in February 1942 after ten years of service in Iraq. Shortly before his death, he had been commended by Britain and Belgium for sheltering their subjects at the legation during the recent disturbances. He was given a state funeral and was buried in the small British civilian cemetery in Baghdad.

Despite the British victory in May 1941, much of what had been accomplished during al-Husri's years as director remained. Iraq now had its own trained archaeologists, and their numbers grew after the war. Lloyd, who had taken an important role in these events, later reflected on what he had witnessed: "Foreign excavators, returning to those countries in the hope of resuming their interrupted work, tended to find that the initiative had passed into the hands of their erstwhile 'hosts.' Locally born excavators now profited from a higher standard of training, and the 'tools of research' had become available in newly founded universities. Under these circumstances it was natural that the most richly productive sites should in future be allotted by local authorities to their own archaeologists."[66]

Decades later, in 1966, the government of Iraq invited Lloyd and the aged al-Husri along with other dignitaries to Baghdad for the grand opening of the new museum on the west bank of the Tigris, on the land that al-Husri had protected from development thirty years earlier. The two former officials sat next to each other at the ceremonies. During the long, flowery speeches, Lloyd's head must have filled with nostalgic thoughts of the vanished era of "Great Excavations" while al-Husri, thoroughly rehabilitated, surely contemplated how well everything had turned out.[67]

# 11. A NEW ERA

For a generation nationalists and foreign archaeologists had been negotiating, often unhappily, the terms under which excavation would continue in the region. The diplomats had weighed in from time to time, siding with their compatriots. And yet step by step the Westerners had been forced to give way. These changes frequently followed a crisis such as that over Sardis, or Persepolis, or the treasure of Tutankhamun, which revealed just how strong the local nationalists had become. Some changes were barely perceptible to outsiders: the demand that foreign archaeologists accept local inspectors or that finds be reported continuously throughout the season. Insignificant as they might seem, these new regulations and restrictions worked to tighten local control. Some observers dismissed these developments, arguing that foreign governments still wielded considerable authority. They were real nonetheless. The transformation that had begun with archaeology would spread to all other areas of responsibility in the early postwar years.

The beginning of World War II marked the end of the period of negotiation in Middle Eastern archaeology. Hereafter archaeological affairs lay almost completely in the hands of local authorities. Secular nationalists such as Hamit Koşay, Ali Asghar Hikmat, and Sati' al-Husri had moved their respective nations steadily toward greater local control, and the war brought a sudden finality to the process. With the outbreak of war, almost every Western archaeologist and expedition withdrew. They left the field to local experts, few though they might be with the exception of Turkey, where Ankara University had been training archaeologists for several years.

George Reisner stayed on at Giza; after decades in Egypt, he was more at home there than in the United States. The effects of old age and illness limited his work, however, and when he died in 1942 years of research notes remained unpublished. Étienne Drioton continued as director of antiquities, but his influence declined steadily in tandem with that of his staunchest supporter, King Faruq. The legal export of antiquities had ceased a full decade before the 1952 revolution.

In Iran and Iraq it was still possible for Western expeditions to be rewarded with duplicates already in national museums, but even there controls had become stricter. In Tehran André Godard continued to direct the Antiquities Service with its focus on Persepolis, but he faced constant challenges to his authority. Despite the fact that he was director general, he did not exercise complete control over his own subordinates. In the mid-1930s, when Muhammad Taghi Mostafavi, one of the first Iranians in the service and the man who would replace Godard in 1952, was transferred to Isfahan, the official notice from Minister of Public Instruction Ali Asghar Hikmat clearly set out the ambiguous nature of the Frenchman's authority. The letter read in part: "In technical matters you must take your instructions from Monsieur Godard, but in administrative matters you will be subject to the chief of education in Isfahan." Such challenges would have increased as more Iranians trained in archaeology entered the service in subsequent years.[1]

In Iraq we have a clear statement regarding the impact of the war on the Antiquities Service. Naji al-Asli, formerly of the Foreign Ministry, became director after Satiʿ al-Husri was sent into exile. Although al-Asli would welcome Western archaeologists back into Iraq when the war ended, he also made clear what his future objectives would be. The mantle of authority had been assumed by the Iraqis, and while they would certainly continue the great work of the past in the pre-Islamic field, at the same time, he remarked, "emphasis must be laid on the cultural heritage bequeathed to us by our Arab ancestors." Special attention would be given to the Abbasid period and "to those aspects of Islamic archaeology which in the past have understandably received less attention from Western scholars." Thus the program would be a continuation of what al-Husri had begun a decade earlier. Although al-Asli did not mention the former director, al-Husri would surely have supported everything in the new director's statement, except, perhaps, for "understandably."[2]

Seton Lloyd served as expert advisor to the department during the war, and although he criticized the political motives of the former director, he also emphasized the positive changes that had taken place in Iraqi archaeology, albeit without giving credit to al-Husri. He praised the fact that the department was undertaking excavations over the *"whole range of historic periods."* He looked forward to the day when Western archaeologists would return, and he stressed the vital importance of *"co-operation between Iraqi and foreign excavators."*[3]

While local experts continued to pursue their archaeological interests with little thought to the departed Westerners, many of the latter found rewarding wartime employment at home. In the United States the government called on the expertise of the returned archaeologists, seeking their assistance in preparing maps and other information on the region and in some cases sending them into the field to collect intelligence. Hardly anyone was overlooked, for they often spoke the local languages, enjoyed excellent contacts, and knew the geography as well as the local inhabitants. They became valued collaborators in the U.S. government's war effort. Such had been the role of European archaeologists in the previous war, but in 1917 there had been few American citizens with the necessary training and experience to be of similar service. Now there were many more, and they were eager to help.

Henry Field provides a good example. He was a leading anthropologist and archaeologist who had worked throughout the region during the interwar years. He went immediately to work for William Donovan, director of the OSS, providing information and propaganda suggestions for the Middle East and Southwest Asia. In March 1941, nine months before Pearl Harbor, he provided Donovan with copies of recent travel reports from Turkey, Iraq, and Iran. Like others in his field, he retained his government contacts into the cold war years, keeping the Central Intelligence Agency, successor to the OSS, informed on his expeditions to Iraq, Iran, and the Persian Gulf region.[4]

In a government-sponsored radio interview early in the war, Field explained that Arabs would reject the Nazis' overtures because Hitler had set himself up as a kind of prophet, and this was anathema to Muslims. American archaeologists were seen as good neighbors, he believed, because they provided work in the region and looked after their workers. The Arabs, he remarked, were delighted to see them come.[5]

He provided a list of specialists on Iraq, Iran, and Turkey who might work for intelligence. These included Herzfeld, Ephraim Speiser, and Calvin McEwan. McEwan spent much of the war in northern Syria ostensibly doing "archaeological" reconnaissance for the Oriental Institute and an unnamed benefactor, clearly Donovan. Iran, too, had its archaeologists serving as undercover agents. Donald Wilber, Pope's former associate, and Joseph Upton, representative of the Metropolitan, worked for the OSS there throughout the war. John Wilson, McEwan's chief at the Oriental Institute, went to work early in 1942 as head of the section on Near Eastern research in the Office of the Coordinator of Information. First he studied whether the Germans would be able to cross the delta quickly toward the Suez Canal if they were to break through Allied lines at El-Alamein. Later he was asked to suggest guidelines for establishing an antiquities service in the kingdom of Saudi Arabia.[6]

When the war ended most of the archaeologists returned to peacetime pursuits. It was several years, however, before they could reestablish contacts in the Middle East and make preparations for working there again. In fact, few Western expeditions returned to the region before 1949.

Part of the preparation was undertaken by John Wilson, who, over a period of three months, January through March 1946, visited Egypt, Palestine, Syria, Iraq, Lebanon, and Turkey. His trip immediately calls to mind Breasted's journey twenty-five years earlier. Like his predecessor, Wilson wanted to survey conditions in the postwar Middle East, with an eye toward reestablishing the Oriental Institute in the region.

He encountered some significant differences. Wilson could no longer engage in the wholesale purchase of antiquities, which had been commonplace in 1919 and which had made Breasted's journey so rewarding. This activity was no longer acceptable. Nor did he stop in Britain to meet with top leaders. That easy access of the interwar years was rapidly disappearing as government bureaucracies mushroomed to meet cold war challenges. Western archaeologists and their institutional representatives were now expected to negotiate directly with the agents of local governments. No longer could foreign archaeologists use their diplomats as intermediaries, as the Americans had done with William Hornibrook, Paul Knabenshue, Joseph Grew, and many others. This now would likely prove ineffective and even harmful to their interests.

Wilson found everywhere a dramatic increase in costs, as much as 400 percent, over those of the prewar period. This posed a serious financial problem for foreign institutions, and the Oriental Institute was no exception. No John D. Rockefeller Jr. came to its assistance in the post–World War II years, and finding adequate funds seemed at times a hopeless task.[7]

Wherever he went, Wilson proposed cooperative efforts among American institutions. He became depressed about the situation in Egypt, where, he claimed, "xenophobia and political intrigue were so marked that the entire atmosphere was one of frustration." The Egyptians clearly controlled all aspects of their archaeology, and Drioton's authority had been "checked by the force of Egyptian nationalism." Yet Wilson recommended a photographic copying expedition because many monuments had been excavated but imperfectly recorded. This could draw on the combined resources of the Boston Museum of Fine Arts, the Metropolitan, the University Museum, the Oriental Institute, and any

**Figure 11.1.**  (*l. to r.*) Iraqi official, Seton Lloyd, John Wilson, Naji al-Asli (director of antiquities), Fuad Safar, and Taha Baqir at Aqar Quf ziggurat, 1946. Courtesy of the Oriental Institute of the University of Chicago.

other interested institutions. Half the photographers would, of course, be Egyptians.[8]

In Iraq he found conditions for renewed excavation much more favorable than in Egypt, and he praised the work of Naji al-Asli, Fuad Safar, and Taha Baqir and the British expert, Lloyd. Once again Wilson urged a new cooperation of institutions, American, British, and Iraqi, to carry out renewed fieldwork. He proposed setting up an archaeological training center in Baghdad, offering cuneiform studies and field excavation methods, using professors competent in the languages and cultural history of ancient Mesopotamia on a short-term basis.

Although he did not travel to Iran, he cited a report sent to him by an unidentified American archaeologist, certainly Wilber or Upton, who believed that Godard's contract there was unlikely to be renewed given recent unfavorable agitation and critical comment in the parliament and the press.[9]

Interestingly, Syria and Lebanon, where the nationalists had been kept from power and French rule was just ending, lagged far behind the four countries studied here. They had almost no trained local archaeologists.

Wilson's final report, which he shared with the State Department, opened with a general statement that more clearly than anything else from that period revealed how much Middle Eastern archaeology had changed since Breasted's sojourn in 1920:

> Now nationalism works against any kind of exploitation. Many of the Near Eastern countries are mature enough to take responsible care of their monuments and antiquities. And the services of antiquities are increasingly coming under the more effective control of locals. It makes good scholarly sense to say that archaeology must be international and not unilateral. It makes good working sense to say that the best continuing conditions may be effected in an atmosphere of cooperation between westerners and orientals.[10]

These admissions did not come without regrets and concerns, but they represented a recognition of the times and an abandonment of any thought of turning back. As Seton Lloyd admitted, perhaps reluctantly, "It was rational that the most richly productive sites should in future be allotted by local authorities to their own archaeologists." And they were.[11]

# 12. REFLECTIONS

Over the decades since the close of World War II, problems relating to archaeology and antiquities have persisted in the Middle East. They did not disappear with the transfer of archaeological affairs into the hands of local nationalists. Sometimes there was bickering among internal factions, each with its own agenda. Sometimes crises arose, as they often had during the interwar years, between Westerners and local governments.

Stolen antiquities made headlines again in 1987, when the Turkish government filed a lawsuit against the Metropolitan Museum of Art. Peasants digging illegally in the vicinity of Sardis in the early 1960s had uncovered beautiful objects in the burial tumuli that dotted the plain. These clandestine digs yielded wonderful examples of Lydian art, which were quickly smuggled abroad. Many of these, labeled "Eastern Aegean" to disguise their origin, found their way into the collection of the Metropolitan. In 1984 the museum, unwisely it turned out, placed a number of the rare items, from the so-called Lydian Hoard, on display. Faced with threats of exposure and pressed by many in the art world, the museum reluctantly agreed to return the treasure to Turkey at its own expense in October 1993. These items went on display as soon as they arrived from the United States. Thus ended Sardis II.[1]

In the Republic of Turkey recently there has been an upsurge in Ottoman studies, but over the past sixty years excavations have centered on the classical period. Many young Turkish archaeologists continued to receive their advanced training from specialists in Europe and the United States, and thus, like their mentors, they focused on the pre-Islamic period.

In Egypt, too, there are events today that remind one of the long-ago days of Lacau and Breasted. A new Egyptian Museum has not yet been built, and given the increasing demands on the state's meager budget, plans for construction of the Grand Egyptian Museum near the Giza Pyramids are making little progress. The century-old structure, wedged between Tahrir Square, the Nile Hilton, and the river itself, has had to suffice all these years. Many of the display rooms are drab, with antiquities poorly displayed; there is almost no climate control. Yet to see the glorious treasure of Tutankhamun all together makes one appreciate not only the great wealth and power of the New Kingdom but also the efforts of the Egyptian nationalists, who insisted that this greatest of all ancient treasures must not be divided and dispersed.

On a brighter note, the Islamic Museum, with its unsurpassed collection, is at last being totally renovated. The Mahmud Mukhtar Museum has been remodeled as well. Two new smaller museums have been established under the authority of the Ministry of Culture. They are a delight to visit. The Museum of Islamic Ceramics in Zamalek, a prosperous neighborhood in Cairo, boasts a magnificent collection from throughout the Islamic Middle East. Each piece is well displayed, and the nineteenth-century princely home, which houses the pottery, provides a perfect setting. The other museum, designed by the Brooklyn Museum of New York, is the Luxor Museum. The antiquities are carefully displayed, clearly identified, and well lighted. These two are noteworthy and mark the new generation of museums in Egypt. Zahi Hawass, Egypt's dynamic director of antiquities, explains that these will be part of a group of teaching centers around the country developed to interest young people in their history and culture, to teach them "to love ancient Egypt and be proud of their ancestors."[2]

Tensions that developed in Egypt in the 1930s between the Arab-Islamists and the Pharaonists have faded, but suspicions remain, especially for those who worry that the advance of one means the eclipse of the other. This briefly became an issue during the presidency of Anwar Sadat (r. 1970–1981), who many claimed was aping the ancient rulers with his palaces and luxurious lifestyle. When Khalid Islambuli assassinated Sadat at a military parade on October 6, 1981, he cried out, "We have killed Pharaoh!" drawing on powerful imagery from the Qur'an.

In a far corner of the al-Rifa'i Mosque in Cairo lies the grave of Muhammad Riza Shah Pahlavi (r. 1941–1979), the last shah of Iran and a close friend of Sadat's. This spot, where his father's body had been interred for several years after his death in 1944, has become a pilgrimage site for Iranian exiles in recent years. They leave flowers and the occasional poem on his tomb in this distant land.

During his long reign, Muhammad Riza Pahlavi praised the glories of the ancient, pre-Islamic dynasties, even as he modernized and secularized the nation. Iranian schoolbooks emphasized in word and picture the accomplishments of the ancients. The shah even announced a new calendar based on the twenty-five centuries of empire rather than the fourteen centuries of Islam. All of this culminated in October 1971 with an international celebration, honoring the 2,500th anniversary of the establishment of monarchy in Iran. Invited monarchs and heads of state gathered at Persepolis to join in the elaborate ceremonies, which were remarkably expensive. It was a catered affair with food, drink, and wait staff all flown in from Maxim's in Paris. Prominent guests stayed in lavish pavilions erected at the site. A vast parade of Iranian soldiers, each contingent dressed in the uniforms of a different dynasty reaching back to the Achaemenids, marched past the reviewing stand.

Earlier the shah had opened the ceremonies with an address at the tomb of Cyrus the Great, founder of the Achaemenid dynasty, at nearby Pasagardae. In his eulogy the shah made clear the enduring relationship between ancient and modern Iran: "Cyrus, great king, king of kings, Achaemenian king, king of the land of Iran, from me, king of kings of Iran and from my nation, I send greetings. . . . Cyrus, we have gathered here today at your eternal tomb to tell you: sleep in peace because we are awake and we will always be awake to look after our proud inheritance."[3]

The extravagance of the events may have provided the proverbial last straw. Although the organization that went into the activities taking place at Persepolis was at first sight impressive, many Iranians viewed it quite differently, grumbling about the huge waste of money and ridiculing the pomp and pageantry. To make matters worse, most Iranians were excluded from the events, having to watch them from afar on television.

Illustrating once again the contested nature of memory and commemoration, Islamic revolutionary authorities quickly put an end to the glorification of the ancients. The Pahlavis had promoted such views for half a century, but orthodox Muslims, who traditionally scorned the pre-Islamic era as the "Age of Ignorance," sought to impose their own official memory. Textbooks were rewritten to reflect important Islamic heroes, and for a while the monuments themselves became neglected once again. Leaders of the revolution were suspicious of archaeology; to them it seemed the discipline had only served the shah's court "to glorify despotism and justify royal oppression." The Department of Archaeology at Tehran University was temporarily closed (1979–1982).[4]

Ali Shariati, whose writings provided a theoretical foundation for the coming revolution in the 1970s, had stated clearly the rejectionist point of view when he announced that the people were "left unmoved by the heroes, geniuses, myths and monuments of these ancient empires." They remembered nothing from that distant past, he claimed, and did not want to learn about it. For them to return to their roots meant, "not a redis-covery of pre-Islamic Iran, but a return to . . . Islamic, especially Shi-ite, roots."[5]

It took ten years for Iranian archaeology to escape from this criticism. A new agency set up in 1985, the Iranian Cultural Heritage Organization (ICHO), incorporated all the different departments previously respon-sible for archaeological endeavors in Iran.[6]

A strong indication that the Islamic regime's attitude had softened came with the visit of President Ali Akbar Hashemi-Rafsanjani to Persepolis in April 1991. He wrote the following in the guest book there: "Visiting the incredible remains at Persepolis provokes considerable national pride in every individual. By seeing these remains, our people will discover their own capabilities and the cultural background of their country, and will believe that they will recover their historical role in the future to uphold upon this talent and foundation, the blazing torch of Islam to light the path of other nations." This official embrace of the full sweep of Iranian history marked an important turning point; it was similar to what had already taken place in Turkey and Egypt. Today the regime is spending considerable sums on a number of sites, both Islamic (Sultanieh, Isfahan) and pre-Islamic (Persepolis, Choqa Zanbil).[7]

Iraq has followed a somewhat similar path. Since the revolution of July 1958, which swept aside the pro-Western regime of Nuri al-Said, the gov-ernment in Baghdad has used archaeology for its own purposes. Floats in the first anniversary parade, celebrating the revolution, drew most of their themes from pre-Islamic history. This tendency became blurred dur-ing the early years of Baath Party rule after 1968, when the regime at-tempted "to embrace a Mesopotamian heritage without abandoning the Baath's commitment to Arab nationalism." After Saddam Hussein became president in 1979, he issued a stamp commemorating the work of Satiʿ al-Husri.[8]

After that time, however, Hussein turned more toward pre-Islamic symbols. Expensive reconstruction and rebuilding of Babylon (1987–1988), at an estimated cost of $100 million, became a main focus for Iraqi national identity. He had bricks stamped with his name just as the Neo-Babylonian ruler, Nebuchadnezzar (604–562 B.C.E.), had done. Archaeo-logical museums were established in all parts of the country. To bring the entire past of Iraq under one tent, Taha Bakir and others revived the old understanding that all Semites, and therefore the Mesopotamians as well, originated from the Arabs in the Arabian peninsula. After 1979 this became the orthodox interpretation, despite the fact that little evidence existed to substantiate the claim.[9]

In November 1990 Saddam Hussein used this understanding of the past to justify in part the invasion of Kuwait. "You know as Arabs," he claimed, "that Iraq's civilization is 6,000 years old. Is it possible for a civilization which is 6,000 years old to have been isolated from the sea? A part of Iraq's land was cut off by English scissors."[10]

Saddam Hussein became increasingly identified as the "New Nebuchadnezzar." The connection became so fixed in people's minds that in the uprisings against him in 1991, mobs attacked and destroyed the local museums set up by the state to strengthen the historical link between the ancient past and the present regime.

Events since March 2003 have brought to the fore once again many of the issues with which this study has been concerned. Looting of archaeological sites began long before the current war; by the mid-1990s, facing increasing hardships under UN sanctions, Iraqis were sending a stream of artifacts to the black markets in London, New York, and Tokyo. Although much of this was random and unorganized, there is growing evidence that some robbers at least showed great sophistication, acting on specific purchase requests from international crime syndicates. When the Baghdad Museum was attacked in April 2003, some of the looters went directly after those antiquities for which they had orders. According to a recent documentary, much of what was taken then has not been recovered. Contrary to the claims of American occupation authorities, who reopened the museum for one day only to showcase returned antiquities, most of those on display came from storage areas that had been undisturbed by the looting.[11]

Although the museum has received a great deal of attention, and justly so, hundreds of sites around the country have been subjected to illegal digging over the past two years. Some looters come well armed, and multinational troops have been reluctant to take them on. Sometimes foreign soldiers, faced with too many challenges, are just not interested. And thus much of the historical record continues to be destroyed.[12]

While Turkey, Egypt, and Iran are successfully blending many of the influences from their long histories, it remains to be seen how the new Iraq will reshape its identity.

# NOTES

## Abbreviations

| | |
|---|---|
| AA | Ann Arbor |
| AAA | American Archives of Art |
| ASOR | American Schools of Oriental Research |
| AUP | Arthur Upham Pope |
| BL | Bentley Library |
| BMFA | Boston Museum of Fine Arts |
| BPF | Baghdad Post Files |
| CB | Charles Breasted |
| CEAV | Committee for the Excavation of Antioch and Vicinity |
| CMA | Cleveland Museum of Art |
| DAA | Department of Art and Archaeology |
| DEA | Department of Egyptian Art |
| DOCF | Director's Office Correspondence File |
| EPF | Egypt Post Files |
| EI | Educational Interests subseries |
| FDRL | Franklin Delano Roosevelt Library |
| FMA | Fogg Museum of Art |
| FO | Foreign Office |
| FWK | Francis W. Kelsey |
| GAR | George A. Reisner |
| HCB | Howard Crosley Butler |
| HF | Henri Frankfort |
| HL | Houghton Library |
| HU | Harvard University |
| *JARCE* | *Journal of the American Research Center in Egypt* |
| JB/JHB | James Breasted/James Henry Breasted |
| MBP | Mark Bristol Papers |
| MESA | Middle East Studies Association |
| MFA | Ministry of Foreign Affairs |
| MMOA | Metropolitan Museum of Art |
| MPI | Ministry of Public Instruction |
| NA | National Archives |
| NEA | Near East Affairs |
| NYPL | New York Public Library |

OHS     Oregon Historical Society
OI      Oriental Institute
OMR     Office of the Messrs Rockefeller
OSS     Office of Strategic Services
PRO     Public Record Office
PU      Princeton University
RAC     Rockefeller Archives Center
RFA     Rockefeller Family Archives
RG      Record Group
SC      Sardis Correspondence
SS      Secretary of State
TPF     Tehran Post Files
TuPF    Turkish Post Files
UC      University of Chicago
UM      University of Michigan
UMA     University Museum Archive
UP      University of Pennsylvania
WMFA    Worcester Museum of Fine Arts

## Introduction

1. "Control" meant issuing permits, determining conditions under which excavations would take place, setting rules for divisions. It often did not include determining which sites would be excavated. This, of course, was significant for "how one goes about hewing the land tells us something about what kinds of objects archaeologists deem to be significant (to be worthy of being observed)." Nadia Abu El-Haj, *Facts on the Ground: Archaeological Practice and Territorial Self-Fashioning in Israeli Society* (Chicago, 2001), 131. As more local archaeologists completed their specialized education and training, they were able to focus on neglected historical periods.

2. G. Ernest Wright, "The Phenomenon of American Archaeology in the Near East," in James A. Sanders, ed., *Near Eastern Archaeology in the Twentieth Century: Essays in Honor of Nelson Glueck* (Garden City, NY, 1970), 16.

3. Neil Asher Silberman, "Fitting the Pieces Together: The Power and Politics of Archaeology in the Modern Middle East," World Archaeological Congress, University of Cape Town, 10–14 January 1999, 13; available at www.wac.uct.ac.za/wac4/silberman.

4. Donald Malcom Reid, *Whose Pharaohs? Archaeology, Museums, and Egyptian National Identity from Napoleon to World War I* (Berkeley and Los Angeles, 2002), 30–31. The statue of Shahpur I was repaired during the reign of Muhammad Riza Pahlavi (1941–1979). Ali Mousavi, "Persepolis in Retrospect: Histories of Discovery and Archaeological Exploration at the Ruins of Ancient Parseh," *Ars Orientalis* 32 (2002): 3 [Wilson Select Plus database].

5. "Syrian Expedition," folder 806, Oriental Institute (OI) publication, 1937, box 111, Educational Interests subseries, Office of the Messrs Rockefeller (OMR), Record Group (RG) 2, Rockefeller Family Archives (RFA), Rockefeller Archive Center, Sleepy Hollow, NY (RAC).

6. 15 May 1925, Breasted to Fosdick, folder 824, box 112, Educational Interests (EI) subseries, OMR, RG2, RFA, RAC.

7. 4 November 1937, John Wilson to David Stevens, folder 274, University of Chicago, OI, box 18, International Education Board series, RAC.

8. Israel Gershoni and James Jankowski, eds., *Rethinking Nationalism in the Arab Middle East* (New York, 1997), ix, xix, 14. Israel Gershoni and James Jankowski, *Commemorating the Nation: Collective Memory, Public Commemoration, and National Identity in Twentieth-Century Egypt* (Chicago, 2004), 10, 16.

9. 5 September 1933, *Al-Balagh* (Cairo). Sami Shawkat, *Hadhih Ahdafuna* [These Are Our Goals] (Baghdad, 1939), 43.

10. 25 November 1899, Robert Garrett diary, 3: 33, Baltimore Museum of Art, Baltimore, MD. "Syrian Expedition," folder 806, OI, 1937, box 111, EI subseries, RG2, OMR, RFA, RAC.

11. 24 July 1935, Fairdyke note, CE32/3018-3034, Director's correspondence, British Museum Archives, London.

12. See, for example, John R. Gillis, editor, *Commemorations: The Politics of National Identity* (Princeton, 1994); Flora Kaplan, *Museums and the Making of "Ourselves": The Role of Objects in National Identity* (London, 1994); Ivan Karp and Steven D. Levine, *Exhibiting Cultures: The Poetics and Politics of Museum Display* (Washington, DC, 1991); Daniel J. Sherman and Irit Rogoff, *Museum Culture: Histories, Discourses, Spectacles* (London, 1994); Wendy M. K. Shaw, *Possessors and Possessed: Museums, Archaeology, and the Visualization of History in the Late Ottoman Empire* (Berkeley and Los Angeles, 2003).

13. Asli Gur, "Anatolia: Cradle of Civilizations," paper presented at Middle East Studies Association conference (MESA), San Francisco, 2001.

14. Wendy M. K. Shaw, "Islamic Arts in the Ottoman Imperial Museum, 1889–1923," *Ars Orientalis* 30 (2000): 1 [Wilson Select Plus database]. "Maronite" refers to a Christian sect in Lebanon in communion with the Roman Catholic Church.

15. Lawrence Davidson, "Imagining Palestine: Archaeology and Popular Perceptions of Palestine in the First Decade of the Mandate," 21, paper presented at MESA, Washington, DC, 1995.

16. Kimberly Hart, "Ideas about Tradition and Modernity in Two Turkish Villages," paper presented at MESA, 2001. Abu El-Haj, *Facts on the Ground*, 50, 256.

17. Gershoni and Jankowski, *Commemorating the Nation*, 116. Interview with Andre and Yedda Godard, no. 26, Ullens Archive Audio Collection, Visual Collections, Fine Arts Library, Harvard University, Cambridge, MA (HU).

18. 8 April 1914, James Breasted (JB) to George Hale, George Ellery Hale papers, microfilm roll #5, Millikan Library, California Institute of Technology, Pasadena, CA.

19. 25 February 1924, Secretary of State Hughes to R. V. D. Magoffin, President, Archaeological Institute of America, box 1, F. W. Kelsey (FWK) papers, Bentley Library (BL), University of Michigan (UM), Ann Arbor (AA). 1 May 1931, Memo to File, U.S., Government of, Director's Confidential File, OI Archives, University of Chicago (UC).

20. See, for example, the following works: Warren Cohen, *Empire without Tears*

(1987); Frank Costigliola, *Awkward Dominion* (1984); and Emily Rosenberg, *Spreading the American Dream: American Economic and Cultural Expansion, 1890–1945* (New York, 1982).

21. 25 May 1907, Henry Gates to James Breasted, Letterbooks, RG1, John D. Rockefeller papers, RFA, RAC.

## 1. End of the Old Order

1. Kemal H. Karpat, "Kossuth in Turkey: The Impact of Hungarian Refugees in the Ottoman Empire, 1849–1851," *Hungarian Heritage Review* 19 (March 1990): 23. Ayşe Özdemir, "A History of Turkish Archaeology from the 19th Century to the End of the Single Party Period" (M.A. thesis, Bogazici University, Istanbul, 2001), 36.

2. Kemal H. Karpat, *The Politicization of Islam: Reconstructing Identity, State, Faith, and Community in the Late Ottoman State* (New York, 2001), 364. Özdemir, "History of Turkish Archaeology," 42, 52.

3. Lutfi Levonian, *The Turkish Press: Selections from the Turkish Press Showing Events and Opinions, 1925–1932* (Athens, 1932), 189.

4. Karpat argues, however, that after the beginning of the twentieth century the sultans referred to themselves as Turks: *The Politicization of Islam*, 394. Eleanor Bisbee, *The New Turks: Pioneers of the Republic, 1920–1950* (Philadelphia, 1951), 151; Harold G. Nicolson, *Curzon: The Last Phase, 1919–1925: A Study in Postwar Diplomacy* (New York, 1934), 69, 96.

5. Jean-Louis Bacque-Grammont and Jean-Paul Roux, *Mustafa Kemal Ataturk et la Turquie nouvelle* (Paris, 1982), 60. Donald E. Webster, *The Turkey of Ataturk: Social Process in the Turkish Reformation* (Philadelphia, 1939), 182. Antecedents to this society can be found in the late-Ottoman period, beginning in 1909: Karpat, *Politicization of Islam*, 366–367.

6. Özdemir, "History of Turkish Archaeology," 88.

7. *Türk Tarih Kongresi, 1932* [The Turkish History Conference] (Istanbul, 1932), 6, 14. For the role of the nationalist Yusuf Akçura at the conference, see Karpat, *The Politicization of Islam*, 390, 397.

8. Recent work by Ilker Aytürk of Brandeis University suggests that the theory provided a means of ending the radical purge of foreign words. If each word emanated from a Turkish root, there could be no justification for removing it from the language. The name, he believes, was related to the archaeologists' recent discovery of Hittite sun discs, which fired the imagination of Turkish nationalists. See "The Sun-Language Theory: Nationalism, Religion and Language Reform in Atatürk's Turkey," paper presented at MESA, Washington, DC, November 2002. Interview with Hans Güterbock, 21 July 1993, Chicago.

9. Interview with Professor Oluş Arik, 15 November 1999, Ankara; Interview with Professor Ekram Akurgal, 11 December 1999, Izmir. 29 December 1934, *Ankara*. Stephen Ronart, *Die Türkei von Heute* [Turkey Today] (Amsterdam, 1936), 144–145.

10. *Cumhuriyet Dönem, Türkiye Ansiklopedisi* [The Republican Era, Encyclopedia of Turkey] (Ankara, 1983), 9:2467. Güterbock interview.

11. Afet Inan, *A History of the Turkish Revolution and Turkish Republic*, trans. Ahmet E. Uysal (Ankara, 1981), 199. *Ankara Üniversitesi Haftasi, Kars, July 22–28, 1942* [Ankara University Week Seminar] (Ankara: Turkish Historical Society Press, 1944), 28. For a similar sentiment, see Karpat, *The Politicization of Islam*, 407.

12. *Türkiye Ansiklopedisi*, 1:76. Gul Ersin Kundakçi, "19 Yüzyilda Anadolu Arkeolojisne ve Eskiçağ Tarihine Genel Yaklaşim" [19th-Century Anatolian Archaeology and Prehistoric History, a General Approach], 13th Turkish Historical Congress, 4–8 October 1999, Ankara.

13. Erendiz Atasü, *The Other Side of the Mountain* (London, 2000), 40–41.

14. Suzanne L. Marchand, *Down from Olympus: Archaeology and Philhellenism in Germany, 1750–1970* (Princeton, 1996), 94–96.

15. Abdullah Martal and Recep Yildirim, "Osmanli Yönetiminin Arkeolojik Eserlere Bakiş Açisi" [A Point of View on the Ottoman Government's Archaeological Work], 13th Turkish Historical Conference, Ankara.

16. Shaw, "Islamic Arts in the Ottoman Imperial Museum," 6 [Wilson Select Plus database].

17. Ibid., 8 [Wilson Select Plus database].

18. 29 March, 26 September 1923, F/17/17244, Ministry of Public Instruction (MPI), Archives National, Paris.

19. Ibid. 19 September 1921, Turquie P1643, Levant 1918–1940, Ministry of Foreign Affairs (MFA) Archive, Quay d'Orsay, Paris.

20. Thomas Scheffler, "The Kaiser in Baalbek: Tourism, Archaeology and the Politics of Imagination," paper presented at MESA, December 1998. These efforts, although considerably reduced, would continue after the war. Marchand, *Down from Olympus*, 281, 283, 284, 287.

21. Marchand, *Down from Olympus*, 204–205, 212, 213, 216. Mschatta was originally believed to be the work of the Sasanian dynasty (226–641 C.E.), but scholars have recently determined that the Umayyads (661–749 C.E.) built it.

22. 18.149.41.1930, Prime Ministerial Archive, Ankara.

23. Interview with Professor Oluş Arik, 15 November 1999, Ankara.

## 2. The Sardis Affair

1. Ann Waldron, "Digging up the Past," *Princeton Alumni Weekly* (11 February 1980): 17. Waldron mistakenly wrote "Arabic" for what clearly should have been "Aramaic."

2. 21 December 1911, Macy to Butler, Howard Crosley Butler Papers (HCB), Sardis Correspondence, 1910–1919 (SC), Department of Art and Archaeology (DAA), Princeton University (PU).

3. 1913, Report of the American Excavation at Sardis, HCB, SC, DAA, PU.

4. 28 February 1919, F/17/17244, MPI, Archives National, Paris. Marchand, *Down from Olympus*, 199. 19 September 1921, Pernot to Ministry of Foreign Affairs, Turquie, P1643, Levant, 1918–1940, MFA Archive, Quay d'Orsay, Paris.

5. 10 February 1921, Toynbee to Professor Hill, HCB, SC, 1919–1922, DAA, PU. February–March 1921, William Ransted Berry, Report on Sardis, HCB, SC, 1919–1922, DAA, PU.

6. 12 March 1921, Berry to Butler, HCB, SC, 1919–1922. February–March 1921, Report on Sardis, SC, 1919–1922, DAA, PU.
7. 14 December 1921, Butler to Papafrango, HCB, SC, 1919–1922, DAA, PU.
8. n.d., Capps to Sterghiades, HCB, SC, 1919–1922. 7 March 1922, Capps to Hill, 31 March 1922. Capps to Papafrango, HCB, SC, 1919–1922. 19 April 1922, McCormick to Butler, HCB, SC, 1919–1922, DAA, PU.
9. 14 May 1922, Shear to Butler, HCB, SC. 24 July 1922, Horton to Butler, HCB, SC, DAA, PU.
10. 10 April 1922, Edward Robinson to Butler, HCB, SC. 22 April 1922, Butler to Robinson, HCB, SC, DAA, PU.
11. 18 April 1922, Butler to Henry Fairchild Osborn, HCB, SC. 21 April 1922, Osborn to Butler, HCB, SC, DAA, PU.
12. 16 October 1922, Board of Metropolitan Museum of Art (MMOA) to State Department, 867.927/8, RG59, National Archives (NA). 27 January 1923, 867.927/17, RG 59, NA.
13. 8 April 1924, H. Feizy to Kelsey, box 1, FWK papers, Kelsey Museum, BL, UM, AA.
14. 16 December 1922, Francis W. Kelsey to Charles Evans Hughes, Box 17, FWK papers, Kelsey Museum, BL, UM, AA.
15. Waldo Heinrichs, *American Ambassador: Joseph C. Grew and the Development of the United States Diplomatic Tradition* (New York, 1966), 71.
16. 25 January 1924, Kelsey to Robinson, box 1, FWK papers, Kelsey Museum, BL, UM, AA. 27 April 1924, box 1, FWK papers, Kelsey Museum, BL, UM, AA. 16–30 April 1924, Memorandum No. 2, box 1, FWK papers, Kelsey Museum, BL, UM, AA.
17. 7 January 1924, J. Butler Wright to William Buckler, 892.7, RG84, Turkish Post Files (TuPF), NA.
18. 21, 23 January 1924, Buckler to Bristol, TuPF, 892.7, RG84, NA. 22 January 1924, Buckler to Macy, TuPF, 892.7, RG84. 16 February 1924, Buckler to Bristol, TuPF, 892.7, RG84.
19. 19 March 1924, Diary, Mark Bristol Papers (MBP), Houghton Library (HL), HU. 27, 28 April 1924, Diary, MBP, HL, HU.
20. 28 May 1924, box 42, General Correspondence, MBP, HL, HU, 28 May–29 June 1924, W. Buckler to G. Buckler, box 3, General Correspondence, William H. Buckler papers, Yale University, New Haven.
21. 23 May 1924, J. P. Morgan Jr. to Buckler, box 21, Letters, J. P. Morgan Jr. papers, Pierpoint-Morgan Library, New York City.
22. 11 June 1924, Macy to Allen W. Dulles, TuPF, 892.7, RG84, NA.
23. Arif Mufid Mansel, "Halil Ethem ve Sard Eserleri" [Halil Ethem and the Sardis Antiquities], in *Halil Ethem: Hatira Kitabi* [In Memory of Halil Ethem] (Ankara, 1948), 2:10.
24. Ibid., 11.
25. 11 January 1926, Sardis Committee to Bristol, TuPF, 892.7, RG84. 18 March 1924, Macy to Bristol, TuPF, 892.7, RG84.
26. 5 February 1926, Kelsey to Dulles, box 2, FWK papers, Kelsey Museum, BL, UM, AA. 10 April 1927, Halil Bey to Bristol, TuPF, 892.7, RG84.
27. 16 October 1923, Shaw to Dr. Chiera, TuPF, 892.7, RG84. 13 October 1926, Bristol to Macy, TuPF, 892.7, RG84.

28. Charles Evans Hughes, "Recent Questions and Negotiations," *American Journal of International Law* 18 (April 1924): 237, 241.
29. 14 March 1924, J. Callander to Kelsey, box 1, FWK papers, Kelsey Museum, BL, UM, AA.
30. James W. Gerard, "The Senate Should Reject the Treaty" (November 1923), box 78, The Turkish Treaty, 1926, FWK papers, Kelsey Museum, BL, UM, AA. George W. Horton, *The Blight of Asia* (Indianapolis, 1926), 268–271.
31. 30 April 1931, H. H. Van der Osten to James Breasted (JB), Von der Osten File, Director's Office Correspondence File (DOCF) for 1931, OI Archives, UC.

## 3. Heirs of the Hittites

1. Hans Henning Von der Osten, *Explorations in Asia Minor* (rpt. New York, 1971), 128.
2. 1 May 1927, Von der Osten to JB, Von der Osten File, DOCF for 1927, OI Archives, UC.
3. 10 March 1927, Von der Osten to D. D. Luckenbill, Von der Osten File, DOCF, 1927, OI Archives, UC.
4. 18–31 October 1928, 867.9111/234, RG 59, NA, College Park, MD.
5. 19 January 1928, JB to Joseph Grew, U.S., Government of, DOCF, 1928, OI Archives, UC. 1 May 1931, Memorandum for JHB's Confidential Files, U.S., Government of, DOCF, 1931, JB papers, OI Archives, UC.
6. 2 May 1931, JB to Von der Osten, Von der Osten File, DOCF, 1931, OI Archives, UC.
7. 17 August 1931, Taft to President Hoover, 867.927/59, RG9, NA.
8. 17 May 1930, Von der Osten Memorandum, Von der Osten File, DOCF, 1930, OI Archives, UC.
9. Ibid.
10. Ibid.
11. Ibid.
12. Ibid.
13. 5 June 1930, Patterson to Secretary of State (SS), 867.927/48, RG59, NA.
14. June 1930, Memorandum on Visit of Gazi, Von der Osten File, DOCF, 1930, OI Archives, UC.
15. 7 April 1932, JB to CB, Charles Breasted File, DOCF, 1932, OI Archives, UC.
16. 2 May 1931, Von der Osten File, DOCF, 1931, OI Archives, UC.
17. 18 January 1930, JB to Von der Osten, Von der Osten File, DOCF, 1930, OI Archives, UC.
18. Interview with Professor Tahsin Özgüç, 4 December 1999, Ankara. 5 October 1930, 892.7, RG84, TuPF, 1930, NA.
19. 7 July 1930, JB to VDO, Von der Osten File, DOCF, 1930, OI Archives, UC.
20. 26 May 1932, Turkey, Government of, DOCF, 1932, OI Archives, UC.
21. 23 August 1931, JB to CB, Charles Breasted File, DOCF, 1931, OI Archives, UC.
22. Interview with Dr. Hans Güterbock, 21 July 1993, Chicago.
23. 16 June 1926, box 73, Expeditions, 1924–1925, FWK papers, Kelsey Museum, BL, UM, AA. Folder 236, University of Chicago/Oriental Institute, 1934, box 17, series 216, Illinois, RG1.1, RAF, RAC.

24. 12 April, 16 June 1934, *Ankara*.
25. Özdemir, "History of Turkish Archaeology," 93, 94. Interviews with Prof. Ekrem Akurgal, 11 December 1999, Izmir; and Prof. Sedat Alp, 4 November 1999, Ankara.
26. Muazzez Çiğ, "Atatürk and the Beginning of Cuneiform Studies in Turkey," *Journal of Cuneiform Studies* 402 (Autumn 1988): 212–213.
27. Hamit Zubeyr (Koşay), *Tarihi Abidelerimizi Koruyalim* [Let Us Preserve Our Historical Monuments] (Ankara, 1932), 1.
28. Ekrem Akurgal, *Ancient Civilizations and Ruins of Turkey*, 8th ed. (Istanbul, 1993), 317.
29. 19 October, 14 November 1935, 16 April 1936, *Ankara*.
30. 27 July 1935, *Ankara*.
31. Hamit Zübeyr, *Tarihi*, 7. 4 April 1930, *Akcham* (Istanbul).
32. Hamit Zübeyr, *Tarihi*, 8. Özdemir, "History of Turkish Archaeology," 92, 110–111. Barak Aharon Salmoni, "Pedagogies of Patriotism: Teaching Socio-Political Community in Twentieth-Century Turkish and Egyptian Education" (Ph.D. diss., Harvard University, 2002), 797, 798.
33. 29 July 1937, 867.41/90, RG59, NA.
34. Özdemir, "History of Turkish Archaeology," 118.
35. December 1937, *La Turquie Kemaliste*, no. 21–22 (Ankara), 7. 30 September 1937, *Ankara*.
36. 7 October 1937, 867.927, RG59, NA. 30 September 1937, *Ankara*.
37. 29 September 1937, box 1, no. 79, Carl Blegen papers, University of Cincinnati, Cincinnati, Ohio.
38. Turgut Özal, *Turkey in Europe and Europe in Turkey*, rev. ed. (Nicosia, 1991), 6–11, 20–33, 38–39, 46–47, 270–271. Apparently, officials in the Foreign Ministry wrote the book, but Özal "reviewed it closely." Karpat, *The Politicization of Islam*, 472.
39. *Türk Tarih Kongresi, 1932* [Turkish History Conference] (Istanbul, 1932), 11; Hasan Cemil Çambel, "Atatürk ve Tarih" [Atatürk and History], *Belleten Türk Tarih Kurumu* 13 (1939): 71–72.
40. Philip Khoury, *Syria and the French Mandate: The Politics of Arab Nationalism, 1920–1945* (Princeton, 1987), 513.
41. 1 December 1938, *Ankara*.
42. Özdemir, "History of Turkish Archaeology," 128.
43. Agatha Christie Mallowan, *Come Tell Me How You Live* (New York, 1946), 185–191.
44. 12 May 1923, 890d.927/4, RG59, NA. 29 January, 9 February, 1 March 1927, 890d.927/11, RG59, NA.
45. 19 March 1936, Wright to Wilson, 2 April 1936, Wilson to Wright, DOCF, 1936, OI Archives, UC.
46. 1931, Dodge to Francis Henry Taylor, Antioch Excavation, General Correspondence, 1931–1932, Worcester Museum of Fine Arts, Worcester, MA (WMFA).
47. 11 December 1936, Minutes, Committee for the Excavation of Antioch and Vicinity (CEAV), DAA, PU. 7 November 1938, Morey to Taylor, folder: Antioch, lists, etc., Antioch Expedition, General Correspondence, 1931–1932, WMFA.

48. 890d.927/24, RG59, NA.
49. 14 April 1936, 890d.927/24, RG59, NA. 17 April 1936, 890d.927/25, RG59, NA. 9 September 1936, 890d.927/36, RG 59, NA.
50. May, 6 June, 6 July, 1936, Marriner to SS, 890d.927/38/39, RG59, NA.
51. Folder 245, University of Chicago/Oriental Institute, box 18, RG1.1, RFA, RAC.
52. 26 February 1937, 892.7, RG84, TuPF, 1937, NA.
53. 7 October 1937, Hitti to Morey, Antioch, Miscellaneous Correspondence, 1937, DAA, PU.
54. Bisbee, *The New Turks*, 64. Seda Altug, "Antioch between Colonial and National Dominations: The Sanjak of Alexandretta under the French Mandate (1920–1939)," 4–5, paper presented at the Middle East Studies Conference, 6–9 November 2003, Anchorage, AK. Erik J. Zurcher, *Turkey: A Modern History*, 3d ed. (New York, 2004), 180.
55. Khoury, *Syria and the French Mandate*, 509–510. Andrew Mango, *Atatürk* (Woodstock, NY, 1999), 520.
56. Khoury, *Syria and the French Mandate*, 513.
57. 27 April 1938, Dodge to Campbell, Antioch: Miscellaneous Correspondence, 1938, CEAV, DAA, PU. 6 June 1938, Campbell to Morey, Antioch: Miscellaneous Correspondence, 1938, CEAV, DAA, PU.
58. 10 June 1938, Morey to Hull, CEAV, DAA, PU. The Oriental Institute's concession would end in September 1941 and Princeton's in January 1943. 23 June 1939, 890d.927/115, RG59, NA.
59. 10 January 1939, Antioch: Mosaics, Miscellaneous Notes and Lists, CEAV, DAA, PU.
60. 12 April 1939, Campbell to Prof. Richard Stillwell, Antioch, Correspondence, 1939, CEAV, DAA, PU. FO 371/13822O E2259/362/44, 28 February 1939, FO 371/23280, Public Record Office, Richmond (PRO); 7 April 1924, Woolley to Director British Museum, CE32/320–351, British Museum Archives, London.
61. September 1939, Campbell to Morey, Antioch: Mosaics, Miscellaneous Notes and Lists, CEAV, DAA, PU.
62. Ibid.
63. Ibid. 18.149.130.1939, Prime Ministerial Archive, Ankara.
64. Antioch: Mosaics, Miscellaneous Notes and Lists, CEAV, DAA, PU.
65. Interview with Prof. Tahsin Özgüç, 4 December 1999, Ankara. Tahsin Özgüç, "Ataturk et l'Archeologie," in *Mémorial Atatürk: Études d'archeologie et de philologie anatoliennes* (Paris, 1982), 8. Özdemir, "History of Turkish Archaeology," 20.

## 4. Egypt Awakening

1. Reid, *Whose Pharaohs?*, 218.
2. Annual Report of the Service des Antiquités (Cairo, 1907), 7.
3. Ibid. (1913), 192; (1914), 13, 19.
4. 2 March 1934, Peterson to Dr. Ruthven, box 5, Institute of Archaeological Research, Kelsey Museum, BL, UM, AA. 5 March 1935, Peterson to Lacau, box 5, Enoch Peterson papers, Kelsey Museum, BL, UM, AA.

5. "Reisner autobiography," 3, George A. Reisner (GAR) papers, Boston Museum of Fine Arts (BMFA).

6. Ibid, 7.

7. 4 November 1908, 23 July 1912, Reisner to Lane, GAR papers, microfilm, American Archives of Art (AAA).

8. 27 January 1914, Frederic A. Whiting to H. W. Kent (Metropolitan), RG1 Director's Office Files, Whiting, Cleveland Museum of Art Archive (CMA). "Chronology of Reisner's Career" (1937), 7, GAR papers, BMFA. 26 November 1915, Reisner to BMFA, GAR papers, microfilm, AAA.

9. 30 November 1919, Breasted to Frances Breasted, Reconnaissance Trip to the Near East, 1919–1920, JHB papers, OI Archives, UC. 2 November 1919, Breasted to "Dearest Ones," Reconnaissance Trip, JHB papers, OI Archives. Breasted was referring to the vicious race riot that took place in his hometown the previous summer.

10. 15 April 1919, Clarence S. Fisher to Gordon, Curatorial Files: Egypt, 1914–1919, Egyptian Section—Clarence Fisher, University Museum Archive (UMA), University of Pennsylvania, Philadelphia (UP).

11. October 1924, JHB to Morrow, Mo-Mz, DOCF, 1924, OI Archives, UC.

12. 27 December 1921, Ernest S. Thomas to JB, DOCF, 1921, OI Archives, UC.

13. 10 April 1919, 15 July 1920, Howard Carter to Whiting and 2 December 1920, Kent to Whiting, Director's Files, box 33, 445 a-e, Howard Carter, CMA. T. G. H. James, *Howard Carter: The Path to Tutankhamun* (London, 1992), 188–189, 198–199.

14. 11 February 1924, Robinson to Lythgoe, "Antiquities Law, 1922–1923," Department of Egyptian Art, MMOA.

15. On Carter's dealing, see also James, *Howard Carter*, 152–157.

16. 2 February 1924, JB to J. D. Rockefeller Jr., Hale papers, roll 5 microfilm, California Institute of Technology, Pasadena.

17. 16 September 1923, JB to Hale, Hale papers.

18. Guy Brunton, "Howard Carter Obituary," *Service des Antiquités* (Cairo, 1939), 39:52–53.

19. 12 July 1927, Lacau to Director, Egypt Exploration Society Correspondence, Toledo Museum of Art, Toledo, Ohio.

20. 19 February 1924, *Egyptian Mail.*

21. 24 February 1924, CB to E. H. Dennis, Charles Breasted Material Relating to the Tomb of Tutankhamun, Tomb Dispute, November 1923–March 1924, JHB papers, OI Archives, UC. See also 7 March 1924, *Chicago Daily News*, 15 March 1923, *Boston Transcript.*

22. 14 February 1924, S. Craig to SS, RG59, 883.927, NA.

23. 3 April 1924, Winlock to Carter, folder: Tutankhamun, Carter files, Department of Egyptian Art (DEA), MMOA.

24. 19 February 1924, *Nizam.* 23 February 1924, *Al-Balagh.* 22 February 1924, *Muqattam.*

25. Beth Baron, *Egypt as a Woman: Nationalism, Gender, and Politics* (Berkeley and Los Angeles, 2005), 67–68. A working model of the statue of Saʿd Zaghlul is on display at the recently renovated Mahmoud Mukhtar museum in Gezira, Cairo. For details of Mukhtar's career, see Gershoni and Jankowski, *Commemorating the Nation*, 1–140.

26. Baron, *Egypt as a Woman*, 64, 70, 199.
27. Salmoni, "Pedagogies of Patriotism," 823–824, 863, 891, 1111.
28. M. M. Badawi, *A Critical Introduction to Modern Arabic Poetry* (New York, 1975), 40, 109; Arafan Shaheed, "Shawqi wa Misr Al-Fira'uniyyah" [Shawqi and Pharaonic Egypt], *Fusul* 3 (Cairo, 1983): 322–358. 1 February 1923, *Al-Muqtataf*, 62, no. 2. Louis Awad, *The Literature of Ideas in Egypt* (Atlanta, 1986), 149; Salama Musa, *The Education of Salama Musa* (Leiden, 1961), 139. Baron, *Egypt as a Woman*, 30, 59–60.
29. 27 November 1929, *Al-Siyasa al-Usbu'iah*. David Semah, *Four Egyptian Literary Critics* (Leiden, 1974), 78–79.
30. 24 November 1924, Alan Gardiner to Prime Minister, Foreign Office (FO) 371/10061, PRO, Kew.
31. Wafik Raouf, *Nouveau regard sur le nationalisme Arabe: Ba'th et Nasserism (Paris, 1984)*, 127. James Jankowski, *Egypt's Young Rebels* (Stanford, 1975), 44–45; Michael Wood, "The Use of the Pharaonic Past in Modern Egyptian Nationalism," *Journal of the American Research Center in Egypt (JARCE)* 35: 179–196. Gershoni and Jankowski, *Commemorating the Nation*, 71.
32. Sayyid Qutb later became a radical Islamist, whom Nasser executed in 1966. Naguib Mahfouz, *Thebes at War*, trans. Humphrey Davies (Cairo, 2003), vi, viii. Tawfik al-Hakim, *Return of the Spirit*, trans. William M. Hutchins (Washington, DC, 1990), 179, 272. Taha Husayn, *The Future of Culture in Egypt*, trans. Sidney Glazer (Washington, DC, 1954), 2.
33. Ralph M. Coury, "The Politics of the Funereal: The Tomb of Sa'd Zaghlul," *JARCE* 29 (1992): 191–200.
34. 5 September 1933, *Al-Balagh;* Semah, *Four Egyptian Literary Critics*, 80; Marcel Colombe, *L'Évolution de l'Égypte, 1924–1950* (Paris, 1951), 125. Salmoni, "Pedagogies of Patriotism," 1004.
35. 1 February 1924, FO 371/10055, PRO.
36. Guy Brunton, "Obituary of George A. Reisner," *Service des Antiquités* 41 (1942): 11–15. 22 November 1922, GAR papers, microfilm, AAA.
37. 9 October 1924, Reisner to Fairbanks, GAR papers, AAA.
38. 9 October 1924, Reisner to Hawes, GAR papers, AAA.
39. 22 November 1922, GAR papers, AAA.
40. 19 June 1919, Reisner to Fairbanks; 21 May 1919, Memorandum, 3, GAR papers, AAA.
41. 23 February 1924, Howell to SS, Egypt Internal Affairs, 1920–1929, RG59, 883.927/36, NA.
42. 5 April 1924, Howell to SS, RG59, 883.927/39, NA.
43. 22 March 1924, JB to Hale, Folder N, Material Relating to the Tomb of Tutankhamun, JHB papers, OI Archives, UC.
44. 3 June 1924, JB to Frances, Source Material for *Pioneer to the Past*, JHB papers, OI Archives, UC. 19 August 1923, JB to CB Source Material for *Pioneer to the Past*, JHB papers, OI Archives, UC.
45. October 1924, 13 January 1925, JB to CB, Breasted, Charles, JHB papers, OI Archives, UC. 13 January 1925, JB to CB, Source Material for *Pioneer to the Past*, JHB papers, OI Archives, UC.
46. 7 November 1929, JB to CB, Source Material for *Pioneer to the Past*, 1929, JHB

papers, OI Archives, UC. 11 October 1924, JB to Morrow, Mo-Mz, DOCF, 1924, OI Archives, UC.

47. 22 March 1924, JB to Hale, Folder N, "Material Relating to the Tomb of Tutankhamun," JHB papers, OI Archives, UC.
48. JB to Herrick, "Material," JHB papers, OI Archives, UC.
49. James, *Howard Carter*, 332.
50. Ibid. 9 October 1924, Reisner to Hawes, AAA; 30 January 1925, Gaillard to Foreign Minister, E90, Égypte, Afrique 1918–1940, MFA Archives, Quai d'Orsay, Paris.
51. James, *Howard Carter*, 362. 7 January 1926, *Le Reveil* [Cairo].
52. James, *Howard Carter*, 388–389. Items returned included 1 greeny blue glass headrest [worth several thousand £ sterling], 1 large shawabbi, blue faience, 1 pair shawabbi, lapis colored (6½ in. high), 1 small libation vase, blue faience, 1 small sepulchral dummy cup, blue faience, 1 ankle amulet, 8 gold-headed nails, 3 gold ornaments from harness, 1 metal tennon (9½ × 2½ in.), 25, 29 November 1939, FO371/23355, PRO. Apparently, Faruq kept these items. The glass headrest was part of his estate and was finally returned to the Egyptian Museum in 1960. For a picture of the headrest, see Zahi Hawass, *Tutankhamun and the Golden Age of the Pharoahs* (Washington, DC, 2005), 236–237.
53. 25 September 1919, JB to CB, August–October 1919, Reconnaissance Trip to Near East, 1919–1920, JHB papers, OI Archives, UC.
54. 8 April 1920, 25 March, 4 April 1921, box 1, Leslie Hall Diaries, Oregon Historical Society, Portland (OHS). 20 December 1922, Hall to Pop, box 1, Leslie Hall papers, OHS.
55. 15 December 1921, FO371, E7891/7891/16, PRO.
56. 27 October 1928, E90, Égypte, Afrique, 1918–1940, MFA, Quai d'Orsay, Paris.
57. 19 April 1923, E90, Égytpe MFA; 3 October 1918, 21 April 1922, F/17/13604, MPI, NA. 15 May 1923, F/17/17242, MPI. 6 May 1923, Foucart to Minister, F/17/13604, MPI, Archives National, Paris.
58. 29 November 1922, Gordon to Fisher, C. S. Fisher Correspondence, 1922–1923, Egyptian Section—Clarence Fisher, UMA.
59. Alpha Correspondence, Chiha, Youssef Bey, box 4, Director's Office—G. B. Gordon, UMA.
60. 27 December 1922, Gordon to Fisher, C. S. Fisher Correspondence, 1922–1923, Egyptian Section—Clarence Fisher, UMA.
61. 5 November 1923, ibid.
62. 16 January 1923, Robert De Forest to Lythgoe, 26 January 1923, Hughes to De Forest, Antiquities Law, 1922–1923, Department of Egyptian Art (DEA), MMOA.
63. 25 February 1924, JB to Alan Gardiner, Folder G, "Material Relating to the Tomb of Tutankhamun," JHB papers, OI Archives, UC.
64. 6 March 1924, JB to Frances, Source material for *Pioneer to the Past*, 1924, JHB papers, OI Archives, UC.
65. 31 March 1923, Robinson to Hughes, RG59, 883.927/19; 4 April 1923, Phillips to Magoffin, RG59, 883.927/8, NA.
66. 7 June 1923, Marie N. Buckman to Godwin, Egypt Exploration Society Correspondence, Toledo Museum of Art, Ohio.

67. 1 February 1924, Reisner to Fairbanks, GAR papers, AAA; 2 May 1924, Griffith to Hall, Correspondence of E. L. Griffith (1920–1923), Egypt Exploration Society Archive, London.
68. 23 January 1924, Lythgoe to Robinson, RG59, 883.927/34, NA.
69. 13 February 1924, JB to Lacau, folder E, JHB papers, OI Archives, UC. 27 February 1924, JB to Sa'd Zaghlul, folder G, JHB papers, OI Archives, UC. 29 May 1924, RG59, 883.927/43, NA.
70. 23 February 1925, Lacau to Board of Trustees, Antiquities Law, 1925, DEA, MMOA.
71. 16 May 1925, folder M, 19 May 1925, folder B, JB to Reisner, JHB papers, OI Archives, UC. 18 May 1925, Root to Robinson, RG59, 883.927/56. 24 December 1925, Memorandum of Conversation, RG59, 883.927/87, NA.
72. 6 March 1926, Reisner to Howell, RG84, Egyptian Post Files (EPF), 1926, 892.7, NA.
73. 30 March 1925, Lythgoe to Robinson, 14 November 1925, Winlock to Lythgoe, Antiquities Law, 1925, DEA, MMOA. 26 April 1937, Lampson to Eden, FO371/20916/137118, PRO.
74. 26 May 1926, Howell to SS, RG59, 883.927/120. 3 August 1926, RG84, EPF, 1926, 892.7, NA. 23 April 1926, Winlock to Harkness, 14 May 1926, Howell to Winlock, 25, 30 May 1926, Winlock to Lythgoe, 26 May 1926, Aide-Mémoire, Antiquities Law, 1926–1927, DEA, MMOA.

## 5. Housing Egypt's Treasures

1. 4 February 1934, Engelbach to JB, Egypt, Government of, DOCF, 1934, OI Archives, UC.
2. 17 September 1923, *Times of Mesopotamia*. 23 February 1925, JB to Hale, Hale papers.
3. See also Jeffrey Abt, "Toward a Historian's Laboratory: The Breasted-Rockefeller Museum Projects in Egypt, Palestine and America," *JARCE* 33 (1996): 174–175. 28 October 1924, John D. Rockefeller Jr. to Fosdick, folder 258, Cairo Museum, Cultural Interests series, RG2, Family, RAC. February 1925, McCormick to John D. Rockefeller Jr., ibid.
4. Abt, "Toward a Historian's Laboratory," 175.
5. For details, see Abt, "Toward a Historian's Laboratory," 176.
6. 18 February 1925, Selby minutes, FO371/10897, J88/88/16, 19 May 1925, FO371/10897, J1411/88/16, PRO. 4 May 1925, JB to Hale, Hale papers.
7. 20 April 1925, Lythgoe to Osborn, Archaeology Law, 1925, DEA, MMOA.
8. 8 May 1925, Hale to JB, Hale papers.
9. 2 May 1925, JB to Kenyon, British Museum File, folder B, DOCF, 1925, OI Archives, UC.
10. 27 June 1925, JB to Kenyon, British Museum File, folder B, DOCF, 1925, OI Archives, UC. 23 June 1925, JB to Fosdick, Correspondence, Curtis, Fosdick and Belknap, Material Related to the Cairo Museum Project, JHB papers, OI Archives, UC.
11. June 1925, Personal Diary, JHB papers, OI Archives, UC.
12. 5 March 1925, Tottenham to JB, Correspondence: T, Museum Project, JHB

papers, OI Archives, UC. 26 May 1925, JB to Bosworth, Correspondence: Welles Bosworth, Museum Project, JHB papers, OI Archives, UC. 26 June 1925, Personal Diary, JHB papers, OI Archives, UC. A. J. P. Taylor, *English History, 1914–1945* (New York, 1965), 216, 222. 26 June 1925, Personal Diary, JHB papers, OI Archives, UC.

13. 13 July 1925, Murray to JB, Correspondence: G, Museum Project, JHB papers, OI Archives, UC.

14. 30 November 1925, Rockefeller to JB, Correspondence: Rockefeller, 1925, Museum Project, JHB papers, OI Archives, UC.

15. 17 November 1925, JB to Frances, Source Material for *Pioneer to the Past*, JHB papers, OI Archives. 23 February 1926, JB to Hale, Hale papers.

16. January 1926, Personal Diary, JHB papers, OI Archives, UC.

17. 20 July 1925, JB to Hale, Hale papers.

18. John D. Rockefeller Jr. to King Fuad, folder 258, box 18, Cairo Museum, Cultural Interests series, RG2, Family, RAC. January 1926, Personal Diary, JHB papers, OI Archives, UC.

19. 13 January 1926, JB to Frances, Source Material for *Pioneer to the Past*, 1926, JHB papers, OI Archives, UC.

20. 10 March 1926, Belknap Report, Museum Project, JHB papers, OI Archives, UC. 10 February 1926, Bosworth to John D. Rockefeller Jr., folder 258, box 25, Cairo Museum, Cultural Interests series, RG2, Family, RAC.

21. 15 February 1926, *Al-Ahram*.

22. 26 February 1926, CB to JB, Museum Project, JHB papers, OI Archives, UC.

23. 19 February 1926, *New York Times*.

24. 8 February 1926, Firth to JB, Museum Project, JHB papers, OI Archives, UC.

25. 10 February 1926, JB to Firth, Museum Project, JHB papers, OI Archives, UC.

26. 17 March 1926, Firth to JB, Museum Project, JHB papers, OI Archives, UC.

27. Reisner to Fairbanks, Director's Correspondence, 1901–1954, BMFA, microfilm 2477, 2478, AAA.

28. 15 March 1926, Howell to SS, 883.927/107, RG59, NA. 2 March 1926, JB to Howell, Museum Project, JHB papers, OI Archives, UC.

29. 20 February, 13 March 1926, Gaillard to Minister of Foreign Affairs, E90, Égypte, Afrique 1918–1940, MFA Archive, Quai d'Orsay, Paris.

30. 16 May 1926, George Merzbach Bey to JB, Museum Project, JHB papers, OI Archives, UC; 19 March 1926, Lacau to Gaillard, N174, Cairo Embassy, Service des Antiquités, Archives Diplomatiques Nantes.

31. 11 April 1926, *New York World*. 14 April, 4 May 1926, *New York Sun*.

32. 16 February 1926, Lythgoe to Winlock, Antiquities Law, 1926–1927, DEA, MMOA.

33. 8 February 1926, JB to Fosdick, Correspondence: Curtis, Fosdick and Belknap, 1926, Museum Project, JHB papers, OI Archives, UC. 23 February 1926, JB to Mrs. Rockefeller, folder: Tutankhamun: Important Letters and Notes, JHB papers, OI Archives, UC. 4 March 1926, JB to John D. Rockefeller Jr., folder 258, box 25, Cairo Museum, Cultural Interests series, RG2, Family, RAC. 10 March 1926, Belknap report, Correspondence, Curtis, Fosdick and Belknap, Museum Project, JHB papers, OI Archives, UC. 20 February 1926, JB to Herrick, Museum Project, JHB papers, OI Archives, UC.

34. 24 March 1926, JB to John D. Rockefeller Jr., Rockefeller Correspondence, JHB papers, OI Archives, UC.
35. Ibid.
36. 6 April 1926, JB to Winlock, Antiquities Law, 1926–1927, DEA, MMOA. 1 May 1926, "Government Communique on Rockefeller Gift to Egypt," folder 258, box 25, Cairo Museum, Cultural Interests series, RG2, Family, RAC; Abt, "Toward a Historian's Laboratory," 187–188.
37. 23 September 1926, Fosdick to JB, Correspondence, Curtis, Fosdick and Belknap, 1926, Museum Project, JHB papers, OI Archives, UC. 5 October 1926, JB to Fosdick, Correspondence, Curtis, Fosdick and Belknap, 1926, Museum Project, JHB papers, OI Archives, UC.
38. 6 March 1927, JB to Fosdick, Museum Project, JHB papers, OI Archives, UC. 12 May 1927, Report on Cairo Museum Project, JHB papers, OI Archives, UC.
39. 1 March 1928, JB to Hale, Hale papers.
40. 2 April 1933, Personal Diary, JHB papers, OI Archives, UC; 2 October 1934, JB to Hale, Hale papers.
41. 21 October 1926, JB to Lucy Aldrich, Correspondence, folder A: Museum Project, JHB papers, OI Archives, UC. 1 September 1921, JB to Hale, Hale papers.
42. 14 January 1927, JB to Fosdick, Correspondence, Curtis, Fosdick and Belknap, 1927, 19 January 1926, JB to CB, Museum Project, JHB papers, OI Archives, UC. 1 March 1926, Winlock to Lythgoe, Museum Project, JHB papers, OI Archives, UC.
43. 19 January 1927, JB to CB, Source Material for *Pioneer to the Past*, JHB papers, OI Archives, UC. 11 May 1927, JB to Bosworth, Correspondence, Welles Bosworth, 1927, Museum Project, JHB papers, OI Archives, UC.
44. 9 February 1927, Fosdick to JB, Correspondence, Curtis, Fosdick and Belknap, 1927, Museum Project, JHB papers, OI Archives, UC. 3 August 1927, Fosdick to Thomas, folder 263, box 25, Jerusalem Museum, Cultural Interests series, RG2, Family, RAC. Abt, "Toward a Historian's Laboratory," 188–190.
45. 6 February 1929, Travel Records, folder 378, box 42, John D. Rockefeller Jr., Personal Papers, OMR, RG2, RAC. February 1929, Personal Diary, JHB papers, OI Archives, UC.
46. 19 January 1929, Travel Records, folder 378, box 42, John D. Rockefeller Jr., Personal Papers, OMR, RG2, RAC.
47. 6 March 1952, CB to John D. Rockefeller Jr., folder 362, box 108B75, Dr. James Breasted files, Friends and Services series, OMR, RG2, RAC.
48. For continuing interest, see December 1996, *Al-Ahram* (English Weekly).
49. FO371/13139/1928, 17 June 1929, FO371/13878, 18 October 1929, E90, Égypte, Afrique 1918–1940, MFA, Quai d'Orsay, Paris.
50. 23 October, 7 December 1923, 24 September 1925, 25 February 1928, E90, Égypte, MFA Archive, Paris; 20 May 1928, Peterson to Sanders, box 5, Correspondence, 1928, Institute for Archaeological Research, Kelsey Museum, BL, UM, AA.
51. 12 October 1928, 6 July 1929, Commission de l'Institut de Caire, F/17/13602, MPI, Archives National, Paris. 5 October 1929, Reisner to Mortland, GAR

papers, BMFA. 21 May 1932, Peterson to Campbell Bonner, Enoch Peterson Papers, box 1, Kelsey Museum, BL, UM, AA.

52. Comité de Conservation des Monuments de l'Art Arabe, Exercice 1925–1926, *Procès-verbaux des séances* (Cairo, 1933), 58–62.

53. 25 November 1932, Égypte 128, Afrique, 1928–1940, MFA, Paris.

54. 5 April 1932, Jardine to SS, 883.927/147, RG59, NA.

55. Donald Malcolm Reid, "Indigenous Archaeology: The Decolonization of a Profession?" *Journal of the American Oriental Society* 105, no. 2 (1985): 237, 241, 246. 21 April 1924, Foucart to Director of Public Instruction, F/17/13604, MPI, Archives National, Paris.

56. 25 November 1932, Égypte 128, Afrique, 1928–1940, MFA, Paris.

57. 14, 17 March 1936, *Al-Balagh*. 21 March 1936, *Rose El-Youssef*. 30 March 1936, *Al-Ahram*.

58. FO371/19094/1935, PRO. 25 May, 18, 29 July 1935, Secretary of French Ambassador to Director of Public Instruction, F/17/17241, MPI, Archives National, Paris. November 1935, Jogruet to Minister of Public Instruction, F/17/17241, MPI, Archives National, Paris. 25 March 1932, Reisner to Jardine, 883.927/147, RG59, NA.

59. 27 March, 6, 24 April, 7, 15, 28 May, 1936, *Al-Balagh*. 9 June 1936, *Al-Siyasa*.

60. 27 March, 10 April, 18 May, 1936, E128, Égypte, MFA, Paris.

61. 8 June 1936, E128, Égypte, MFA, Paris.

62. Ibid. P. J. Vatikiotis, *The Modern History of Egypt*, Asia-Africa series (New York, 1969), 288. 10 June 1936, E128, Egypte, MFA, Paris. 9 June 1936, *Rose El-Youssef*.

63. Donald Reid, "Imperialism, Nationalism and Archaeology in Modern Egypt," talk given at University of Chicago, 24 January 1997. 10 March 1937, Égypte 128, MFA, Paris. 24 November 1936, Jogruet to Director of Public Instruction, F/17/17241, MPI, Archives National, Paris.

64. 12 June 1936, Bert Fish to SS, 883.927/162, RG59, NA. 3 June 1998, interview with T. G. H. James, London.

65. 25 May, 6 December 1938, Reisner to Harold, GAR papers, BMFA.

66. 1 March 1937, Egypte 128, MFA, Paris. 7 December 1937, Lansing to Fish, 892.7, EPF, 1937, RG84, NA. 20 November 1937, Murray to John Wilson, 883.927/166, 19 January 1938, 883.927/170, RG59, NA.

67. 15 June 1939, FO371/23354, 21 July 1939, Lampson to Lord Halifax, FO371/23355, PRO. 29 July 1944, Tuck to SS, EPF, 1944, 892.7, RG84, NA. A recent Egyptian government publication states that a major reason for his dismissal was his refusal to return to the king certain antiquities in the museum, which Faruq claimed belonged to his family. "Selim Hassan: Egyptian Civilization Lover," *Egypt* 34 (Winter 2004): 16.

68. 12 March 1941, Embassy of France in Cairo, 174, MFA, Vichy, Archives Diplomatiques Nantes, 3 August 1939, FO371/23355, PRO.

69. 15 March 1941, Francis Allen to G. H. Edgell, GAR papers, AAA.

70. 6 April 1937, 2 June 1938, Drioton to Peterson, Institute of Archaeological Research, box 2, Kelsey Museum, BL, UM, AA. 6 February 1939, Drioton to Peterson, Enoch Peterson papers, box 5, Kelsey Museum, BL, UM, AA. 26 August 1937, Gueraud to Peterson, Institute of Archaeological Research,

box 5, Kelsey Museum, BL, UM, AA. 9 February 1946, John Wilson to Henri Frankfort, Henri Frankfort File, DOCF, 1946, OI Archives, UC.
71. *Annales* 62 (Cairo, 1977); 63 (Cairo, 1979).

## 6. France's Closed Door

1. Iran: Persepolis, Persepolis Correspondence, P3-1 Persepolis Miscellaneous, OI, UC. October 1897, F/17/17250, MPI, Archives National, Paris.
2. Davood Karimlu, ed., *Taraj-i mirat-i milli*, vol. 2, *Hiyat-i faransavi, 1341–1354* [Plunder of the National Heritage, vol. 2, The French Mission, 1923-1935], Iran and Imperialism 3 (Tehran: Center for Documents and Diplomatic History, 2001), 59, 60, 63, 65. 29 May 1923, Perse 66, Asie 1918-1940, MFA, Paris. 9 November 1923, F/17/17247, MPI, Archives National, Paris.
3. 6 May 1925, F/17/17247, MPI, Archives National, Paris. 29 November 1916, Vosuq ad-Dauleh to Lecomte, 1 December 1916, Lecomte to Briand, F/17/17245, MPI, Archives National, Paris.
4. *Asr-i Pahlavi* [The Pahlavi Period] (Tehran, 1967), 279.
5. Mostofa Vaziri, *Iran as Imagined Nation: The Construction of National Identity* (New York, 1993), 106-107. 23 January 1925, *Iran.* Ali Asghar Hikmat, *Siy khaterat az asr-i farkhandeh Pahlavi* [Thirty Years of Memories from the Golden Age of the Pahlavis] (Tehran, 1976), 141.
6. Firoozeh Kashani-Sabet, *Frontier Fictions: Shaping the Iranian Nation, 1804–1946* (Princeton, 1999), 18, 45, 200. Ali M. Ansari, *Modern Iran since 1921: The Pahlavis and After* (New York, 2003), 15. Juan Cole, "Marking Boundaries, Marking Time: The Iranian Past and the Construction of the Self by Qajar Thinkers," *Iranian Studies* 39, nos. 1-2 (Winter–Spring 1996): 38-41. Ironically, some members of the ruling dynasty appear to have adopted, at least superficially, this glorification of ancient Iran, giving their sons the names of heroes of old such as Farhad and Jamshid. The founder of the dynasty, Aga Muhammad Shah, an avid reader of Ferdowsi's *Shahnameh*, wore some of the dress and a crown modeled on those of ancient Iranian rulers at his coronation in 1796. His nephew, Fath Ali Shah, copied the ancient practice of carving reliefs and inscriptions on rock faces. Ali Gheissari, *Iranian Intellectuals in the 20th Century* (Austin, 1998), 19. Abbas Amanat, "The Kayanid Crown and Qajar Reclaiming of Royal Authority," *Iranian Studies* 34, nos. 1-4 (2001): 22. Mohammad Tavakoli-Targhi, *Refashioning Iran: Orientalism, Occidentalism and Historiography* (New York, 2001), 98, 101.
7. Kashani-Sabet, *Frontier Fictions*, 103. Evan Siegel, Review of *Die Politische Offentlichkeit Iranisch-Aserbaidschans wahrend der Konstitutionellen Revolution im Spiegel der Tabriser Zeitung Azarbayjan*, *Iranian Studies* 37, no. 1 (March 2004): 184.
8. Kashani-Sabet, *Frontier Fictions*, 176. Rosita Forbes, *Conflict: Angora to Afghanistan* (New York, 1931), 127. Ansari, *Modern Iran since 1921*, 32. Ardashir was the founder of the Sasanian dynasty.
9. 12 July 1923, Henri Massé, F/17/17278, MPI, Archives National, Paris. Vaziri, *Iran as Imagined Nation*, 156.
10. Seyd Mohammad Taghi Mostafavi, *Talash dar rah-i khidmat be athar-i milli*

*va omid be ayande* [Struggles in the Service of the National Monuments and Hopes for the Future] (Tehran, 1955), 12–13, 36.

11. Karimlu, *Taraj-i mirat-i milli*, vol. 2, 69, 73.

12. Jay Gluck and Noel Silver, eds., *Surveyors of Persian Art: A Documentary Biography of Arthur Upham Pope and Phyllis Ackerman* (Ashiya, Japan, 1996), 84, 122, 154, 162–163, 165, 168–170. 10 October 1925, Copley Amory to State Department, 891.927/22, RG59, NA.

13. Gluck, *Surveyors of Persian Art*, 2, 84–85.

14. Ibid., 84, 93–110.

15. This was clearly a slap at the Qajars, whose origins were Turkish. Gluck, *Surveyors of Persian Art*, 2, 85, 90. M. Reza Ghods, "Iranian Nationalism and Reza Shah," *Middle Eastern Studies* 27, no. 1 (January 1991): 43.

16. 12 March 1925, Murray to State Department, 891.927/4, April 1925, Murray to State Department, 891.927/5, 6 May 1925, Murray to State Department, 891.927/10, RG59, NA.

17. 16 May 1926, Ala to Pope, box 1, General Correspondence, 1926–1929, Personal Correspondence, 1926–1927, Arthur Upham Pope (AUP) papers, New York Public Library, New York City (NYPL). 24 September 1926, Pope to Murray, Box 1, General Correspondence, 1926–1929, Personal Correspondence, 1926–1927, AUP papers, NYPL. Pope has been accused of using these exhibitions to sell his own antiquities and those belonging to various dealers. Oscar White Muscarella, "The Pope and the Bitter Fanatic," in Abbas Alizadeh et al., eds., *The Iranian World: Essays on Iranian Art and Archaeology* (Tehran, 1999), 10–11.

18. 3 May 1925, Murray to State Department, 891.927/8, RG59, NA. 13 May 1925, Murray to State Department, 891.927/13, RG59, NA.

19. 28 May 1925, Murray to State Department, 891.927/14, RG59, NA.

20. 6 May 1925, F/17/17247, MPI, Archives National, Paris.

21. 20 April 1925, F/17/17253, MPI, Archives National, Paris. 1 April 1925, Bozoni to Herriot, F/17/17247, MPI, Archives National, Paris.

22. Rapport de Mission, 1926, F/17/17253, MPI, NA, Paris. 30 November 1929, Wilden to MFA, F/17/17247, MPI, Archives National, Paris. Rapport de Mission, 1931, F/17/17256, MPI, Archives National, Paris.

23. Karimlu, *Taraj-i mirat-i milli*, vol. 2, 160, 164.

24. 6 July 1925, F/17/17245, MPI, Archives National, Paris.

25. 10 November 1925, Pope to Murray, 891.927/26, RG59. 4 June 1926, Pope to Langdon Warner, Box 1, General Correspondence, 1926–1929, Personal Corresp. "V–Z," AUP papers, NYPL. 29 April 1926, Pope to Murray, box 1, General Correspondence, 1926–1929, Personal Correspondence, "Unsorted," AUP papers, NYPL.

26. Karimlu, *Taraj-i mirat-i milli*, vol. 2, 103. 29 September 1926, 891.927/32, RG59, NA. 24 December 1926, Maugras to MFA, F/17/17245, MPI, Archives National, Paris. Talinn Grigor, "Recultivating 'Good Taste': The Early Pahlavi Modernists and Their Society for National Heritage," *Iranian Studies* 37, no. 1 (March 2004): 30, 42.

27. Grigor, "Recultivating 'Good Taste,' " 30, 42.

28. Iran Persepolis, P3-1 Persepolis Miscellaneous, DOCF, OI Archives, UC.

18 October 1927, Ballereau to MFA, F/17/17245, MPI, Archives National, Paris. Mostafavi, *Talash dar rah-i khidmat*, 37.

29. 18 October 1927, Ballereau to MFA, F/17/17245, MPI, Archives National, Paris.

30. 18 January, 18 November 1927, Commission Consultative des Fouilles Archeologiques en Perse, F/17/17250, MPI, Archives National, Paris.

31. 13 December 1928, Wilden to MFA, Perse 66, Asie, 1918–1940, MFA, Paris.

32. 10 June 1929, 891.927/43, RG59, NA. 5 March 1930, Herzfeld to Hart, 891.927/50, RG59, NA.

33. Grigor, "Recultivating 'Good Taste,' " 18, 20, 25.

34. Mohammad Gholi Majd argues that ending the French monopoly worked against Iran's interests by opening the whole country to plundering American expeditions. He does not discuss widespread local pillaging of sites and the loss of all historical records, as well as antiquities, wherever these occurred. *The Great American Plunder of Persia's Antiquities, 1925–1941* (Lanham, MD, 2003), 16, 70.

## 7. Winning Persepolis

1. Mousavi, "Persepolis in Retrospect," 2–4 [Wilson Select Plus database].

2. Ernst Herzfeld, "Rapport sur l'état des ruines de Persepolis et propositions pour leur conservation," in *Archeoliogische Mitteilungen aus Iran*, vol. 1 (reprint, New York, 1966), 18–19, 34, 36.

3. Ibid, 38.

4. 10 October 1929, Herzfeld to Jayne, Alpha Correspondence, Persian Exhibition, 1929–1931 (Pope, Arthur U.), Director's Office, H. H. F. Jayne, UMA, UP.

5. 28 September 1929, Pope to Jayne, Alpha Correspondence, Persian Exhibition, Director's Office, H. H. F. Jayne, UM, UP.

6. 9 September 1929, Williamson to Jayne, 892.7, Tehran Post Files (TPF), RG84, NA.

7. 17 August 1929, Pope to Jayne, Persian Exhibition, 1929–1931 (Pope, Arthur U.), Director's Office, H. H. F. Jayne, UMA, UP.

8. 11 November 1929, Jayne to Herzfeld, Director's Office—Jayne, UMA, UP.

9. 22 August 1930, Jayne to Pope, box 1, General Correspondence, Tepe Hissar, UMA, UP. 23 April 1931, Pope to Myron Smith, Persian Institute, Director's Office, Jayne, UMA, UP. It is instructive to note that the director of the Boston Museum of Fine Arts was attempting to purchase antiquities from Pope while his representative in Egypt, George Reisner, was railing against such purchases there.

10. Ezzatolah O. Negahban, "Fifth International Congress of Iranian Art and Archaeology," *Bastan Chenassi va Honar-e Iran* 1 (Winter 1969): 10.

11. André Godard, "Les récentes fouilles archéologiques," *Athar-e Iran* 8 (1934): 111.

12. 8 October 1929, Pope to Ala, Persian Institute, Director's Office, Jayne, UMA, UP. 9 October 1929, Pope to Jayne, Persian Institute, Director's Office, Jayne, UMA, UP.

13. 26 February, 30 March 1929, Herzfeld to Becker, Herzfeld Papers, N-126, Sackler Gallery, Smithsonian Institution, Washington, DC.
14. 14 December 1929, Williamson to Jayne, Persian Exhibition, 1929–1931, Director's Office, Jayne, UMA, UP.
15. 20 December 1930, Hugh Millard to David Williamson, box 1, General Correspondence, Tepe Hissar, UMA, UP. 11 May 1931, Murray to Hart, 891.927, Persepolis/35, RG59, NA.
16. February 1931, Wulsin to Jayne, Alpha Correspondence, 1929–1940, Director's Office, Jayne, UMA, UP.
17. 19 December 1930, W. R. Castle to James Breasted, 23 December Breasted to Castle, Persepolis: Concession, Iran, Government of, DOCF, 1930, OI Archives, UC.
18. 7 February 1931, Breasted to Herzfeld, Persepolis: Concession, Iran, Government of, DOCF, 1931, OI Archives, UC. 12 December 1931, JB to Hale, 16 January 1933, JB to Hale, Hale papers.
19. 28 November 1930, Wulsin to Jayne, F. Wulsin File, Director's Office, Jayne, UM, UP. 8 November 1930, Mirzayantz to Pope, box 2, General Correspondence, 1930–1934, Personal Correspondence "Mirzayantz," AUP papers, NYPL.
20. 3 November 1927, Pope to Cutler S. Bonesteel, Box 1, General Correspondence, 1926–29, Personal Correspondence, "B," AUP papers, NYPL. 13 August 1926, Pope to Mrs. W. H. Crocker, box 1, General Correspondence, 1926–1929, Personal Papers, 1926–27, "C," AUP papers, NYPL.
21. 14 June 1930, Hart to SS, 891.927/55, RG59, NA.
22. Davood Karimlu, ed., *Taraj-i mirat-i milli*, vol. 4, *Hayathayi almani va amrika'i, 1899–1940* [Plunder of National Heritage, vol. 4, The German and American Missions, 1899–1940] *Iran and Imperialism 5* (Tehran, 2001), 80–85.
23. Keeling 1930–31, Box 2, International Exhibition of Persian Art, AUP papers, NYPL.
24. 14 April 1930, Pope to Taghizadeh, box 2, General Correspondence 1930–1934, Personal Correspondence 1930–1931, AUP papers, NYPL. 13 June 1930, Wulsin to Jayne, Persian Exhibition, Alpha Correspondence, Director's Office, Jayne, UMA, UP.
25. 15 June 1931, Herzfeld to Jayne, General Correspondence, Tepe Hissar, UMA, UP.
26. 29 December 1932, Breasted to Murray, State Department File, U.S., Government of, DOCF, 1932, OI Archives, UC.
27. 9 November 1933, Ala (Minister of Court) to Herzfeld, 891.927, Persepolis/70, RG59, NA.
28. 26 February 1929, Herzfeld to Becker, N-126, Herzfeld papers, Sackler Gallery, Smithsonian Institution, Washington, DC.
29. 30 December 1931, Hart to SS, 891.927/140, RG59, NA.
30. Hikmat, *Siy khaterat az asr-i farkhandeh Pahlavi*, 114. 25 January 1934, 891.927, Persepolis/72, RG59, NA. Ahmad Mahrad, *Die deutsch-persischen Beziehungen von 1918–1933* (Frankfurt, 1974), 320–322. See also Reza Aslan, "The Epic of Iran," *New York Times Book Review* (30 April 2006): 27.
31. 6 December 1933, *Iran-i Bastan*, 9; 30 September 1934, *Iran-i Bastan*, 7; 30 No-

vember 1937, *Journal de Tehran*. Kamyar Abdi, "Nationalism, Politics and the Development of Archaeology in Iran," *American Journal of Archaeology* 105 (2001): 60. Vaziri, *Iran as Imagined Nation*, 195.

32. Kashani-Sabet, *Frontier Fictions*, 186, 199, 200, 201. Abdi, "Nationalism," 56.
33. 8 April 1937, *Journal de Tehran*.
34. 6 April 1936, 27 September 1935, *Journal de Tehran*.
35. 20 March 1938, 17 August 1938, *Journal de Tehran*.
36. Ansari, *Modern Iran since 1921*, 33.
37. 16 May 1931, Wulsin to Jayne, box 1, General Correspondence, Turang Tepe, UMA, UP; 26 November 1932, Richards to Herzfeld, Miscellaneous folder, U.S., Government of, DOCF, 1932, OI Archives, UC.
38. 1 May 1934, JB to CB, Charles Breasted File, Director's Confidential File, 1934, OI Archives, UC.
39. Ibid.
40. 16 May 1934, Murray to Hornibrook, 891.927Persepolis/74, RG59, NA.
41. 26 May 1934, Hornibrook to SS, 891.927Persepolis/81, RG59, NA.
42. 10 July 1934, Breasted to Murray, 891.927Persepolis/87, RG59, NA.
43. Ibid.
44. Ibid. 30 July 1934, JB to CB, Charles Breasted File, Director's Confidential File, 1934, OI Archives, UC.
45. Karimlu, *Taraj-i mirat-i milli*, vol. 2, 61, 91. 10 October 1929, Herzfeld to Jayne, Persian Exhibition, Director's Office, Jayne, UMA, UP.
46. 6 August 1934, Murray to Hornibrook, 891.927Persepolis/104, RG59, NA. 7 August 1934, CB to JB, Charles Breasted File, Director's Confidential File, 1934, OI Archives, UC.
47. 18 August 1934, CB to JB, Charles Breasted File, Director's Confidential File, 1934, OI Archives, UC.
48. 3 September 1934, Hornibrook to SS, 891.927Persepolis/132, RG59, NA.
49. 6 September 1934, State Department File, U.S., Government of, DOCF, 1934, OI Archives, UC. 11 September 1934, 891.927Persepolis/151, RG59, NA.
50. 17 September 1934, Hornibrook to SS, 891.927Persepolis/199, RG59, NA. 9 October 1934, Breasted to Murray, 891.927Persepolis/1891/2, RG59, NA.
51. 17 October 1934, Hornibrook to SS, 891.927Persepolis/231, RG59, NA.
52. 17 November 1934, Expedition, Agreement and Concession File, Iran, Government of, DOCF, 1934, OI Archives, UC.
53. 24 September 1934, Murray to Hornibrook, 891.927Persepolis/176, RG59, NA.
54. 2 October 1934, JB to Hale, Hale papers.
55. 1 February 1935, Murray to Hornibrook, 891.927Persepolis/295, RG59, NA.
56. May 1933, Personal Diary, JHB papers, OI Archives, UC. Emphasis in original.
57. 6 August 1934, Murray to Hornibrook, 891.927Persepolis/104, RG59, NA. 20 July 1934, JB to Murray, 891.927Persepolis/91, RG59, NA. 23 August 1934, CB to Herzfeld, 891.927Persepolis, RG59, NA.
58. 19 October 1934, Hornibrook to Murray, 892.7, TPF, RG84, NA. 8, 10 January 1935, Hornibrook to SS, 891.927Persepolis, RG59, NA. 3 October 1934, Hornibrook to SS, 891.927Persepolis/215, RG59, NA.

59. Grigor, "Recultivating 'Good Taste,' " 36–39.
60. Marzieh Yazdani, ed., *Asnad hayathayi bastan shenasi dar Iran, 1254–1345* [Records on the Archaeological Missions in Iran, 1875–1966] (Tehran, 2001), 193–195. 23 September 1934, Hornibrook to SS, 891.927Persepolis/269, RG59, NA.
61. 23 September 1934, Hornibrook to SS, 891.927Persepolis/269, RG59, NA. Yazdani, *Asnad hayathayi bastan shenasi dar Iran*, 200–202.
62. Karimloo, ed., *Taraj-i mirat-i milli*, vol. 4, 62, 93. Yazdani, *Asnad hayathayi bastan shenasi dar Iran*, 94. Today there is a gallery named for Rabenou in the Israel Museum, Jerusalem. He donated a large part of his collection of Iranian art and antiquities to the museum in the early 1960s and provided funds for the construction of a gallery of Islamic art. 1 March 2004, communication from the museum.
63. 13 September 1934, Murray to Hornibrook, 891.927Persepolis/154, RG59, NA.
64. 27 December 1934, Hornibrook to SS, 891.927Persepolis/292, RG59, NA.
65. 18 January 1935, JB to Hekmat, 891.927Persepolis/288, RG59, NA. 11 February 1935, Hekmat to Hornibrook, Concession, Iran, Government of, DOCF, 1935, OI Archives, UC.
66. 29 January 1935, JB to CB, Chicago, University of, Oriental Institute, Charles Breasted, DOCF, 1935, OI Archives, UC. 1 February 1935, Herzfeld to JB, Chicago, University of, Oriental Institute, Herzfeld, DOCF, 1935, OI Archives, UC.
67. Jack M. Balcer, "Erich Friedrich Schmidt, 13 September 1897–3 October 1964," *Achaemenid History* 7 (1991): 164–165. 28 December 1937, Maugras to Herzfeld, N-131, File B, Personal Correspondence, Herzfeld papers, Sackler Gallery, Smithsonian Institution, Washington, DC. Donald Wilber, *Adventures in the Middle East: Excursions and Incursions* (Princeton, 1986), 50.
68. Balcer, "Erich Friedrich Schmidt," 167. 27 January 1941, Herzfeld to Wilson, "I" folder, DOCF, 1941, OI Archives, UC. 14 December 1946, Herzfeld to Frau Sarre, File B: Personal Correspondence, N-131, Herzfeld papers, Sackler Gallery, Smithsonian Institution, Washington, DC.
69. 11 January 1935, Hornibrook to Murray, DOCF, 1935, OI Archives, UC. 20 February 1935, Hornibrook to SS, 891.927Persepolis, RG59, NA. 10 January 1935, Hornibrook to SS, 891.927Persepolois, RG59, NA.
70. 21 January 1935, Hornibrook to SS, 891.927Persepolis, RG59, NA.
71. 27 August 1934, Murray to JB, State Department, Wallace Murray, U.S., Government of, DOCF, 1934, OI Archives, UC.
72. 7 June 1934, Hornibrook to SS, 891.927Persepolis/86, RG59, NA. Karimlu, *Taraj-i mirat-i milli*, vol. 4, 63.
73. 27 August 1934, Murray to JB, State Department, Wallace Murray, U.S., Government of, DOCF, 1934, OI Archives, UC.
74. 7 September 1934, Murray to Hornibrook, 891.927Persepolis/216, RG59, NA.
75. 14 November 1935, Murray to Hornibrook, 892.7, TPF, RG84, NA. 9 January 1935, Murray to Phillips 891.927Persepolis, RG59, NA. 1 February 1935, Murray to Hornibrook, 891.927Persepolis/295, RG59, NA.

**8. Troubles over Iran**

1. 2 February 1935, Erich Schmidt to CB, Chicago, University of, Oriental Institute, Schmidt, Erich F., DOCF, 1935, OI Archives, UC. 9 March 1935, CB to Erich Schmidt, Iran, Government of, 1935, DOCF, 1935, OI Archives, UC.
2. 14 March 1935, Hornibrook to SS, Concession, Iran, Government of, OI Archives, UC.
3. 3 May 1935, Childs to Murray, 891.927Persepolis/379, RG59, NA. 4 August 1933, JB to Hale, Hale papers.
4. 15 June 1935, Schmidt to CB, Iran, Government of, DOCF, 1935, OI Archives, UC. 7 July 1935, Schmidt to CB, Chicago, University of, Oriental Institute, Schmidt, E. F., DOCF, 1935, OI Archives, UC.
5. 3 May 1935, Childs to Murray, 891.927Persepolis/379, RG59, NA. 21 December 1937, *Journal de Tehran*.
6. 14 June 1935, Childs to SS, 891.927/243, RG59, NA.
7. 18 May 1935, Schmidt to CB, Chicago, University of, Oriental Institute, Schmidt, E. F., DOCF, 1935, OI Archives, UC.
8. 30 May 1935, Childs to SS, 891.927/247, RG59, NA. 18 May 1935, Schmidt to CB, Chicago, University of, Oriental Institute, Schmidt, E. F., DOCF, 1935, OI Archives, UC. 30 June 1935, Hornibrook to Murray, 891.927/253, RG59, NA. 5 July 1935, Schmidt to Foroughi, Iran, Government of, DOCF, 1935, OI Archives, UC.
9. 15 July 1935, CB to Schmidt, Expedition, Iran, Government of, DOCF, 1935, OI Archives, UC.
10. 30 June 1935, Hornibrook to Murray, 891.927/253, RG59, NA.
11. 5 August 1935, Hornibrook to SS, Expedition, Iran, Government of, DOCF, 1935, OI Archives, UC; 22 May 1935, Childs to SS, 891.927/248, RG59, NA, College Park, MD. 8 August 1935, Hornibrook to Murray, 892.7, TPF, RG84, NA.
12. 23 September 1935, *Journal de Tehran*. 3 October 1935, Hornibrook to Murray, 891.927/265, RG59, NA. 31 July 1935, *Journal de Tehran*.
13. 3 October 1935, Hornibrook to SS, 892.7, TPF, RG84, NA. 15 July 1935, Hornibrook to SS, 891.927/255, RG59, NA. 6 November 1935, Hornibrook to SS, 891.927/269, RG59, NA.
14. Breasted, *Pioneer to the Past*, 412–413.
15. 16 January 1933, JB to Hale, Hale papers.
16. 19 September 1935, CB to Schmidt, Iran, Government of, DOCF, 1935, OI Archives, UC. 1 March 1935, JB to John D. Rockefeller Jr., folder 241, box 18, Series 216, Projects, RG2, OMR, RAC. 4 March 1935, Thomas B. Appleget diary, box 4, RG12.1 Diaries, RFA, RAC.
17. 12 August 1935, JB to David Stevens, folder 241, box 18, Series 216, Illinois, Projects, RG2, OMR, RAC. 26 November 1935, John D. Rockefeller Jr. to Breasted, folder 811, box 111, EI subseries, OMR, RG2, Family, RAC.
18. 16 December 1935, Stevens and Wilson Interview, Chicago, folder 243, box 18, University of Chicago — OI, RG1.1, RFA, RCA.
19. 31 January 1936, CB to Murray, U.S., Government of, DOCF, 1936, OI Ar-

chives, UC. 7 February 1936, Murray to Wilson, 891.927Persepolis/406, 5 February 1936, Murray to Phillips, 891.927Persepolis/405, RG59, NA.

20. 15 April 1936, Merriam to SS, 891.927/273, RG59, NA.
21. Karimlu, *Taraj-i mirat-i milli*, vol. 4, 156–157.
22. Ibid. 29 May 1936, Merriam to SS, 891.927/278, RG59, NA. 25 August 1936, Murray to Merriam, 892.7, TPF 1936, RG84, NA.
23. 18 June 1936, Pope to Hekmat, E. F. Schmidt, Misc. Corresp. with AUP, 1936–1939, DOCF, 1936, OI Archives, UC.
24. Donald Wilber, *Riza Shah Pahlavi: The Resurrection and Reconstruction of Iran* (Hicksville, NY, 1975), 179.
25. 20 June 1935, Hekmat to Schmidt, "I" folder, DOCF, 1935, OI Archives, UC. 23 June 1935, Schmidt to Hekmat, "I" folder, DOCF, 1935, OI Archives, UC.
26. 25 June 1936, Merriam to Murray, 891.927Persepolis/422, RG 59, NA.
27. 27 July 1936, Pope to Hekmat, E. F. Schmidt, Misc. Corresp. with AUP, 1936–1939, DOCF, 1936, OI Archives, UC. 25 August 1936, Schmidt to Pope, EFS, Misc. Corresp. with AUP, 1936–1939, DOCF, 1936, OI Archives, UC.
28. 15 November 1936, Schmidt to Howard Matthews (Executive Secretary, Oriental Institute), Iran, Government of, DOCF, 1936, OI Archives, UC.
29. Ibid. 2 December 1936, Wilson to Schmidt, E. F. Schmidt File, DOCF, 1936, OI Archives, UC. 2 December 1936, Memo of Conversation, Murray and Schmidt, 891.927Persepolis/426, RG59, NA.
30. 7 December 1936, Murray to Wilson, 10 December 1936, Wilson to Murray, U.S., Government of, DOCF, 1936, OI Archives, UC.
31. 1 October 1936, Merriam to Murray, 891.927/286, RG59, NA.
32. 14 December 1936, Murray to Merriam, 892.7, TPF 1936, RG84, NA.
33. 31 March 1937, Schmidt to Wilson, E. F. Schmidt File, DOCF, 1937, OI Archives, UC.
34. Ibid.
35. Ibid. 30 April 1937, Wilson to Schmidt, E. F. Schmidt File, DOCF, 1937, OI Archives, UC.
36. 5 April 1937, Schmidt to Hekmat, Persepolis Correspondence, Department of Antiquities, File PS-4, E. F. Schmidt File, DOCF, 1937, OI Archives, UC. May 1937, Hekmat to Schmidt, 20 May 1937, Schmidt to Hekmat, Persepolis Correspondence, Department of Antiquities, File PS-4, E. F. Schmidt File, DOCF, 1937, OI Archives, UC. 6 June 1937, Schmidt to Hekmat, Persepolis Correspondence, Department of Antiquities, File PS-4, E. F. Schmidt File, DOCF, 1937, OI Archives, UC.
37. 2 June 1937, Murray to SS, 891.927Persepolis/459, RG59, NA.
38. 15 December 1937, Schmidt to Wilson, E. F. Schmidt File, DOCF, 1937, OI Archives, UC. 3 February 1938, Schmidt to Pope, Misc. Corresp. with AUP, 1936–1939, E. F. Schmidt File, DOCF, 1938, OI Archives, UC.
39. 26 April 1935, Childs to SS, 891.402/18, RG59, NA.
40. 26 March 1932, Wadsworth to SS, 891.927/142, 3 May 1933, 891.4061/4, RG59, NA. Hikmat, *Siy khaterat az asr-i farkhandeh Pahlavi*, 57.
41. Grigor, "Recultivating 'Good Taste,'" 41.
42. Tir [July] 1939, *Iran Imruz* [Iran Today].
43. 3 February 1936, Pope to Schmidt, Misc. Corresp. with AUP, 1936–1939, E. F.

Schmidt File, DOCF, 1936, OI Archives, UC. 16 December 1937, Pope to Schmidt, Misc. Correspondence with AUP, 1936–1939, E. F. Schmidt File, DOCF, 1936, OI Archives, UC. 20 December 1937, Pope to Donald Wilber, box 4, General Correspondence, 1937–1951, Personal Correspondence, 1937, OI Archives, UC.

44. 30 August 1937, Pope to Byron, box 3, 25 August 1937, Pope to Stein, box 4, AUP papers, NYPL.

45. 23 November 1949, box 11, Asia Institute, Subject file E-P, 1949, Iran, Shah Reception, AUP papers, NYPL.

46. Persepolis Correspondence, January 1938–December 1939, P-3-6, E. F. Schmidt File, DOCF, 1938, OI Archives, UC.

47. 23 August 1943, Memo of Conversation, Merriam and Schmidt, 891.927Persepolis/501, RG59, NA.

48. 15 October 1937, Myron B. Smith to Katherine Smith, No. 28, Correspondence with Department of Antiquities, M. B. Smith Papers, Sackler Gallery, Smithsonian Institution, Washington, DC. Balcer, "Erich Friedrich Schmidt," 157–158.

49. 4 February 1941, Dreyfus to SS, 891.927Persepolis/487, RG59, NA. 6 March 1941, Dreyfus to SS, 892.7, TPF 1941, RG84, NA.

50. In May 1941 Riza Shah had ordered the ministers of foreign affairs and public instruction to resolve the issue. Yazdani, *Records on the Archaeological Missions in Iran*, 216, 225. A special thanks to John Larson, archivist at the Oriental Institute, for his help locating the information regarding the sinking.

51. Grigor, "Recultivating 'Good Taste,' " 44.


## 9. Archaeology as Usual

1. Mogens Trolle Larsen, *The Conquest of Assyria: Excavations in an Antique Land, 1840–1860* (New York, 1996). 9–10 July 1994, *International Herald Tribune*, 6.

2. Bruce Kuklick, *Puritans in Babylon: The Ancient Near East and American Intellectual Life, 1880–1930* (Princeton, 1996), 110.

3. Janet Wallach, *Desert Queen* (New York, 1996), 289.

4. Ibid., 199, 326.

5. 21 April 1920, Kenyon to Gordon, box 1, Ur Expedition, UMA, UP. 28 October 1918, CE32/377, Director's Correspondence, Records of the British Museum, London.

6. 29 April 1920/10-16/20, Gordon to Secretary of State for India, no. 160, Letterbook no. 27, UMA, UP.

7. 3 November 1920, Kenyon to Gordon, box 1, Correspondence, 1920–1921, Ur Expedition, UMA, UP; 6 November 1920, British Museum to India Office, FO371/5318/E3089/113144, PRO.

8. 7 April 1920, JB to Frances, JHB papers, OI Archive, UC. 12 May 1920, Personal Diary, JHB papers, OI Archive, UC.

9. 12 May 1920, Personal Diary, JHB papers, OI Archive, UC.

10. 4 March 1921, Kenyon to Gordon, box 1, Correspondence, 1920–21, Ur Expedition, UMA, UP. 25 January 1922, Lawrence to Gordon, Correspondence

"L," Director's Office—G. B. Gordon, UMA, UP. 18 November 1921, Kenyon to Gordon, box 1, Correspondence, 1920–21, Ur Expedition, UMA, UP.

11. 22 August 1922, Kenyon to Gordon, Woolley-Gordon Correspondence, 1922, box 1, Ur Expedition, UMA, UP.

12. 2 November 1922, Woolley to Gordon, Woolley-Gordon Correspondence, 1922, box 1, Ur Expedition, UMA, UP.

13. 18 November 1922, 15 January, 26 February 1923, Woolley to Gordon, Woolley-Gordon Correspondence, 1922, 1923, box 1, Ur Expedition, UMA, UP.

14. 24 May 1924, Woolley to Gordon, Woolley-Gordon Correspondence, 1924, box 1, Ur Expedition, UMA, UP.

15. Wallach, *Desert Queen*, 355.

16. 12 November 1925, JB to Frances, Source Material for *Pioneer to the Past*, JHB papers, OI Archive, UC. 28 March 1926, Woolley to Gordon, Woolley-Gordon Correspondence, 1926, box 1, Ur Expedition, UMA, UP.

17. 15 January 1923, Woolley to Gordon, Woolley-Gordon Correspondence, 1923, box 1, Ur Expedition, UMA, UP. 10 August 1923, Gordon to Kenyon, Ur Excavations, 1923–1925, CE32/509–526, Records of the British Museum, London. FO371/1894C/1935, PRO.

18. Max Mallowan, *Mallowan's Memoirs* (London, 1977), 47.

19. Brian Fagan, *Return to Babylon: Travelers, Archaeologists, and Monuments in Mesopotamia* (Boston, 1979), 254–269. 30 January 1928, Woolley to Jayne, box 2, Ur, UMA, UP. 19 March 1930, Woolley to Jayne, box 2, Ur, UMA, UP. 25 February 1928, Woolley to Gordon, Correspondence 1927–1932, box 2, Ur, UMA, UP. 7 March 1928, Chiera to Lyon, Expedition to Kirkuk, 1927–1928, Chiera Corresp. II, Fogg Museum of Art (FMA), Cambridge, MA. 31 January 1929, Robert Pfeiffer to Lyon, Expedition to Kirkuk, 1928–1929, FMA, Cambridge, MA. 6 April 1929, Starr to Forbes, Expedition to Kirkuk, FMA, Cambridge, MA.

20. 6 April 1929, Starr to Forbes, Expedition to Kirkuk, FMA, Cambridge, MA.

21. 18 December 1926, El-Askeri to Directors, American Schools of Oriental Research (ASOR), DOCF, 1926, OI Archives, UC.

22. 30 May 1928, JB to Fosdick, DOCF, 1928, OI Archives, UC. Emphasis in original.

23. 19 October 1928, Thomas Appleget to Colonel Woods, folder 823, box 112, EI series, OMR, RG2, RFA, RAC.

24. 10 October 1929, JB Memorandum, Iraq, Government of, DOCF, 1929, OI Archives, UC.

25. 24 October 1930, Bache to Jayne, box 1, Nuzi Expedition, UMA, UP; emphasis in original. The critics could not deny, however, that members of the institute's expeditions were generally healthier than those at other excavations.

26. 10 September 1929, JB to Hale, Hale papers. 29 October 1929, JB to CB, Charles Breasted File, DOCF, 1929, OI Archives, UC.

27. 2 January 1930, JB to Appleget, folder 823, box 112, EI series, OMR, RG2, RAC.

28. 21 January 1930, French Consul to Minister of Foreign Affairs, 23 August 1930, Dussaud to Minister of Foreign Affairs, Irak 85, Levant 1930–1940,

MFA, Paris. 18 January 1930, Starr to Jayne, box 1, Correspondence, Nuzi, UMA, UP.

29. 1 November 1930, Speiser to Jayne, box 1, Tell Billa, UMA, UP. 8 April 1931, Woolley to Jayne, box 2, Correspondence 1927–1932, Ur, UMA, UP. 4 March 1932, Speiser to Jayne, box 1, Reports, 1930–1932, Tell Billa, UMA, UP.

30. June 1930, Speiser to George Barton, Expedition to Kirkuk, 1930–1931, FMA, Cambridge, MA. 23 July 1930, Richard Starr and Lyon to Sydney Smith, Sachs files, FMA, Paris.

31. 23 February 1931, Speiser to Barton, box 1, Reports 1930–1932, Tel Billa, UMA, UP. 15 September 1929, Sydney Smith to JB, Concessions, Iraq, Government of, DOCF, 1929, OI Archives, UC.

32. M. Farouk-Sluglett and Peter Sluglett, *Iraq since 1958* (London, 1990), 17.

33. Ibid., 76.

34. Abu Khaldun Sati‘ al-Husri, *Mudhakkirati fi al-Iraq* [My Memories of Iraq] (Beirut, 1967), 2:479–486. See also Shawkat, *Hadhih Ahdafuna*, 43; Muhammad Mahdi Kubbah, *Muzakkirati fi samim al-ihdath* [Memoirs of Essential Events] (Beirut, 1965), 55.

35. Reeva Simon, *Iraq between Two World Wars: The Creation and Implementation of a National Ideology* (New York, 1986), 77.

36. Ibid., 100. Reeva Simon, "The Teaching of History in Iraq before the Rashid Ali Coup of 1941," *Middle Eastern Studies* 22 (1986): 44.

37. Talib Mushtaq, *Awraq Ayyami, 1908–1958* [Pages of My Days] (Beirut, 1968), 5, 60, 133–134. Simon, *Iraq between Two World Wars*, 32.

38. Simon, *Iraq between Two World Wars*, 83.

39. Phoebe Marr, "The Development of a Nationalist Ideology in Iraq, 1920–1941," *Muslim World* 75, no. 2 (April 1985): 95–97.

40. Al-Husri, *Mudhakkirati*, 2:399–402.

41. Ibid., 2:403–404.

## 10. The Reign of Sati‘ al-Husri

1. Simon, *Iraq between Two World Wars*, 123.

2. 13 August 1933, Forbes to Foreign Office, FO624/1/412, PRO.

3. 1 August 1933, George Hill to Jayne, box 4, Ur, UMA, UP. 22 August 1933, Frankfort to JB, Henri Frankfort File, DOCF, 1933, OI Archives, UC. 13 August 1933, Forbes to FO, FO624/1/412, PRO. 1 June 1932, Speiser to Barton, box 1, Tepe Gawra, UMA, UP. 24 September 1933, Jordan to Bach, box 1, Correspondence with Department of Antiquities, 1933–1938, Tell Billa, UMA, UP. 3 October 1933, HF to JB, Henri Frankfort File, DOCF, 1933, OI Archives, UC.

4. 5 October 1933, FO to Humphreys, FO624/1/412, PRO.

5. 1 August 1933, Hill to Jayne, box 4, Ur, UMA, UP. 11 August 1933, Hill to JB, British Museum File, DOCF, 1933, OI Archives, UC. 5 September 1933, Frankfort to JB, Henri Frankfort File, DOCF, 1933, OI Archives, UC.

6. 27 September 1933, JB to Wallace Murray, 30 September, 6 November 1933, Murray to JB, U.S., Government of, DOCF, 1933, OI Archives, UC.

7. 15 September 1933, JB to Hill, 4 October 1933, Hill to JB, British Museum File,

DOCF, 1933, OI Archives, UC. 15 September 1933, JB to HF, Henri Frankfort File, DOCF, 1933, OI Archives, UC.

8. 12 September 1933, HF to JB, 18 September 1933, JB to HF, Henri Frankfort File, DOCF, 1933, OI Archives, UC.

9. 27 September 1933, JB to Hill, British Museum File, DOCF, 1933, OI Archives, UC.

10. 2 January 1930, JB to Thomas Appleget, folder 823, box 112, Educational Interests Series, OMR, RG2, RAC. 13 October 1933, JB to HF, Henri Frankfort File, DOCF, 1933, OI Archives, UC.

11. 6, 20 November 1933, Murray to JB, U.S., Government of, DOCF, 1933, OI Archives, UC. 8 November, 7 December 1933, JB to Murray, U.S., Government of, DOCF, 1933, OI Archives, UC.

12. 26 October 1933, Knabenshue to SS, 890G.927/64, RG59, NA. 19 October 1933, JB to Murray, U.S., Government of, DOCF, 1933, OI Archives, UC.

13. 8 December 1933, JB to Murray, U.S., Government of, DOCF, 1933, OI Archives, UC. 13 December 1933, Woolley to Jayne, box 2, Correspondence, 1927–1932, Ur, UMA, UP. 30 October 1933, Minutes of Commission of Excavation in Western Asia, F/17/17244, MPI, Archives National, Paris.

14. 5 March 1934, HF to JB, Henri Frankfort File, DOCF, 1934, OI Archives, UC. 21 July 1934, Bache to Barton, box 1, Tepe Gawra, UMA, UP. 13 March 1934, HF to JB, Henri Frankfort File, DOCF, 1934, OI Archives, UC.

15. July 1934, Memorandum of Oxford Dons to John Simon, FO371/17871/E4933/1831/93, PRO. 28 August 1934, FO371/17871/5682/1831/93, PRO.

16. 13 March 1934, HF to JB, Henri Frankfort File, DOCF, 1934, OI Archives, UC. 28 March 1934, HF to JB, 17 April 1934, JB to HF, Henri Frankfort File, DOCF, 1934, OI Archives, UC. 25 March 1934, HF to Knabenshue, 11 April 1934, Knabenshue to SS, 892.7, Baghdad Post Files (BPF), RG84, NA.

17. 6 August, 4 October 1934, JB to HF, Henri Frankfort File, DOCF, 1934, OI Archives, UC.

18. 4 October 1934, JB to HF, Henri Frankfort File, DOCF, 1934, OI Archives, UC.

19. 21 September 1934, HF to JB, Henri Frankfort File, DOCF, 1934, OI Archives, UC. 18 October 1934, "Sati Beg al Hasri" [sic], FO371/17871/E6594/1831/93, PRO.

20. Al-Husri, *Mudhakkirati*, 2:407.

21. Ibid., 2:408–411.

22. Ibid.

23. Ibid., 413.

24. Ibid., 413–414. n.d., Satiʿ al-Husri to HF, Henri Frankfort File, DOCF, 1934, OI Archives, UC.

25. 3 November 1934, Burrows to Knabenshue, 892.7, RG84, NA. 15 November 1934, Andrae to Frankfort, 28 November 1934, Frankfort to Andrae, Henri Frankfort File, DOCF, 1934, OI Archives, UC. 22 December 1934, JB to HF, Henri Frankfort File, DOCF, 1934, OI Archives, UC. 10 January 1935, Speiser to Bache, box 1, Tepe Gawra, UMA, UP. 16 February 1935, Bache to Jayne, Letter Reports of 3rd season, Tepe Gawra, UMA, UP.

26. Al-Husri, *Mudhakkirati*, 2:415–418.

27. 21 February 1935, HF to JB, Henri Frankfort File, DOCF, 1935, OI Archives, UC.
28. 19 February 1935, JB to Murray, 890G.927, RG59, NA. 27 February 1935, Phillips to Knabenshue, 892.7, BPF, RG84, NA.
29. 2 February 1931, Speiser to Jayne, box 1, General Correspondence, Tell Billa, UMA, UP.
30. 7 March 1935, Knabenshue to SS, 890G.927, RG59, NA.
31. Ibid. Al-Husri, *Mudhakkirati*, 2:419.
32. Al-Husri, *Mudhakkirati*, 2:419.
33. 4 April 1935, Satiʿ al-Husri to JB, Iraq, Government of, DOCF, 1935, OI Archives, UC.
34. Al-Husri, *Mudhakkirati*, 2:420. 7 March 1935, HF to JB, Henri Frankfort File, DOCF, 1935, OI Archives, UC.
35. 7 March 1935, Knabenshue to SS, 890G.927/113, RG59, NA. 1 March 1935, Knabenshue to SS, 892.7, BPF, 1935, RG84, NA.
36. 22 March 1935, JB to Murray, U.S., Government of, DOCF, 1935, OI Archives, UC.
37. 8 March 1935, JB to Murray, 890G.927/110, RG59, NA. 7 March 1935, HF to JB, Henri Frankfort File, DOCF, 1935, OI Archives, UC.
38. 1 May 1935, JB to Satiʿ al-Husri, Iraq, Government of, DOCF, 1935, OI Archives, UC.
39. Al-Husri, *Mudhakkirati*, 2:424–425.
40. FO371/1894C/*Al-Bilad*/163, PRO.
41. FO371/1894C/*Al-Bilad*/159, PRO. 24 September 1936, Saty to Woolley, CE 32/6, Director's Correspondence, British Museum Archives, London. 25 February 1935, FO371/18946.
42. Nadeem Naimy, *The Lebanese Prophets of New York* (Beirut, 1985), 91–92.
43. 24 May 1935, F. Grobba to Knabenshue, 892.7, RG84, NA.
44. 1935, "Rihani Case," 1–4, 892.7, RG59, NA.
45. 23 May 1935, Rihani to Knabenshue, 892.7, RG84, NA.
46. 22 October 1936, John Wilson to Ambrose Lansing, Henri Frankfort File, DOCF, 1936, OI Archives, UC.
47. 21 February 1936, Bache to Jayne, box 1, General Correspondence, 1931–1943, Tepe Gawra, UMA, UP. 1 April 1936, Saty to Bache, box 1, Tepe Gawra, UMA, UP.
48. Seleucia, 1936–37, Report, box 6, Kelsey Museum, Institute of Archaeological Research, BL, UM, AA. 21 February 1937, Peterson to Robbins, Enoch Peterson papers, box 1, Kelsey Museum, BL, UM, AA.
49. 17 January 1936, Wilson to HF, Henri Frankfort File, DOCF, 1936, OI Archives, UC. 22 October 1936, Wilson to Lansing, Henri Frankfort File, DOCF, 1936, OI Archives, UC.
50. 29 October 1936, Jayne to Lansing, Metropolitan Museum, Director's Office —H. H. Jayne, UMA, UP.
51. 25 February 1937, Speiser to Jayne, box 1, Khafaje Expedition, 23 March 1937, Speiser to Jayne, box 1, Tepe Gawra, UMA, UP. 26 November 1937, 23 March 1940, Delougaz to Jayne, Alphabetical Correspondence, box 9, Director's Office—Jayne, Khafaje, UMA, UP.

52. Al-Husri, *Mudhakkirati*, 2:448.

53. Ibid., 487–490.

54. 27 December 1934, Knabenshue to SS, 890G.927/90, RG59, NA.

55. Al-Husri, *Mudhakkirati*, 2:442–444.

56. Ibid., 434–437.

57. 6 May 1923, N-83, p. 36, Herzfeld Papers, Sackler Gallery, Smithsonian Institution, Washington, DC. 12 March 1928, Kenyon to Shuckburgh, CO730132/9, PRO.

58. 1921, FO371/E2642/384/93/6362, PRO.

59. Ibid. 1935, CE 32/2075-2084/2, CE 32/2085-2097, Director's Correspondence, British Museum Archives, London.

60. Al-Husri, *Mudhakkirati*, 2:438–441.

61. 20 January 1940, Wilson to Satiʿ, "I" File, DOCF, 1940, OI Archives, UC.

62. 6 March 1940, Satiʿ to Wilson, "I" File, DOCF, 1940, OI Archives, UC.

63. Agatha Christie, *An Autobiography* (New York, 1977), 451. 19 May 1939, Sidney Smith to Frankfort, Henri Frankfort File, DOCF, 1939, OI Archives, UC. Ghazi, who liked fast cars, died in an automobile accident. According to the local rumor mill, the British had sabotaged his vehicle.

64. 2 April 1936, Dussaud to Marx, 487.2, Mandat en Syrie, Archives Diplomatiques Nantes. 1 January 1939, *Al-Akhbar* (Baghdad).

65. Al-Husri, *Mudhakkirati*, 2:518–521.

66. Seton Lloyd, *The Interval: A Life in Archaeology* (Oxford, 1986), 176.

67. Ibid., 175–176.

## 11. A New Era

1. S. Malek Shahmirzadi, "Ishareh-i Mukhtasar bar Tahavul Bastanshinasy dar Iran" [A Review of the Development of Archaeology in Iran], *Asar* 12–14 (1986): 140.

2. Naji al-Asli, "Foreword," *Sumer: A Journal of Archaeology in Iraq* 1, no. 1 (January 1945): 3–4.

3. 27 May 1943, Report on "Post War Archaeology," by Seton Lloyd, Antioch, Miscellaneous Correspondence, 1940–, Department of Art and Archaeology, Princeton University. Emphasis in original.

4. Letters on Iran, 1940, box 27-G, Henry Field papers, Franklin Delano Roosevelt Library (FDRL), Hyde Park, NY. 1951, box 44, Henry Field papers, FDRL, Hyde Park, NY.

5. Personal Correspondence, vol. 30, 1920-1950, Henry Field Papers, FDRL, Hyde Park, NY.

6. 1942, box 44, Henry Field papers, FDRL, Hyde Park, NY. Wilber, *Adventures in the Middle East*, 105. Syria, Government of, DOCF, 1942, OI Archives, UC. John Wilson, *Thousands of Years: An Archaeologist's Search for Ancient Egypt* (New York, 1972), 89. 16 February 1942, Wilson to Karl Twitchell, Personal Correspondence, vol. 30, 1920-1950, Henry Field papers, FDRL, Hyde Park, NY.

7. 14 February 1946, Wilson to Millar Burrows, box 2, subject file, 1920–1952, Records of Office of NEA, Lot File no. 54D 403, RG59, NA.

8. 30 January 1946, Wilson to Dows Dunham [BMFA], box 2, subject file, 1920–1952, Records of Office of NEA, Lot File no. 54D 403, RG59, NA.
9. 27 March 1946, box 2, subject file, 1920–1952, Records of Office of NEA, Lot File no. 54D 403, RG59, NA.
10. Wilson Report, n.d., box 2, subject file, 1920–1952, Records of Office of NEA, Lot File no. 54D 403, RG59, NA.
11. Lloyd, *The Interval*, 176.

## 12. Reflections

1. Ilknur Özgen and Jean Öztürk, *Heritage Recovered: The Lydian Treasure* (Istanbul, 1996); Thomas Hoving, *Making the Mummies Dance: Inside the Metropolitan Museum of Art* (New York, 1993), 101, 217. Anyone wishing to view the Lydian antiquities returned from the Metropolitan in 1926 (Sardis I) would have to be very patient. Apparently, they are all in storage in what the director of the Istanbul Museum refers to as the treasury, and one can only gain access to them by obtaining permission from the Ministry of Culture in Ankara.
2. Zahi Hawass, *Hidden Treasures of Ancient Egypt: Unearthing the Masterpieces of Egyptian History* (Washington, DC, 2004), 14.
3. Ansari, *Modern Iran since 1921*, 173.
4. Abdi, "Nationalism," 70, Patience J. Higgins and Pirouz Shoar-Ghaffari, "Changing Perceptions of Iranian Identity in Elementary Textbooks," in Elizabeth Fernea, ed., *Children of the Middle East* (Austin, 1995), 346–350.
5. Abdi, "Nationalism," 67–68.
6. Ibid., 71.
7. Ibid., 72. Abdulkarim Soroush, *Reason, Freedom and Democracy in Islam* (Oxford, 2000), 156.
8. Donald M. Reid, "The Postage Stamp: A Window on Saddam Hussein's Iraq," *Middle East Journal* 47, no. 1 (Winter 1993): 84.
9. Amatzia Baram, "A Case of an Imported Identity: The Modernizing Secular Ruling Elites of Iraq and the Conception of Mesopotamian-inspired Territorial Nationalism, 1922–1992," 23, 30 [draft in author's possession]. Rannfrid I. Thelle, "The Conquest of the Past: Archaeology and Historiographic Representation of Ancient Mesopotamia in Relief," paper delivered at MESA, 6–9 November 2003, Anchorage, AK, 8–9. See also Jabra Ibrahim Jabra, *Princesses' Street: Baghdad Memories*, trans. Issa J. Boullata (Fayetteville, AR, 2005), 42.
10. Baram, "A Case of an Imported Identity," 34.
11. 23 June, 8 December 1996, *New York Times;* 9–10 July 1994, *International Herald Tribune*. "Robbing the Cradle: Iraq's Antiquities" (2003), Robin Benger, director, Canadian Broadcasting Corporation.
12. 4 April 2004, 18 December 2005, *New York Times*, 10 July 2003, "Edmund Andrews Interview," *Fresh Air*, National Public Radio.

# BIBLIOGRAPHY

## Unpublished Primary Sources

### United States

Archives of American Art, Smithsonian Institution, Washington, DC
    Director's Correspondence, 1901–1954, Boston Museum of Fine Arts [microfilm]
    George Reisner Papers [microfilm]
Baltimore Museum of Art, Baltimore, Maryland
    Robert Garrett Diary
Bentley Library, University of Michigan, Ann Arbor
    Francis W. Kelsey Papers
    Enoch Peterson Papers
    Kelsey Museum of Archaeology
Boston Museum of Fine Arts
    George A. Reisner Papers
California Institute of Technology, Pasadena
    George Hale Papers [microfilm]
Cleveland Museum of Art
    RG1, Director's Office Files
Fine Arts Library, Harvard University, Cambridge, Massachusetts
    Ullens Archive Audio Collection, Visual Collections
        Interview with André and Yedda Godard
Fogg Museum of Art, Cambridge, Massachusetts
    Expedition to Kirkuk
    Sachs Files
Franklin Delano Roosevelt Library, Hyde Park, New York
    Henry Field Papers
Houghton Library, Harvard University, Cambridge, Massachusetts
    Mark Bristol Papers
Metropolitan Museum of Art, Department of Egyptian Art
    Antiquities Law, 1922–1923, 1925, 1926–1927
    Carter Files
National Archives, College Park, Maryland
    General Records of the Department of State (RG59)
    Baghdad Post Files (RG84)

Egyptian Post Files (RG84)
Tehran Post Files (RG84)
Turkey Post Files (RG84)
New York Public Library, New York, New York
Arthur Upham Pope Papers
Oregon Historical Society, Portland
Leslie Hall Papers
Oriental Institute, University of Chicago, Chicago, Illinois
James H. Breasted Papers
Charles Breasted File
Concessions
Correspondence of Henri Frankfort
Director's Confidential File
Director's Correspondence File
Director's Office Correspondence
Government of Egypt
Iran, Persepolis
Persepolis Concession
Turkish Government File
Von der Osten File
Pierpont Morgan Library, New York, New York
J. P. Morgan Jr. Papers
Princeton University, Department of Art and Archaeology
Antioch, Miscellaneous Correspondence
Committee for the Excavation of Antioch and Vicinity
Howard Crosley Butler Papers
Rockefeller Archive Center, Sleepy Hollow, New York
Rockefeller Family Archives
John D. Rockefeller Papers, RG1
Letterbook series
Office of the Messrs Rockefeller, RG2
Cultural Interests series
Educational Interests series
Friends and Services series, Dr. James Breasted files
John D. Rockefeller Jr. Personal Papers
Rockefeller Foundation Archives
Record Group 1.1 Projects
Series 216, Illinois
Record Group 12.1 Diaries
International Education Board Archives
Sackler Gallery, Smithsonian Institution, Washington, DC
Ernst Herzfeld Papers
Myron B. Smith Papers
Toledo Museum of Art, Toledo, Ohio
Egypt Exploration Society Correspondence
University of Cincinnati, Cincinnati, Ohio
Carl Blegen Papers

University Museum Archive, University of Pennsylvania, Philadelphia
  Egypt Section—Clarence Fisher
  Director's Office—H. H. F. Jayne
  Director's Office—G. B. Gordon
  Near East Section
  Khafaje Expedition
  Nuzi Expedition
  Tell Billa Expedition
  Tepe Gawra Expedition
  Tepe Hissar Expedition
  Turang Tepe Expedition
  Ur Expedition
Worcester Museum of Fine Arts, Worcester, Massachusetts
  Antioch Expedition, General Correspondence, 1931–1932
Yale University, Sterling Memorial Library
  William H. Buckler Papers

### Egypt

National Library
Library of the American Research Center in Egypt
American University Cairo
  Rare Books and Special Collections Library

### France

Archives Diplomatiques, Nantes
  Cairo Embassy, Service des Antiquités
  Embassy of France in Cairo, Ministry of Foreign Affairs, Vichy
  Mandat en Syrie
Ministry of Foreign Affairs Archive, Quai d'Orsay, Paris
  Égypte, Afrique 1918–1940
  Irak, Levant 1930–1940
  Perse, Asie 1918–1940
  Turquie, Levant 1918–1940
Archives National, Paris
  Ministry of Public Instruction

### Great Britain

British Museum Archives, London
  Excavations, 1846–1955 (CE32)
Egypt Exploration Society Archive, London
  Correspondence of E. L. Griffith (1920–1923)
Public Record Office, Kew
  Colonial Office CO730132/9

Political Correspondence of the Foreign Office (FO371)
High Commission and Consulate, Iraq (FO624)

### Iran

Center for Documents and Diplomatic History, Foreign Ministry, Tehran
National Archives, Tehran

### Turkey

Prime Ministerial Archive, Ankara
National Library, Ankara

### Interviews with the Author

| | |
|---|---|
| Ekrem Akurgal | Hans Güterbock |
| Sedat Alp | T. G. H. James |
| Oluş Arik | Tahsin Özgüç |

### Published Primary Sources

*Ankara Universitesi Haftasi, Kars, July 22–28, 1942* [Ankara University Week Seminar]. Ankara: Turkish Historical Society Press, 1944.

Al-Asli, Naji. "Foreword." *Sumer: A Journal of Archaeology in Iraq* 1, no. 1 (January 1945).

*Annual Report of the Service des Antiquités.* Cairo, 1907, 1913, 1914, 1939.

Breasted, Charles. "Exploring the Secrets of Persepolis." *National Geographic Magazine* 64, no. 4 (October 1933): 381–420.

Breasted, James. "The University of Chicago Expedition to the Near East, 1919–1920." *University Record* 7, no. 1 (1922): 6–25.

Burgoyne, Elizabeth. *Gertrude Bell from Her Personal Papers*, vol. 2, *1914–1926*. London, 1961.

Dawn, Ernest. "The Formation of Pan-Arab Ideology in the Interwar Years." *International Journal of Middle East Studies* 20 (1988): 167–191.

Godard, André. "Les récentes fouilles archéologiques." *Revue des Artes Asiatiques* 8 (1934): 111–115.

———. "Activités diverses du Service des Antiquités en Iran." *Revue des Artes Asiatiques* 10 (1936): 165–167.

Herzfeld, Ernst. "Rapport sur l'état des ruines de Persepolis et propositions pour leur conservation." *Archeoliogische Mitteilungen aus Iran*, vol. 1. Reprint, New York, 1966.

Karimlu, Davood, ed. *Taraj-i mirat-i milli*, vol. 2, *Hiyat-i faransavi, 1341–1354* [Plunder of the National Heritage, vol. 2, The French Mission, 1923–1935]. Iran and Imperialism 3. Tehran, 2001.

———. *Taraj-i mirat-i milli*, vol. 4, *Hayathayi almani va amrika'i, 1899–1940* [Plunder of National Heritage, vol. 4, The German and American Missions, 1899–1940]. Iran and Imperialism 5. Tehran, 2001.

Maslahat al-Athar [Antiquities Service]. *Rapport du Service des Antiquités (1906–1916)*. Cairo.
Sadiqi-pur, Abd al-Riza, ed. *Yadgar-i guzashteh: Majmu'eh-yi sukhanraniha-yi a'lahazrat-i faqid Riza Shah Kabir* [Memorial of the Past: Collection of the Speeches of His Late Majesty Riza Shah the Great]. Tehran, 1346 [1967].
Shawkat, Sami. *Hadhih Ahdafuna* [These Are Our Goals]. Baghdad, 1939.
*Türk Tarih Kongresi, 1932* [The Turkish History Conference]. Istanbul, 1932.
Yazdani, Marzieh, ed. *Asnad hayathayi bastan shenasi dar Iran, 1254–1345* [Records on the Archaeological Missions in Iran, 1875-1966]. Tehran, 2001.

## Memoirs

Childs, J. Rives. *Foreign Service Farewell: My Years in the Near East.* Charlottes-ville, 1969.
Christie, Agatha. *An Autobiography.* New York, 1977.
Gardiner, Alan H. *My Working Years.* London, 1963.
Hidayat, Mahdi-Quli. *Khatirat va Khatarat* [Memories and Dangers]. Tehran, 1329 [1950].
Hikmat, Ali Asghar. *Siy khaterat az asr-i farkhandeh Pahlavi* [Thirty Years of Memories from the Golden Age of the Pahlavis]. Tehran, 1976.
Al-Hashimi, Taha. *Mudhakkirat* [Memoirs], vol. 1, *1919–1943.* Beirut, 1967.
Al-Husri, Abu Khaldun Sati'. *Mudhakkirati fi al-Iraq* [My Memories of Iraq]. 2 vols. Beirut, 1967.
Jabra, Jabra Ibrahim. *Princesses' Street: Baghdad Memories.* Translated by Issa J. Boulatta. Fayetteville, AR, 2005.
Kubbah, Muhammad Mahdi. *Mudhakkirati fi samim al-ihdath* [Memoirs of Essential Events]. Beirut, 1965.
Lloyd, Seton. *The Interval: A Life in Archaeology.* Oxford, 1986.
Mallowan, Agatha Christie. *Come Tell Me How You Live.* New York, 1946.
Mallowan, Max. *Mallowan's Memoirs.* London, 1977.
Mostafavi, Seyd Mohammad Taghi. *Talash dar rah-i khidmat be athar-i milli va omid be ayande* [Struggles in the Service of the National Monuments and Hopes for the Future]. Tehran, 1955.
Mushtaq, Talib. *Awraq Ayyami, 1908–1958* [Pages of My Days]. Beirut, 1968.
Petrie, William M. F. *Seventy Years in Archaeology.* London, 1931.

## Newspapers

| | |
|---|---|
| *Al-Ahram* | *International Herald Tribune* |
| *Al-Akhbar* | *Iran* |
| *Akcham* | *Iran-i Bastan* |
| *Ankara* | *Iran Imruz* |
| *Al-Balagh* | *Iraq News* |
| *Boston Transcript* | *Itilla'at* |
| *Chicago Daily News* | *Journal de Tehran* |
| *Egyptian Mail* | *Muqattam* |
| *Entekhab* | *Al-Muqtataf* |

*New York Times*  
*Nizam*  
*Le Reveil*  
*Rose El-Youssef*  

*Al-Siyasa*  
*Al-Siyasah al-Usbuʿiah*  
*Times of Mesopotamia*  
*La Turquie Kemaliste*

**Secondary Sources**

Abdi, Kamyar. "Nationalism, Politics and the Development of Archaeology in Iran." *American Journal of Archaeology* 105 (2001): 51–76.

Abt, Jeffrey. "Toward a Historian's Laboratory: The Breasted-Rockefeller Museum Projects in Egypt, Palestine and America." *Journal of the American Research Center in Egypt* 33 (1996): 173–194.

Abu El-Haj, Nadia. *Facts on the Ground: Archaeological Practice and Territorial Self-Fashioning in Israeli Society.* Chicago, 2001.

———. "Reflections on Archaeology and Israeli Settler-Nationhood." *Radical History Review (National Myths in the Middle East)* 86 (Spring 2003): 149–163.

Akurgal, Ekrem. *Ancient Civilizations and Ruins of Turkey.* 8th ed. Istanbul, 1993.

Altug, Seda. "Antioch between Colonial and National Dominations: The Sanjak of Alexandretta under the French Mandate (1920–1939)." Paper presented at the Middle East Studies conference, Anchorage, 6–9 November 2003.

Amanat, Abbas. "The Kayanid Crown and Qajar Reclaiming of Royal Authority." *Iranian Studies* 34, nos. 1–4 (2001): 17–30.

Anderson, Benedict. *Imagined Communities: Reflections on the Origin and Spread of Nationalism.* 2d ed. London, 1991.

Ansari, Ali M. *Modern Iran since 1921: The Pahlavis and After.* New York, 2003.

Antonius, George. *The Arab Awakening: The Story of the Arab National Movement.* 2d ed. London, 1938.

Aslan, Reza. "The Epic of Iran." *New York Times Book Review* (30 April 2006): 27.

Atasü, Erendiz. *The Other Side of the Mountain.* London, 2000.

Aytürk, Ilker. "The Sun-Language Theory: Nationalism, Religion and Language Reform in Ataturk's Turkey." Paper presented at the annual conference of the Middle East Studies Association, Washington, DC, November 2002.

*Asr-i Pahlavi* [The Pahlavi Period]. Tehran, 1967.

Awad, Louis. *The Literature of Ideas in Egypt.* Atlanta, 1986.

Bacque-Grammont, Jean-Louis, and Jean-Paul Roux. *Mustafa Kemal Ataturk et la Turquie nouvelle.* Paris, 1982.

Badawi, M. M. *A Critical Introduction to Modern Arabic Poetry.* New York, 1975.

Balcer, Jack M. "Erich Friedrich Schmidt, 13 September 1897–3 October 1964." *Achaemenid History* 7 (1991): 147–172.

Baram, Amatzia. *Culture, History and Ideology in the Formation of Baʿthist Iraq, 1968–1989.* New York, 1991.

———. "A Case of an Imported Identity: The Modernizing Secular Ruling Elites of Iraq and the Conception of Mesopotamian-Inspired Territorial Nationalism, 1922–1992." [Draft in author's possession.]

Baram, Phillip. *The Department of State in the Middle East.* Philadelphia, 1978.

Baron, Beth. *The Women's Awakening in Egypt: Culture, Society and the Press.* New Haven, 1994.

———. *Egypt as a Woman: Nationalism, Gender, and Politics.* Berkeley and Los Angeles, 2005.

Bell, Gertrude. *Letters of Gertrude Bell.* New York, 1928.

———. *Persian Pictures.* New York, 1928.

Bernhardsson, Magnus. *Reclaiming a Plundered Past: Archaeology and Nation Building in Modern Iraq.* Austin, TX, 2005.

Bisbee, Eleanor. *The New Turks: Pioneers of the Republic, 1920–1950.* Philadelphia, 1951.

Brackman, Arnold. *The Search for the Gold of Tutankhamen.* New York, 1976.

Breasted, Charles. *Pioneer to the Past: The Story of James Henry Breasted, Archaeologist.* Chicago, 1943.

Brunton, Guy. "Howard Carter Obituary." *Service des Antiquités* 39 (1939): 52–53.

———. "Obituary of George A. Reisner." *Service des Antiquités* 41 (1942): 11–15.

Byron, Robert. *The Road to Oxiana.* London, 1937.

Çambel, Hasan Cemil. "Atatürk ve Tarih" [Ataturk and History]. *Belleten Türk Tarih Kurumu* 13 (1939).

Chubb, Mary. *City in the Sand.* New York, 1957.

Çiğ, Muazzez. "Atatürk and the Beginning of Cuneiform Studies in Turkey." *Journal of Cuneiform Studies* 402 (Autumn 1988): 211–216.

Cleveland, William L. *The Making of an Arab Nationalist: Ottomanism and Arabism in the Life and Thought of Sati' Al-Husri.* Princeton, 1971.

Cole, Juan. "Marking Boundaries, Marking Time: The Iranian Past and the Construction of the Self by Qajar Thinkers." *Iranian Studies* 39, nos. 1–2 (Winter-Spring 1996): 35–56.

Colombe, Marcel. *L'Évolution de l'Égypte, 1924–1950.* Paris, 1951.

Comité de Conservation des Monuments de l'Art Arabe, Exercice 1925–1926. *Procès-verbaux des séances.* Cairo, 1933.

Cone, Polly, ed. *Wonderful Things: The Discovery of Tutankhamun's Tomb.* New York, 1976.

Coury, Ralph M. "The Politics of the Funereal: The Tomb of Saad Zaghlul." *Journal of the Research Center in Egypt* 29 (1992): 191–200.

———. *The Making of an Egyptian Arab Nationalist: The Early Years of Azzam Pasha, 1893–1936.* Reading, UK, 1998.

*Cumhuriyet Dönem, Türkiye Ansiklopedisi* [The Republican Era, Encyclopedia of Turkey]. Ankara, 1983.

Daniel, Robert L. *American Philanthropy in the Near East, 1820–1960.* Athens, OH, 1970.

Davidson, Lawrence. "Imagining Palestine: Archaeology and Popular Perceptions of Palestine in the First Decade of the Mandate." Paper presented at the 29th Annual Meeting of the Middle East Studies Association, Washington, DC, 1995.

Davis, Eric. *Memories of State: Politics, History, and Collective Identity in Modern Iraq.* Berkeley and Los Angeles, 2005.

Dawisha, Adeed. *Arab Nationalism in the Twentieth Century: From Triumph to Despair.* Princeton, 2003.

Dawson, Warren R., and Eric P. Uphill. *Who Was Who in Egyptology.* 2d rev. ed. London, 1972.

DeNovo, John A. *American Interests and Policies in the Middle East: 1900–1939*. Minneapolis, 1963.

Deringil, Selim. *The Well-Protected Domains: Ideology and the Legitimation of Power in the Ottoman Empire, 1876–1909*. New York, 1998.

Devereux, Robert, ed. *Ziya Gökalp: Principles of Turkism*. Leiden, 1968.

Dumont, Paul, ed. *La Turquie et la France a l'époque d'Ataturk*. Paris, 1981.

Eley, Geoff, and Ronald Grigor Suny, eds. *Becoming National: A Reader*. Oxford, 1996.

Fabri, C. L. "On the Tracks of Stone Age Man in Persian Baluchistan." *Asia* 34, no. 8 (August 1934): 468–473.

Fagan, Brian. *Return to Babylon: Travelers, Archaeologists, and Monuments in Mesopotamia*. Boston, 1979.

Farhi, Farideh. "Crafting a National Identity amidst Contentious Politics in Contemporary Iran." *Iranian Studies* 38, no. 1 (March 2005): 7–22.

Farouk-Sluglett, M., and Peter Sluglett. *Iraq since 1958*. London, 1990.

Fawcett, Clare, and Philip L. Kohl, eds. *Nationalism, Politics, and the Practice of Archaeology*. New York, 1995.

Forbes, Rosita. *Conflict: Angora to Afghanistan*. New York, 1931.

Gathercole, Peter, and David Lowenthal, eds. *The Politics of the Past*. Boston, 1990.

Gaucher, Gilles, and Alain Schnapp, eds. *Archéologie, pouvoir et sociétés*. Paris, 1984.

Gershoni, Israel, and James Jankowski. *Egypt, Islam and the Arabs: The Search for Egyptian Nationhood, 1900–1930*. New York, 1986.

———, eds. *Rethinking Nationalism in the Arab Middle East*. New York, 1997.

———. *Commemorating the Nation: Collective Memory, Public Commemoration, and National Identity in Twentieth-Century Egypt*. Chicago, 2004.

Gheissari, Ali. *Iranian Intellectuals in the 20th Century*. Austin, TX, 1998.

Ghods, M. Reza. "Iranian Nationalism and Reza Shah." *Middle Eastern Studies* 27, no. 1 (January 1991): 35–45.

Gidiri, A. "Imperialism and Archaeology." *Race: Journal of the Institute of Race Relations* 15, no. 4 (April 1974): 431–459.

Gillis, John R., ed. *Commemorations: The Politics of National Identity*. Princeton, 1994.

Gluck, Jay, and Noel Silver, eds. *Surveyors of Persian Art: A Documentary Biography of Arthur Upham Pope and Phyllis Ackerman*. Ashiya, Japan, 1996.

Goode, James F. "Archaeology and Diplomacy in the Republic of Turkey, 1919–39." In *Turkish-American Relations: Past, Present and Future*, ed. Mustafa Aydin and Çagri Erhan, 49–65. New York, 2004.

Grigor, Talinn. "Recultivating 'Good Taste': The Early Pahlavi Modernists and Their Society for National Heritage." *Iranian Studies* 37, no. 1 (March 2004): 17–45.

Gur, Asli. "Anatolia: Cradle of Civilizations." Paper presented at the Middle East Studies Association conference, San Francisco, 2001.

Haines, Richard. "Erich F. Schmidt." *Journal of Near Eastern Studies* 24, no. 1 (1965): 145–147.

Al-Hakim, Tawfik. *Return of the Spirit*. Trans. William M. Hutchins. Washington, DC, 1990.

Hare, Paul. *Diplomatic Chronicles of the Middle East: A Biography of Ambassador Raymond Hare.* Lanham, MD, 1993.

Hart, Kimberly. "Ideas about Tradition and Modernity in Two Turkish Villages." Paper presented at the Middle East Studies Association conference, San Francisco, 2001.

Hawass, Zahi. *Hidden Treasures of Ancient Egypt: Unearthing the Masterpieces of Egyptian History.* Washington, DC, 2004.

———. *Tutankhamun and the Golden Age of the Pharoahs.* Washington, DC, 2005.

Heinrichs, Waldo. *American Ambassador: Joseph C. Grew and the Development of the United States Diplomatic Tradition.* New York, 1966.

Higgins, Patience J., and Pirouz Shoar-Ghaffari. "Changing Perceptions of Iranian Identity in Elementary Textbooks." In *Children of the Middle East,* ed. Elizabeth Fernea, 346–350. Austin, 1995.

Hobsbawm, Eric, and Terence Ranger, eds. *The Invention of Tradition.* Cambridge, MA, 1983.

Hobsbawm, E. J. *Nations and Nationalism since 1780: Programme, Myth, Reality.* New York, 1990.

Horton, George W. *The Blight of Asia.* Indianapolis, 1926.

Hoving, Thomas. *Making the Mummies Dance: Inside the Metropolitan Museum of Art.* New York, 1993.

Hughes, Charles Evans. "Recent Questions and Negotiations." *American Journal of International Law* 18 (April 1924): 229–245.

Husayn, Taha. *The Future of Culture in Egypt.* Trans. Sidney Glazer. Washington, DC, 1954.

Hutchinson, John, and Anthony D. Smith, eds. *Nationalism.* New York, 1994.

Inan, Afet. *A History of the Turkish Revolution and Turkish Republic.* Trans. Ahmet E. Uysal. Ankara, 1981.

Institute de France. *Célébration du cinquantenaire de l'Institut Français d'Archéologie du Proche-Orient: Séance du vendredi 18 octobre 1996.* Paris, 1996.

Jackh, Ernest, ed. *Background of the Middle East.* Ithaca, 1952.

James, T. G. H., ed. *Excavating in Egypt: The Egypt Exploration Society, 1882–1982.* London, 1982.

———. *The British Museum and Ancient Egypt.* London, 1990.

———. *Howard Carter: The Path to Tutankhamun.* London, 1992.

Jankowski, James. *Egypt's Young Rebels.* Stanford, 1975.

Kaplan, Flora. *Museums and the Making of "Ourselves": The Role of Objects in National Identity.* London, 1994.

Karp, Ivan, and Steven D. Levine. *Exhibiting Cultures: The Poetics and Politics of Museum Display.* Washington, DC, 1991.

Karpat, Kemal H. "Kossuth in Turkey: The Impact of Hungarian Refugees in the Ottoman Empire, 1849–1851." *Hungarian Heritage Review* 19 (March 1990): 18–23.

———. *The Politicization of Islam: Reconstructing Identity, State, Faith, and Community in the Late Ottoman State.* New York, 2001.

Kashani-Sabet, Firoozeh. *Frontier Fictions: Shaping the Iranian Nation, 1804–1946.* Princeton, 1999.

Kenny, L. M. "Sati' al-Husri's Views on Arab Nationalism." *Middle East Journal* 17, no. 3 (1963): 236–256.

Khadduri, Majid. "The Coup d'État of 1936." *Middle East Journal* 3 (1948): 270–292.

Khalidi, Rashid. *The Origins of Arab Nationalism.* New York, 1993.

Khoury, Philip. *Syria and the French Mandate: The Politics of Arab Nationalism, 1920–1945.* Princeton, 1987.

King, Philip J. *American Archaeology in the Middle East.* Baltimore, MD, 1983.

Kinross, Lord. *Ataturk: The Rebirth of a Nation.* London, 1964.

Komaroff, Lisa. "Exhibiting the Middle East: Collections and Perceptions of Islamic Art." *Ars Orientalis* 30 (2000): 1–8.

Krefter, Friedrich. "Mit Ernst Herzfeld in Pasargadae und Persepolis 1928 und 1931–1934." *Archaeologische Mitteilungen aus Iran* 12 (1979): 13–25.

Kuklick, Bruce. *Puritans in Babylon: The Ancient Near East and American Intellectual Life, 1880–1930.* Princeton, 1996.

Kundakçi, Gül Ersin. "19 Yüzyilda Anadolu Arkeolojisne ve Eskiçağ Tarihine Genel Yaklaşim" [19th-Century Anatolian Archaeology and Prehistoric History, a General Approach]. 13th Turkish Historical Congress, 4–8 October 1999, Ankara.

Landau, Jacob M. *Ataturk and the Modernization of Turkey.* Boulder, CO, 1984.

Larsen, Mogens Trolle. *The Conquest of Assyria: Excavations in an Antique Land, 1840–1860.* New York, 1996.

Leclant, M. Jean. "Le chanoine Étienne Drioton (1889–1961)." *Bulletin de la Faculté des Lettres de Strasbourg* (November 1961): 163–167.

———. "Pierre Lacau (1873–1963)." *Archiv für Orientforschung* 21 (1966): 272–273.

———. *Les recherches archéologiques françaises à l'étranger.* Paris, 1984.

Lewis, Bernard. "History-writing and National Revival in Turkey." *Middle Eastern Affairs* 4, nos. 6–7 (June–July 1953): 218–227.

———. *The Emergence of Modern Turkey.* London, 1961.

———. *History Remembered, Recovered, Invented.* Princeton, 1975.

Levonian, Lutfi. *The Turkish Press: Selections from the Turkish Press Showing Events and Opinions, 1925–1932.* Athens, 1932.

———. *The Turkish Press, 1932–1936.* Beirut, 1937.

Lloyd, Seton. *Mesopotamia: Excavations at Sumerian Sites.* London, 1936.

———. *Ruined Cities of Iraq.* London, 1942.

———. *Foundations in the Dust: The Story of Mesopotamian Exploration.* Rev. ed. London, 1980.

Mahfouz, Naguib. *Khufu's Wisdom.* Trans. Raymond Stock. Cairo, 2003.

———. *Thebes at War.* Trans. Humphrey Davies. Cairo, 2003.

Mahrad, Ahmad. *Die deutsch-persischen Beziehungen von 1918–1933.* Frankfurt, 1974.

———. *Iran unter der Herrschaft Reza Schahs.* New York, 1977.

Majd, Mohammad Gholi. *The Great American Plunder of Persia's Antiquities, 1925–1941.* Lanham, MD, 2003.

Mango, Andrew. *Ataturk.* Woodstock, NY, 1999.

Mansel, Arif Mufid. "Halil Edhem ve Sard Eserleri" [Halil Ethem and the Sardis

Antiquities]. In *Halil Ethem: Hatira Kitabi* [In Memory of Halil Ethem], 1–12. Ankara, 1948.

Marchand, Suzanne L. *Down from Olympus: Archaeology and Philhellenism in Germany, 1750–1970*. Princeton, 1996.

Marr, Phoebe. "The Development of a Nationalist Ideology in Iraq, 1920–1941." *Muslim World* 75, no. 2 (April 1985): 85–101.

———. *The Modern History of Iraq*. 2d ed. Boulder, CO, 2004.

Martal, Abdullah and Recep Yildirim, "Osmanli Yönetiminin Arkeolojik Eserlere Bakiş Açisi" [A Point of View on the Ottoman Government's Archaeological Work]. 13th Turkish Historical Conference, Ankara.

Massé, Henri. "André Godard." *Journal Asiatique* 252 (1965): 415–417.

Meskell, Lynn, ed. *Archaeology under Fire: Nationalism, Politics and Heritage in the Eastern Mediterranean and Middle East*. New York, 1998.

El-Moti'i, Lam'i. *Portraits of Eminent Egyptians*. Cairo, 1995.

Mottahedeh, Roy. *The Mantle of the Prophet: Religion and Politics in Iran*. New York, 1985.

Mousavi, Ali. "Persepolis in Retrospect: Histories of Discovery and Archaeological Exploration at the Ruins of Ancient Parseh." *Ars Orientalis* 32 (2002): 209–251.

Mozaheri, Hushang. *Aramgah Kharajian dar Isfahan* [Tombs of Foreigners in Isfahan]. Isfahan, 1379 [1999].

Musa, Salama. *The Education of Salama Musa*. Leiden, 1961.

———. *Mahia Al-Nahdat* [What Is the Revival?]. Cairo, 1993.

Muscarella, Oscar White. "The Pope and the Bitter Fanatic." In *The Iranian World: Essays on Iranian Art and Archaeology*, ed. Abbas Alizadeh et al., 5–12. Tehran, 1999.

Naimy, Nadeem. *The Lebanese Prophets of New York*. Beirut, 1985.

Negahban, Ezzatolah O. "Fifth International Congress of Iranian Art and Archaeology." *Bastan Chenassi va Honar-e Iran* 1 (Winter 1969): 8–10.

Nicolson, Harold G. *Curzon: The Last Phase, 1919–1925: A Study in Postwar Diplomacy*. New York, 1934.

Özal, Turgut. *Turkey in Europe and Europe in Turkey*. Rev. ed. Nicosia, 1991.

Özdemir, Ayşe. "A History of Turkish Archaeology from the 19th Century to the End of the Single Party Period." M.A. thesis, Boğaziçi University, Istanbul, 2001.

Özgen, Ilknur, and Jean Öztürk. *Heritage Recovered: The Lydian Treasure*. Istanbul, 1996.

Özgüç, Tahsin. "Ataturk et l'archéologie." In *Mémorial Ataturk: Études d'archéologie et de philologie anatoliennes*, 5–8. Paris, 1982.

Parla, Taha. *The Social and Political Thought of Ziya Gökalp, 1876–1924*. Leiden, 1985.

Perkins, Ann. "American Archaeology in the Near and Middle East." In *Background of the Middle East*, ed. Ernest Jackh, 211–218. Ithaca, 1952.

Pope, Arthur Upham. "The International Congress for Persian Art and Archaeology." *Bastan Chenassi va Honar-i Iran* 1 (Winter 1969): 3–7.

Al-Qazzaz, Ayad. "The Power Elite in Iraq, 1920–58." *Muslim World* 61 (1971): 267–282.

Raouf, Wafik. *Nouveau regard sur le nationalisme Arabe: Ba'th et Nasserism.* Paris, 1984.

Reid, Donald Malcolm. "Indigenous Egyptology: The Decolonization of a Profession?" *Journal of the American Oriental Society* 105, no. 2 (1985): 233–246.

———. "Cultural Imperialism and Nationalism: The Struggle to Define and Control the Heritage of Arab Art in Egypt." *International Journal of Middle East Studies* 24 (1992): 57–76.

———. "The Postage Stamp: A Window on Saddam Hussein's Iraq." *Middle East Journal* 47, no. 1 (Winter 1993): 77–89.

———. *Whose Pharaohs? Archaeology, Museums, and Egyptian National Identity from Napoleon to World War I.* Berkeley and Los Angeles, 2002.

Reisner, George A. "The Dead Hand in Egypt." *The Independent* 114 (1925): 318–320.

Richard, Yann. "Le Kemalisme en Iran." *Cahiers du GETC* 3 (Autumn 1987): 60–75.

Ronart, Stephen. *Die Türkei von Heute* [Turkey Today]. Amsterdam, 1936.

Rosenberg, Emily. *Spreading the American Dream: American Economic and Cultural Expansion, 1890–1945.* New York, 1982.

Rustow, Dankwart. "Ataturk's Political Leadership." In *Near Eastern Round Table, 1967–68,* ed. R. Bayly Winder, 143–155. New York, 1969.

Salmoni, Barak Aharon. "Pedagogies of Patriotism: Teaching Socio-Political Community in Twentieth-Century Turkish and Egyptian Education." Ph.D. dissertation, Harvard University, 2002.

Sanders, James A., ed. *Near Eastern Archaeology in the Twentieth Century.* New York, 1970.

Scheffler, Thomas. "The Kaiser in Baalbek: Tourism, Archaeology and the Politics of Imagination." Paper presented at the Middle East Studies Association conference, Chicago, 1998.

Schmidt, Erich. *Flights over Ancient Cities of Iran.* Chicago, 1950.

Schnapp, Alain. "Archéologie, archéologues et nazisme." In *Le racisme mythes et sciences,* ed. Maurice Olender, 289–315. Brussels, 1981.

"Selim Hassan: Egyptian Civilization Lover." *Egypt* 34 (Winter 2004): 16–17.

Semah, David. *Four Egyptian Literary Critics.* Leiden, 1974.

Shaheed, Arafan. "Shawqi wa Misr Al-Fira'uniyyah" [Shawqi and Pharaonic Egypt]. *Fusul* 3 (1983): 322–358.

Shahmirzadi, S. Malek. "Ishareh-i mukhtasar bar tahavul bastanshinasy dar Iran" [A Review of the Development of Archaeology in Iran]. *Asar* 12–14 (1986): 133–160.

Shahrokh, Shahrokh, and Rashna Writer, eds. *The Memoirs of Keikhosrow Shahrokh.* Lewiston, NY, 1994.

Shaw, Stanford, and E. K. Shaw. *History of the Ottoman Empire and Modern Turkey.* 2 vols. Cambridge, 1976–1977.

Shaw, Wendy M. K. "Islamic Arts in the Ottoman Imperial Museum, 1889–1923." *Ars Orientalis* 30 (2000): 55–68.

———. *Possessors and Possessed: Museums, Archaeology, and the Visualization of History in the Late Ottoman Empire.* Berkeley and Los Angeles, 2003.

Sherman, Daniel J. and Irit Rogoff. *Museum Culture: Histories, Discourses, Spectacles.* London, 1994.

Siegel, Evan. Review of *Die Politische Öffentlichkeit Iranisch-Aserbaidschans während der Konstitutionellen Revolution im Spiegel der Tabriser Zeitung Azarbayjan.* *Iranian Studies* 37, no. 1 (March 2004): 182–186.

Silberman, Neil Asher. *Digging for God and Country: Exploration, Archaeology and the Secret Struggle for the Holy Land, 1799–1917.* New York, 1982.

———. *Between Past and Present: Archaeology, Ideology and Nationalism in the Modern Middle East.* New York, 1989.

———. "Fitting the Pieces Together: The Power and Politics of Archaeology in the Modern Middle East." Paper presented at World Archaeological Congress (WAC), University of Cape Town, 10–14 January 1999. Available at www.wac.uct.ac.za/wac4/silberman.

Silverfarb, Daniel. *Britain's Informal Empire in the Middle East: A Case Study of Iraq, 1929–1941.* New York, 1986.

Simon, Reeva. *Iraq between Two World Wars: The Creation and Implementation of a National Ideology.* New York, 1986.

———. "The Teaching of History in Iraq before the Rashid Ali Coup of 1941." *Middle Eastern Studies* 22 (January 1986): 37–51.

Sluglett, Peter. *Britain in Iraq, 1914–1932.* Oxford, 1976.

Smith, Charles D. "The Crisis of Orientation: The Shift of Egyptian Intellectuals to Islamic Subjects in the 1930s." *International Journal of Middle East Studies* 4 (October 1973): 382–410.

———. *Islam and the Search for Social Order in Modern Egypt: A Biography of Muhammad Husayn Haykal.* Albany, NY, 1983.

Soroush, Abdulkarim. *Reason, Freedom and Democracy in Islam.* Oxford, 2000.

Spencer, Robert F. "Cultural Process and Intellectual Current: Durkheim and Ataturk." *American Anthropologist* 60, no. 4 (August 1958): 648–657.

Tachau, Frank. "Language and Politics: Turkish Language Reform." *Review of Politics* 26 (April 1964): 191–204.

Tavakoli-Targhi, Mohammad. *Refashioning Iran: Orientalism, Occidentalism and Historiography.* New York, 2001.

Taylor, A. J. P. *English History, 1914–1945.* New York, 1965.

Thelle, Rannfrid I. "The Conquest of the Past: Archaeology and Historiographic Representation of Ancient Mesopotamia in Relief." Paper delivered at the Middle East Studies Association conference, Anchorage, 6–9 November 2003.

Tibi, Bassam. *Arab Nationalism: A Critical Enquiry.* New York, 1981.

Trask, Roger R. *The U.S. Response to Turkish Nationalism and Reform, 1914–1939.* Minneapolis, 1971.

Trigger, Bruce. *A History of Archaeological Thought.* Cambridge, 1989.

Vatikiotis, P. J. *The Modern History of Egypt.* Asia-Africa series. New York, 1969.

Vaziri, Mostafa. *Iran as Imagined Nation: The Construction of National Identity.* New York, 1993.

Vernoit, Stephen. "The Rise of Islamic Archaeology." *Muqarnas* 14 (1997): 1–10.

Viorst, Milton. "Man of Gamaliya." *New Yorker* (2 July 1990): 32–53.

Von der Osten, Hans Henning. *Explorations in Asia Minor.* Reprint. New York, 1971.

Vyronis, Speros, Jr. *The Turkish State and History: Clio Meets the Grey Wolf.* 2d ed. New Rochelle, NY, 1993.

Waldron, Ann. "Digging up the Past." *Princeton Alumni Weekly* (11 February 1980): 14–20.

Wallach, Janet. *Desert Queen.* New York, 1996.

Walz, Terence. "The American Experience in Egypt: A Retrospective Chronicles Two Centuries of Exploration." *Archaeology* 49, no. 1 (January–February 1996): 70–75.

Webster, Donald E. *The Turkey of Ataturk: Social Process in the Turkish Reformation.* Philadelphia, 1939.

Wendell, Charles. *The Evolution of the Egyptian National Image from Its Origins to Ahmad Lutfi al-Sayyid.* Berkeley and Los Angeles, 1972.

Wilber, Donald. *Riza Shah Pahlavi: The Resurrection and Reconstruction of Iran.* Hicksville, NY, 1975.

———. *Adventures in the Middle East: Excursions and Incursions.* Princeton, 1986.

Wilkinson, Charles K. *The Iranian Expedition, 1936.* New York, 1937.

Willey, Gordon R. *A History of American Archaeology.* London, 1980.

Wilson, John A. "Islamic Culture and Archaeology." *Middle East Journal* 8 (Winter 1954): 1–9.

———. *Signs and Wonders upon Pharaoh.* Chicago, 1964.

———. *Thousands of Years: An Archaeologist's Search for Ancient Egypt.* New York, 1972.

Winstone, H. V. F. *Woolley of Ur: The Life of Sir Leonard Woolley.* London, 1990.

Wood, Michael. "The Use of the Pharaonic Past in Modern Egyptian Nationalism," *Journal of the American Research Center in Egypt* 35 (1998): 179–196.

Wortham, John David. *British Egyptology, 1549–1906.* Newton Abbot, UK, 1972.

Wright, G. Ernest. "The Phenomenon of American Archaeology in the Near East." In *Near Eastern Archaeology in the Twentieth Century: Essays in Honor of Nelson Glueck,* ed. James Sanders, 3–40. Garden City, NY, 1970.

Yazdani, Marzieh. "Archaeological Teams in Iran." *Historical Research Quarterly* [Tehran] (Spring–Summer 1996): 95–100.

Zübeyr, Hamit (Koşay). *Tarihi Abidelerimizi Koruyalim* [Let Us Preserve Our Historical Monuments]. Ankara, 1932.

Zürcher, Erik J. *Turkey: A Modern History.* 3d ed. New York, 2004.

# INDEX

Society for the Independence of
   Hatay, 63
Society for the Preservation of the
   National Heritage, 132, 140, 156,
   160–161, 178, 183
Speiser, Ephraim Avigdor, 58, 59, 197,
   215
Standard Oil, 176
Stark, Freya, 220
Starr, Richard, 194–195
State Department, U.S.: and archae-
   ologists, 46, 228; and diplomats,
   16–18; and Egyptian policy, 88, 97,
   124; and France, 49, 58, 61; and
   Oriental Institute concession in
   Iran, 146–147, 156, 159, 165, 175;
   and Ottoman Empire, 36; and
   Pope, 135; and protest to Bagh-
   dad, 210; and support for Cairo
   Museum project, 103; and Turkey,
   40–41, 42, 45
Stein, Sir Aurel, 181
Stevens, David, 172
Straus, Oscar, 90
Suez Canal, 226
Sulayman Pasha, Abdul Hamid, 118
Sultanieh, 232
Sumer, 10
Sumerians: relations to Turks, 21, 22,
   51, 52; and Ur, 193
Sun-language theory, 22–23
Sunnis, 198
Susa, 127, 128, 129, 130, 136, 137, 138;
   compared to Persepolis, 142; shah's
   visit to, 174
Suwaydi, Tawfik al-, 200–201
Syria: and French mandate, 14, 17,
   34, 105, 228; and the Hatay, 57,
   59, 62–64; as haven for Western
   archaeologists, 206, 210, 215, 219–
   220; influence of, in Iraq, 199; and
   nationalism, 60–61; and Western
   archaeology, 2, 3, 58–59, 189

Taft, Robert A., 45
Taghizadeh, Seyed Hassan, 133, 135,
   149

Takht-i Abu Nasr, 148
Takht-i-Jamshid. *See* Persepolis
Tavalolli, Fereydun, 169
Taymurtash, Abdul Husayn, 133, 138,
   139, 144, 146, 148, 178
Tefik Bey, 46
Tekardağ, Ruhi, 65
Tell Asmar, 196, 206
Tell Billa, 197
Temple of Artemis, 32
Temple of Rome and Augustus, 50
Teos, 26
Tepe Gawra, 214, 215
Tepe Hissar, 148
Third Reich, 52, 55, 152–153
Thrace, 19
Tigris River, 185, 221
Toledo Museum of Art, 79
Tottenham, P. M., 92
Toynbee, Arnold, 34
Treaty of Lausanne, 19, 22, 40, 41
Treaty of Sèvres, 19, 33, 34, 35, 188
Troy, 24, 28, 46, 52
Turang Tepe, 148
Turcology, 20–21
Turcoman, 176
Turkey: and antiquities, 2, 3, 26, 36,
   47, 50, 229; and the Hatay, 57–64;
   and history, 11, 15, 20, 21, 22, 23,
   229; and language reform, 238n8;
   as regional model, 86, 157, 198,
   199; and Turkish Historical So-
   ciety, 22, 50, 52, 55, 66, 238n5; and
   U.S. policy, 37–42; and war with
   Greece, 34, 35
Turkish Language Society, 22–23
Turkish Youth Sports Club, 63
Turkophobia, 21, 22, 41
Tutankhamun ("King Tut"), 2, 3, 5,
   8, 76; and Iran, 157, 164; statue of,
   113; symbolic importance of, 75, 80,
   82, 230
Twain, Mark, 115

Ukhaidar, 217
Ulen Group, 147
Umari, Arshad al-, 218